A ROOM OF HIS OWN

Judaic Traditions in Literature, Music, and Art

Ken Frieden and Harold Bloom, *Series Editors*

A ROOM OF HIS OWN

In Search of the Feminine in the Novels of Saul Bellow

GLORIA L. CRONIN

Syracuse University Press

813.52
B44zc

First Edition 2001
01 02 03 04 05   6 5 4 3 2 1

The paper used in this publication meets the minimum requirements of American
National Standard for Information Sciences—Permanence of Paper for Printed
Library Materials, ANSI Z39.48-1984. ∞

Library of Congress Cataloging-in-Publication Data

Cronin, Gloria L., 1947–
  A room of his own: in search of the feminine in the novels of Saul Bellow /
Gloria L. Cronin—1st ed.
    p. cm.—(Judaic traditions in literature, music, and art)
    Includes bibliographical references and index.
    ISBN 0-8156-2862-5 (alk. paper)—ISBN 0-8156-2863-3 (pbk. : alk. paper)
      1. Bellow, Saul—Knowledge—Psychology. 2. Bellow, Saul—Characters—Men.
3. Men in literature. 4. Masculinity in literature. 5. Femininity in literature. 6.
Gender identity in literature. I. Title. II. Series.

PS3503.E4488 Z619 2000
813'.52—dc21

                                                                00-030087

Manufactured in the United States of America
Page design by Fara Sneddon

For dear friends and colleagues

Gloria L. Cronin is professor of English at Brigham Young University, where she teaches Jewish American, African American, women's, and twentieth-century Anglo-American literatures, critical theory and Anglophone postcolonial literature. She is coeditor of the *Saul Bellow Journal* and associate editor of *Pacific Studies*. Her book-length publications include *Zora Neale Hurston: Critical Essays* (1998), *Conversations with Saul Bellow* (1994), *Tales of Molokai* (1992), *Sixty Other Jewish Fiction Writers: An Annotated Bibliography* (1991), *Jerzy Kozinski: An Annotated Bibliography* (1989), *Saul Bellow in the 1980s* (1989), *Saul Bellow: An Annotated Bibliography*, vols. 3 (1987) and 4 (2000), and the forthcoming *Jewish American and Holocaust Literature: A Late Twentieth-Century Look*.

CONTENTS

ACKNOWLEDGMENTS

I would like to express my deep gratitude to my dear friend and colleague Ben Siegel for all his advice and encouragement across the years, and especially in the writing of this book. I am grateful also to Bert Wilson, my earliest mentor and greatest example of humane learning. My grateful thanks go also to Dini Hansma, Charlene Lind, Lynne Facer, Linda Hunter Adams, Ruth Liljenquist, and Fara Anderson Sneddon for their professional help and moral support.

ABBREVIATIONS AND TEXTS

References are to the following editions of Bellow's novels.

AM	*The Adventures of Augie March*, Viking, 1953
AT	*A Theft*, Penguin, 1989
BC	*The Bellarosa Connection*, Penguin, 1989
DM	*Dangling Man*, Vanguard, 1944
DD	*The Dean's December*, Harper, 1981
HRK	*Henderson the Rain King*, Viking, 1959
HWFIM	*Him With His Foot in His Mouth and Other Stories*, Harper, 1984
H	*Herzog*, Viking, 1964
HG	*Humboldt's Gift*, Viking, 1975
IAAU	*It All Adds Up: From the Dim Past to the Uncertain Future*, Viking, 1994
LA	*The Last Analysis*, Viking, 1965
MDH	*More Die of Heartbreak*, Morrow, 1987
MSP	*Mr. Sammler's Planet*, Viking, 1964
MM	*Mosby's Memoirs*, Viking, 1968
R	*Ravelstein*, Viking, 2000
SD	*Seize the Day*, Viking, 1956
SRMB	*Something to Remember Me By: Three Tales*, Viking, 1991
TA	*The Actual*, Viking, 1997
TJ	*To Jerusalem and Back*, Viking, 1976
TV	*The Victim*, Vanguard, 1947

CHRONOLOGY

A ROOM OF HIS OWN

1

INTRODUCTION

Men have had the advantage of us in telling their own story. The
pen has been in their hands. I will not allow books to prove
anything.
                                        —Jane Austen, *Persuasion*

We are folded up in and into—implicated—even tied up in our
seeing.
        —Mary Ann Caws, "The Female Body in Western Culture"

Traditional readings of Saul Bellow's novels, including many of
my own previously published pieces, have consistently told the
story of Saul Bellow and his male protagonists as defenders of an
embattled Western humanist tradition, enemies alike of nihilists,
existentialists, rationalists, and other touters of the void. Major critics[1] have carefully built the critical narrative of Bellow as an
antimodernist who romantically, even archaically, clings to notions
of soul, human transcendence, and a belief in the universality of the
Western humanist Self. In short, such readings of Bellow and his
protagonists as concerned primarily with continental philosophical
issues have dominated Bellow criticism in the American, British, and
European academies since the 1960s. Although they have paid
mostly accurate tribute to Bellow's liberal humanist and spiritual
convictions about the sacredness of ordinary human life, these critics have foregrounded this debate with continental philosophy so
powerfully that there is still not very much significant post-1970s
contemporary critical conversation on split subjectivity, cultural
locatedness, gender, and issues of difference.
    The universalizing tendencies of liberal humanist criticism and

1

its mental habit of viewing writer, reader, and protagonist as universal nonparticularized constructions of human nature should now give way to critiques that acknowledge the split nature of the subject and the particular effects of the androcentric, monological text. Robert Solomon and Toril Moi have reminded us that the entire history of Western civilization is marked by an attempt to universalize a gendered human nature embedded in illusions of a particular bourgeoisie. Moi writes:

> Traditional humanism . . . is in effect part of patriarchal ideology. At its center is the seamlessly unified self—either individual or collective—which is commonly called "Man." . . . This integrated self is in fact a phallic self, constructed on the model of the self-contained powerful phallus. Gloriously autonomous, it banishes from itself all conflict, contradiction, and ambiguity. History or the text becomes the sole expression of this unique individual: all art becomes nothing but autobiography, a mere window onto the self and the world, with no reality of its own.[2]

In the reading I offer, I will deal with only one area of difference, that of gender. I will attempt to demonstrate that Bellow's androcentric texts represent a search for the absent mother, lover, sister, female friend, female psyche, and anima. It is this figure that eludes all his male protagonists, who search abstractly through the detritus of Western philosophy, ethics, and transcendental thinking in intense and forlorn pursuit of a woman or feminine that they cannot quite apprehend. Hence, their ironic rejection of the literal historical women of their own social milieu and the angry, misogynous depiction of absent, lacking, destructive, stereotypical woman of the very masculine culture in which they are enmeshed. Much of Bellow's irony centers on this hapless misogynous male monologist entrenched in the American codes of male homosociality embarking on a metaphysical quest for the missing feminine. For in the very act of erasing the feminine by constructing only woman, the protagonist and his text re-encode the very conditions of its tantalizing and ultimately pathological absence.

It is not this simple, however. Bellow's deconstructive irony with regard to his own acculturation and the shortcomings of his protagonists' alter egos suggests that these alter egos and their creator all seem to sense the source of the problem. In some cases they even come quite close to peeking behind the mirror of their own masculine subjectivity. It is as if Bellow has used these alter egos systematically, as did William Faulkner, in order to discover his own and society's chief ills and scotomas. Sometimes Bellow and his protagonists catch a glimpse of the elusive feminine figure of the imagination only to be confronted once again with their own limitations. It is as if the Bellow protagonist laments, "Help me catch it, see it, and thus find my own health in a sick universe." Transcendental ideologies fail to enable him to escape the bind of the masculine selfsame as he engages in various spiritual exercises. It is their failures that Bellow is most eager to understand, however, and it is in his comic and ironic analyses of these failures that he comes closest to understanding what the gender barriers are.

For this reason it would be untruthful and reductive to read Bellow only as antifeminist, simply misogynist, or wilfully male in his viewpoint. Although both Bellow and his protagonists are frequently all of these by turns, they do intuit the direction, if not the exact shape, of that feminine which eludes them. They capture our sympathy and engage our intellects and spiritual faculties because of the sheer comedy, irony, and moral seriousness of this pursuit. They brush so close, so often to what eludes them that many readers sense also the almost tangible presence of the feminine absence on which the entire production rests. Ironically, however, she simultaneously exists and dies in the rooms masculine desire creates in the texts. This is not to say that what Bellow's men desire is not thoroughly grounded in masculine symbolic conceptions of woman, but rather to say that, occasionally, they and their creator seem to almost know another space.

Hence, while Bellow's texts are often perpetrators of misogynous stereotypes, they can also be suspicious, analytical deconstructors of them. Some texts do more of one and less of the other. In terms of gender ideology, they show traces of the lost feminine in the desiring of their protagonists. They often play in the margins and erode cultural boundaries. They even examine the epistemological assumptions of consciousness and reality rooted in what, according to Bellow, is a faulty discourse of reality as modernist catastrophe devoid of affective and transcendental elements.

Bellow, however, stops short of a real exploration of the ethics of difference or any real understanding of the failures of his generation's gender ideologies. Bellow's protagonists seem ultimately unable to unravel the central significance of this conundrum and finally, in several of the later novels, simply rail against women. Typically, they make the old patriarchal move and remove themselves from the presence of the female body—chaotic, wicked, and unclean—in favor of the calm cleanliness of books and abstract transcendental thought. It is a move as old as the Jewish patriarchs and more recently of the Christian fathers. Jean Baùdrillard puts it clearly when he notes that women are typically seen as responsible for and guilty of blocking the flow of male desire.[3] In Jacques Derrida's words: "'Woman' may be monstrous, unclean, mad, oriental, profane, or improper, yet she is that which is necessary to the completion of misguided male desire."[4]

Noam Chomsky and Michel Foucault take this discussion even further by showing that the discourse of the human and social sciences does not merely constitute this universal presence but simultaneously constitutes its opposite in the form of some shadowy double.[5] Such an idea has intriguing possibilities for cultural poetics. It also suggests that there is no real way of explicating human nature for either novelist or critic. The positive can be revealed only by writer, critic, social scientist, or reader by posing artificially or culturally constructed images of the normative or a type. Hence, the intent of the human sciences, including reading and criticism—to appreciate the object of discourse, the human subject—becomes subverted.[6]

Luce Irigaray describes these contingencies of history in her brilliant narrative account of the masculine construction of Western selfhood and its colonizations of the feminine.

> Woman in this sexual imaginary is only a more or less obliging prop for the enactment of man's fantasies. . . . For woman is traditionally a use-value for man, an exchange value among men; in other words, a commodity. As such she remains the guardian of material substance, whose price will be established, in terms of the standard of their work and their need/desire, by "subjects": workers, merchants, consumers. Women are marked phallically by their fathers, husbands, procurers. And this branding determines their value in sexual commerce. Woman is never anything but the locus of a more or less competitive exchange between two

4

men, including the competition for the possession of mother earth.[7]

Sexuality in Western art, Irigaray argues, has always been defined against the masculine standard, thus constructing the feminine as absence, lack, silence, atrophy, or deficiency. What are the precise strategies of this masculine mastery of the symbolic economy, she asks. How should we account for its "systematicity," its resourcefulness, and its "reappropriation of the various productions of history" (74)? She concludes:

> This domination of the philosophic logos stems in large part from its power to reduce all others to the economy of the Same. The teleologically constructive project it takes on is always the project of diversion, deflection, reduction of the other in the Same. And, in its greatest generality perhaps, from its power to eradicate the difference between the sexes in systems that are representative of a "masculine subject." Whence the necessity of "reopening" the figures of philosophical discourse—idea, substance, subject, transcendental subjectivity, absolute knowledge—in order to pry out of them what they have borrowed that is feminine, from the feminine, to make them "render up" and give back what they owe the feminine. (74)

She then calls for an examination of the operation of the "grammar" of each figure of discourse, its syntactic laws or requirements, its imaginary configurations, its metaphoric networks, and also, of course, what it does not articulate at the level of utterance: *its silences* (75). Thus, it is woman, the feminine, that nourishes, maintains, and makes possible mimesis for men, for the logos. She suggests a "jamming" of the machinery of the masculine selfsame in the logocentric, symbolic economy in order to understand such a gendered "grammar" and thus better understand the "recto verso" structure of gendered selfhood. It would be, she says, a casting "loose from its moorings" the whole phallocentric project, a returning of the masculine to its own language so that "it could no longer, all by itself, define, circumvent, circumscribe, the properties of anything and everything. That the right to define every value—including the abusive privilege of appropriation—would no longer belong to it" (85).

5

Bellow's woman, so frequently a cutout or icon, is produced by that masculine selfsame which Irigaray argues is the ruling ideology or psychical structure inherent in our culture. In particular, the androcentric realistic novel such as Bellow's functions very much like narrative cinema in that it reveals the manner in which "the unconscious (formed by the dominant order) structures ways of seeing and pleasures in looking" (85). Harold Bloom comments that "American texts will prove resistant to deconstruction" or "analytic associative technique" because "writing in the American grain" affirms the "self over language."[8] Likewise, Alice Jardine notes that the American son as artist is reluctant to let loose of the third person function within representation. This son *portrays* the woman, and hence the mother, as something that must be known. He then expresses rather than constitutes woman as modernity's problem without making her his own. Jardine argues that the "woman-in-effect" in American male fiction, throughout its thematization of gynesis, is close to the foundations of Anglo-American thought itself.[9]

What both Jardine and Irigaray call for is a radical re-evaluation of the masculine text and a radical self-examination of ourselves as gendered readers and critics of gendered discourse. By implication, of course, they suggest that gender is simply the most obvious alterity, that it suggests a host of other others as well, whose traces may be archaeologically recovered if the "grammar" of the phallic Western humanist text can be fathomed. "Without such an interpretation of a general grammar of culture, the feminine (and all other alterities) will never take place in history, except as a reservoir of matter and of speculation."[10]

Such a reading paradigm would of necessity force the reader and critic to examine many alterities in the Bellow text: Bellow himself as masculine as opposed to feminine, American to European, white to black, educated to uneducated, Jewish to Wasp, Western humanist to non-Western.

Within the Bellow text, and for the most part, within the body of Bellow critical narrative, there has really been only one scopic economy—a masculine and liberal humanist one. This study will focus primarily on gender, and in it I will forgo the hubris of supposed *complete* or *all-encompassing* readings and admit that there is only my "interested," partial, and angled reading here.

But what of the nature of this masculine or feminine that this study will examine? And what of the issue of presence? Heidegger, in arguing for "existence before essence," suggests that there is one more step in man's drive for mastery over physis: his potentially gentle, poetic union of techne with physis.[11] My critical reading assumes presence (not essence) behind and within representation of either the feminine or the masculine. Furthermore, it implies that each of these constructs is multiplicitous. It also asserts that Bellow's male protagonists simultaneously erase and search for that lost feminine, maternal ground, or mother, thus creating their own metaphysical imprisonments. To complicate matters further, there is also a discernible ironic and philosophical self-consciousness on Bellow's part (and that of his protagonists) about the limitations of their own textual creations of masculinity, reality, truth, subjectivity, and representation, which must be acknowledged. The human compassion and comic dimensions of the Bellow text ought to call forth both a corresponding compassion and sense of the humor in the postmodern feminist reader because she/he and they (the protagonists and their author) are also bound in the same prison of metaphor, albeit from a different position. Feminist teleology itself is, after all, implicated in the roots of classical logic.

Irigaray has spoken of the "sexual indifference sustaining the truth of all science, the logic of all discourse."[12] Realistically, we can no longer use reading paradigms that enact a corresponding indifference. We might disagree on how such a reading might be done, but surely we are not in disagreement that it should be done. Such a reading needs to construct a topology of gender codes and symbolic strategies operant in the Bellow text, rather than to posit a utopian notion of what they ought to have been.[13]

I intend to explore the conditions of possibility within these texts for the presence of the feminine absence they seem to seek. I will also attempt to explore the presence of that spiritual sensibility which tries to reach beyond the gendered and other paradigms of selfhood enacted in the Bellow text, in order to discover the presence of those profound ethical and spiritual dimensions that make these characters and these texts so much more than the sum of their inevitable scotomas. This kind of critique involves a topological exploration of the movement and transformation of rhetorical and thematic spaces, rather than the identification of fixed lists of definitions about gender identities. Such a reading will, however, recognize the monological androcentric structures within these texts

7

as the chief source of their scopic failures. I am interested in the repeated use of woman in these texts as the enigma that keeps the hermeneutic machinery grinding. My attempt is to add a dimension to Bellow criticism, not by displacing earlier readings or questioning their value, but by suggesting that they too are only partial readings.[14]

Then there are the ethical issues raised by feminist reader response critics who point out the gendered nature not only of the text, but of the reader. In the case of the androcentric monologist text that creates within the text a sympathetic (sometimes misogynous) male narratee and without the text a sympathetic male reader, there is a considerable problem of identification for the female reader. The androcentric text is always a misogynist text because it not only fictionally constructs the male gaze but also all too often invites male readers into the text for spectator sport at the expense of women, thereby producing one more account of a particular kind of masculine erotics.[15]

The same is true of our critical paradigms. Hans Robert Jauss and Michel Foucault both theorize that as readers we intersect with the text along a horizon of expectations formulated by our own respective cultural environments or that "one simply tracks along the course laid out by the general deployment of sexuality."[16] Likely our desires as readers and writers are marked by historicity, and in this case, a historical masculine homosocial erotics. Is it possible then to locate one appeal of the Bellow text in its very production of a masculine gaze, voice, worldview, and erotics for a like-minded masculine reader? This cannot be the whole story, but it is certainly a significant factor.[17] What we see as Bellow readers are the scopic transactions of a classic masculinity. The mirror of the text reflects only the image placed in front of it. This specular image, or optic, is thus composed of man and his self-reflecting other, an image of himself, or the masculine selfsame. Woman is produced and women are thus denied self-representation in this textual economy because they cannot move from being the creations and objects of the male gaze and voice to becoming the subjects looking and speaking back. Buried and blinded by such fixed location, they lose their right to look, to speak, or to be heard. They remain unspecified woman, and rarely women. She cannot cease to operate in this double economy of male homosociality as his self-reflecting other. Hence, what is missing in these homosocial masculine and monologic texts of

Bellow's is what Catherine Clément and Hélène Cixous have called the land of the "elsewhere,"[18] that land, Irigaray would argue, whose shape cannot be mapped by the flat mirror, but which just might be glimpsed in the mysterious reflecting surfaces of the curved speculum.

Obviously, an immasculated female reader of the Bellow text will experience the text much as a male reader would, perhaps barely noticing that to enter into the collusive relationship demanded by the text is to identify against her own gender. As Judith Fetterly observes: "The cultural reality is not emasculation of men by women, but the immasculation of women by men. As readers and teachers and scholars, women are taught to think as men, to identify with a male point of view and to accept as normal and legitimate a male system of values, one of whose central principles is misogyny."[19] She concludes that "powerlessness . . . derives from not only seeing one's experience articulated, clarified, and legitimized in art, but more significantly, . . . [it] results from the endless division of self against self, the consequence of the invocation to identify as male while being reminded that to be male—to be universal—to be American—is to be *not* female."[20]

Should a woman whose image has continually been stolen be asked to perpetuate this complicity as reader? To be a woman reader of such texts means being used against oneself in a masculinist reading paradigm, because such a reading paradigm solicits her complicity in the elevation of male difference into universality and, accordingly, the denigration of female difference into otherness with reciprocity. By this means, the feminine is being produced within a particular gender system. The power of the text is the false consciousness into which women are coopted. Susan Winnett asks: "Would it not stand to reason that men and women read differently, that there must be a fundamental disparity between what they bring to, do to, demand from, and write about texts? And if we do read differently, is it not necessary to figure out how and where we do so?"[21] To reread as a woman is at least to imagine the lady's place; to imagine while reading the place of a woman's body; to be reminded that her identity is also re-remembered in stories of the body.[22]

By reading Bellow as an androcentric writer staging a male homosocial world through the monologic voice of one male narrator, I hope to interrupt the fictional construction of that gaze, reveal its narrative machinery, and refuse collusion with its male narrator, the monologist. This process involves reading the text against itself,

9

not in order to reject it but to identify its gender operations, cultural embeddedness, and culpability in perpetuating certain strategies and codes. More important, it is the kind of reading that may reveal that multiplicity and excess within the text which will enable us to catch a glimpse of the unrepresented masculine, feminine, or other.[23]

What does it mean that Bellow and male writers like him have spoken for woman? Such a reading is a search for that which has been de-emphasized, left out of Western thinking, and for a new historicity that allows it space to come back in. Derrida redefines this feminine alterity by collapsing the categories of Same and Other. He illustrates in almost all of his works that the battle with the Father-Author is his oldest and most consistent topic. By refusing intersubjectivity and paradox, he argues, we cannot move into becoming—move past the fixed sexual identities of inter-subjectivity—subject and object. Refusing to rethink alterity, we enact violence. This is the frequent plight of the Bellow protagonist. Kristeva describes in more sweeping terms this textual alienation of other in the authorial refusal to think in terms of alterity. Her contribution to a feminist ethics of reading is to point out that the other in Western ideology is always the feminine. After all, the feminine is what lies outside of masculine subjectivity. Kristeva, via Jacques Lacan, continues in her discussion of the other as the mother, that she is the first other "with whom 'I'—the son—initiate a dialogue with the mother. Privileged addressee, the mother is above all the other sex: she is therefore doubly justified in constituting this pole of alterity through which the allocation constitutes itself, and which fiction is going to usurp, absorb, and dissolve."[24]

Such a reading is less a matter of recovering identity than of articulating the problems encountered in the Bellow text as it struggles to articulate such gender difference within outworn epistemological models of the old history. I would argue that Saul Bellow (as well as Henry James and William Faulkner) are unique among major white male American novelists for perceiving, reacting to, apprehending, locating, and reinvigorating culture with their attempts at staging difference, even if they often fail. It is as if all three sense a missing presence through its absence to such a degree that it becomes that gendered backing on the mirror of identity which they cannot quite see for not having gone, like Alice, through the looking glass of masculine metaphorization of culture. It is to their credit that they have sensed the lack.

10

2

A ROOM OF HIS OWN

MONOLOGISTS AND MALE
HOMOSOCIALITY

Civilization's first gesture is to hold up a mirror to the Object, but
the object is only seemingly reflected therein; in fact it is the Object
itself which is the mirror, and it is here that the subject is taken in
by the illusion of himself.
—Jean Baùdrillard, *De la seduction*

The Bellow protagonist is unarguably a descendant of the
eighteenth-and nineteenth-century romantic individualists
and, more recently, the great Victorian male autobiographers.
Monologists all, they appear self-created and self-sustaining as they
are seen engaged in solipsistic metaphysical pursuits. They are
narcissists who, in a classic double move, construct their own masculine subjectivity as they portray a world in the likeness of their
own consciousnesses. Bellow, however, always the intellectual
historian, is quite deliberate in revealing the genealogy of his protagonists, whom he usually presents to us as the comic,
ironic inheritors of this tradition. Bellow's nostalgic yet ironic
demythologization fuels much of his comedy.

Built on the Arnoldian and Emersonian models, each of
Bellow's late twentieth-century American Dreamers, when they
are not talking to themselves or other men, are seen fleeing
from destructive women and planning a variety of quasi-
monastic retreats. Specialists in the inward gaze, each is at heart a

11

nineteenth-century spiritual quester trapped both within his own masculinity and within an age that scarcely values his presence. Through these characters, Bellow creates androcentric texts that function in Mikhail Bakhtin's terms as monoglossias whose narrator's voice stages a male homosocial world. Bellow would seem to be reluctantly agreeing with Johann Wolfgang von Goethe's frequent observation that man is a true narcissist because he makes the whole world his mirror.

The classic setting of the Bellow protagonist is a man mentally alone in a study, a room of his own in more senses than one. First there is Joseph, that reader of Enlightenment and romantic literature, who communes mostly alone in a rented room in a rooming house as he writes his journal and complains that he can no longer talk to his wife, family, or male friends. Next there is Asa Leventhal, who is alone in his apartment as well as locked claustrophobically within his own paranoid consciousness. Augie March's is mostly a masculine picaresque world in which he wanders as an isolato at heart, neither entirely withdrawing nor entirely allowing himself to be coopted. Tommy Wilhelm occupies a room in the horrible Hotel Gloriana and is nearly destroyed within this sinister colony of father-destroyers. Eugene Henderson escapes his room for the hypermasculine world of Hemingwayesque adventure in Africa and is last seen alone with the Persian orphan child at the North Pole. Moses Herzog has spent his life in a study trying to write his magnum opus on romanticism. As the novel begins and ends, he is sans wife, child, mistress, family, and friends. He shares his ruined garden space with mice and owls. Charlie Citrine and Von Humboldt Fleisher are seen suffering their way through a painful and dubious blood brotherhood for the entire length of the novel, during which time they are mostly seen alone. Humboldt ends up sick, aged, and alone in his flophouse room, while Charlie ends up standing on his head in a Madrid hotel room, bereft of everyone who has mattered to him. Mr. Sammler, that polite, scholarly "slim jim" from the early modern world of pre–World War II Europe is also seen mostly alone or weighing the impact of the nineteenth-century masculine intellectual tradition that has rendered him slightly less human than he wants to be. Despite this realization that he must connect himself to his kin in genuine love, he is last seen longing for the monastic silence of his room, the texts of Meister Eckhardt, and the voices of the biblical prophets. Dean Corde usually communes alone in a room in Minna's childhood home in Bucharest as he mourns the loss of certain humanistic values due to fascism and violence in both East and West. In a more comic vein, Benn Crader and Kenneth Trachtenberg, that goofy pair of romantic idealists and boon companions, are most at home communing together in Uncle Benn's classic men's-club-style bachelor quarters. Clara Velde and Ithiel Regler seem to reach the high point of their relationship alone in a room while Ithiel studies his dangerous documents and Clara cooks for him, naked but for a pair of clogs. We sense that the unnamed narrator of *The Bellarosa Connection* is alone in the study in his home as he tells us of his significant emotional and spiritual loss of Sorella Fonstein, the one remarkable human being he can find in his phenomenal memory. Harry Trellman, in *A Theft*, feels equally entombed. Ravelstein and Chick are slightly more social. They prefer each other's company, and after that the classroom. Ravelstein accuses Chick of perpetually being "stuck in privacy" (9) and of being in need of rescue. From within rooms of their own, like their forebears, the Victorian male autobiographers— Ruskin, Tennyson, Carlyle, Arnold, Newman, Stevenson, DeQuincy, Gosse, Lewes, and Rossetti—the Bellow autobiographers produce not The World but the world of Western masculine intellectual life.

Through these quasi-journalistic, meditative first-and third-person interior monologues, Bellow's texts create not only his famous monologists but a quasi-monoglossia[1] that enacts a particular kind of gender construction of both masculinity and femininity.[2]

I wish to appropriate Bakhtin's model of the monoglossia, and his language, to both affirm and refute his thesis about the novel. Although in one sense even a monologue contains within it the possibility of these centripetal and colliding centrifugal voices, in another sense it actually does not. That is to say, although there may be a masculine heteroglossia immanent in the monologue, this is only a narrow and gendered form of dialogue. When there is a dominant male voice present in a monologue, the feminine component of otherness is not so discernable and fully voiced. In this particular sense, the androcentric, monologic novel does not so easily reveal femininity as otherness in its language. Rather, it functions in the manner of the monoglossia Bakhtin ascribes to the single voice of the poet.

In the male-authored text that uses first-person or third-person quasi-direct speech representing an interior monologue belonging to a specific male character, full heteroglossia is prevented. The feminine is, in many essential ways, silenced and excluded. I recognize, and will later demonstrate, how the voice of the feminine can occasionally be discerned within the male monologue. It remains mostly true, however, that in the male-voiced novel of monologue and interior monologue, the feminine voice is seriously obscured and, for all practical purposes, lost. Bellow has produced mostly masculine single-voiced texts, not that heteroglossia which would mirror in its language the voice of the feminine and the literally female.

Women in Bellow's texts are more spoken to and about than speaking, more gazed at than gazing back, more marginal than center stage. The monologic Bellow text, like the Victorian male autobiography, is a monoglossia which is almost never semantically open to dialogic forms or other voices. Like the Victorian male autobiography, the Bellow text tends to include women only to objectify and silence them, causing woman in both of these instances to become the overdetermined site of male fantasy and hostility.[3]

The androcentric monoglossia exists all through the cultural history of the West, but it is the Victorian male autobiography that stands as the immediate precursor and model for Bellow's novels. Monologism and its related strategies are inextricably bound up with the nineteenth-century history of individualism and its more recent permutations in late twentieth-century American bourgeois individualism. The myths Bellow's protagonists share with the great Victorian male autobiographers provide evidence of such a genealogy. Most of Bellow's male characters subscribe, however comically and with however much self-irony, to such defunct and often destructive ideas as the myth of the solitary genius, the notion that inwardness equals freedom, the idea that genius requires eccentricity, and the corollary of all these ideas—the myth of the masculine "community of one."[4] Hence, the construction of the monologist as liminal, nostalgic, in retreat from society, a classic misogynist usually engaged almost exclusively in male homosocial community.

Bellow has always been more vitally interested in the American masculine experience. Consider how widely he has attempted to map the history of male power games, charlatans, nutcases, brutes, mad poets, gentle dreamers, crooked intellectuals, bogus religious figures, internationally known intellectuals, refugees, phony reporters, egomaniacs, financial hucksters, writers, legal thieves, mafiosi, lawyers, immigrant populations, and old neighborhood personalities. His pantheon of male characters and male intellectuals of bygone eras cuts across high society, government, the under-world, ethnic neighborhoods, the international scene, a variety of occupational groups, the politically displaced, the homosocial and the homosexual, and several ranges on the educational scale, not to mention both Protestant and Jewish worlds.

By concentrating on the novelistic staging of this seemingly autosufficient male culture, its monocular vision, monologic voice, and inevitable masculine narcissism, Bellow can produce endless symphonic variations on American masculine subjectivity. He has simply not made it his business to imagine femininity far beyond a series of sadly familiar but fictionally usable cultural stereotypes.

His male homosocial world can be examined through the models of male homosociality suggested by Luce Irigaray and Eve Sedgwick. At the base of their theories is the notion of woman as object of exchange within a masculine economy structured around male desire. In her essay "The Blind Spot of an Old Dream of Symmetry,"[5] Irigaray uncovers the workings of this masculine desire for the same—"the desire for the auto . . . the homo . . . the male."[6] "[All] divergences will finally become 'proportions, functions, relations that can be referred back to *sameness*,'"[7] she reasons.

Whereas the world of feminine origins and feminine relation-ships remains largely without representation, Western culture reifies and celebrates that father-son relationship which becomes replicated through time by the genealogy of copies of the masculine selfsame. Irigaray calls this a "stagnant repetition" in which the scene of representation is always fixed by similitude. Speaking of the myth of the universal, she notes that truth and reality in Western culture are images made from images: "offspring, copies, fakes."[8]

Eve Sedgwick, in her influential work *Between Men: English Literature and Male Homosocial Desire*,[9] draws on Claude Levi-Strauss[10] and Gayle Rubin[11] in formulating what is at present our fullest description of the dynamics of male homosociality. I am aware that Sedgwick's description is a primarily British model constructed on a British public school masculinity, but it does have its uses here. Sedgwick contends that nineteenth-and twentieth-century English literature, rightly read, will reveal not only how heterosexuality struc-tures homosexuality, but how actualized or repressed homosexual desire occurs within the text, despite and because of the rupture of the homosocial continuum that mandates heterosexuality.

15

The primary characteristic the Bellow hero shares with the nineteenth-century male autobiographers and other sorts of romantic individualists is his gynophobic tendency toward solipsism and monastic retreat. Bellow's twentieth-century American Dreamers are nearly always alone or engaged with other men, despite their periodic heterosexual erotic adventures. After having their unique speculative powers damaged by either the crassness of the world or destructive women, they seek solitude in which to reengage the spiritual quest. More often than not, like the classic nineteenth-century portrait of "Charles Reade in His Study," which prefaces Martin Danahay's book, the Bellow hero also seeks "a room of his own" where he engages in solitary metaphysical and humanistic contemplation, and in which nearly all traces of a grounding or supportive feminine are barely visible on the margins of his life.

Joseph, in *Dangling Man*, becomes the model for so many of the other protagonists. He is usually seen alone in the small apartment he shares with his working wife, talking to himself while he tries to avoid the larger social world of war and conscription. Though he is occasionally seen interacting with family, it is the male members he prefers to talk to, especially since he and Iva no longer confide in each other. After his brief sojourns out of the apartment, during which he primarily talks to men, he is mostly alone with his reading on the Enlightenment thinkers and romantic individualists. He believes in searching for the truth within and avoiding the contaminating experience of the world of affairs, though he seriously doubts that his inner resources are enough to sustain him. As for sexual affairs, his one dalliance is merely a brief interlude in response to boredom, after which he gladly returns to his room.

Asa Leventhal is also mostly alone in his room sans wife, who for almost the duration of the novel is visiting her parents. He speaks as little as possible to his brother's wife and mother-in-law, both of whom he suspects to be superstitious, hostile, and possibly mad. Thereafter, he talks mostly to other men, including his nemesis, Kirby Allbee. He is rarely happy in his work world of men and welcomes his outings with his young nephew, Philip. Although he does not exactly seek and cherish being alone, he chooses this situation by default because he is paranoid about the physical and emotional hostility of the outside world. It is with relief uncharacteristic of late Bellow heroes that he welcomes his wife at the end of the novel.

Augie is a solipsistic and romantic dreamer who, though he is engaged in the dynamic masculine world of the contemporary picaro, remains uncooptable, unattached, and emotionally celibate. He will engage in the world of affairs to a degree, but he will not immerse himself in its materialistic enterprises like his driven brother, Simon. He has found a space apart while remaining ostensibly within contemporaneity.

Tommy Wilhelm is not so much the solipsist as the child-man shorn of personal connection to a nurturing adult world. Battered in sensibility by a Hobbesian capitalistic world ruled by absurdist alienation ethics, he finally finds his space apart by mourning for others like himself deep in the New York subway and by attending the funeral of an absolute stranger.

Eugene Henderson, after abusing all his women (wives, mistress, daughter, and housekeeper), leaves the American continent in order to escape the insatiable inner voice screaming "I want, I want" and departs for the supposedly primitive innocence of an uncontaminated Africa. His progression throughout the novel is from one state of disencumberment to another. First he divests himself of mistresses, wives, and family at home. Then he pays off the extra native bearers and departs for the inner continent. Next he loses the society of Dahfu and Atti, and with it his chief hope of transcendental awareness. He is last seen, all but alone, dancing for joy on the polar icecap with his small, curly-headed Persian orphan. Though he is anxious to return to Lily and the kids, we suspect we have seen him reach his highpoint of social fulfillment as an orphan boy, alone at the North Pole.

Moses Herzog, much like Joseph, is also a scholar of romanticism and romantic individualism. He is mostly seen ousted from family and community, however, rushing about all over the city, or alone, in a manic state, writing letters to thinkers dead and alive, until he flees from friends, ex-wife, and mistresses all, to the silence of his ruined Ludeyville estate. Here, like latter-day deromanticized Thoreau, he is content to share space with owls and to sleep outside in an old hammock contemplating the magnificence of starry skies. It is monastic retreat from the social, intellectual, and financial chaos of his life.

Charlie Citrine is stamped from the same solipsistic mold as his precursors. Almost blasted in his poetic powers, he recalls the magnificent ruin of Humboldt and seeks to extricate himself from the legal and not-so-legal thieves and con men of the establishment. Finally evading his own squalling, disarrayed soul represented in his doppelgänger, Rinaldo Cantabile, as well as in the deathly temptations of erotic women like Renata, he is seen standing on his head, alone, in a Madrid hotel room. Representative of his spiritual state is the presence of the abandoned child, Roger, whose helplessness and nurturance he is now entirely responsible for. Charlie is last seen trying to reclaim that male homosocial family from the remnants of hangers-on from his original pseudofamily of childhood.

Artur Sammler is Bellow's most entrenched denizen of a "room of his own." Sammler has spent his life in the study, so to speak, with the exception of his experience during the Nazi Holocaust. Even then, he spends much of his time hiding in a tomb, sans light and human companionship. Now, despite his awareness of the goodness of such people as Elya Gruner and the belated realization that truth is to be found in social complicity, Sammler is terribly compelled, through historical precedent and personal habit, to stay in his own room reading only the writings of Meister Eckhardt and the prophets of the Bible. Previously, he enjoyed only the company of the handsome, manly, and intellectual Arkin. He is in misogynistic flight from contaminating women and misanthropic flight from violent and predatory men.

Dean Albert Corde seems almost a younger and less misanthropic version of Mr. Sammler. Like most men trained in the humanities, he is a would-be romantic individualist who is appalled by the atrocities of his age. We see him mostly alone in a room he shares with his wife, Minna. Keeping warm under her afghan, he is surrounded by a community of women from whom he is sexually and socially isolated as he considers the world of male fascists (political, scientific, and criminal) on both sides of the iron curtain. He is last seen watching himself as if in a mirror as he drives down Lakeshore Drive alone in his car.

Uncle Benn Crader and Kenneth Trachtenberg are also monastically inclined scholars whose metaphysical ruminations demand a room of their own. Kenneth still lives in a dorm with graduate students, while Uncle Benn occupies what are now bachelor quarters with plants and leather clubman's furniture. Both belong in the long tradition of Bellow's American Dreamers for whom too much erotic, financial, and social engagement damages their metaphysical powers. Certainly, both are happiest with their celibate community

18

of two, or else quite alone, away from damaged and damaging women. A virtual summa on romantic idealism and the male homosocial world, this novel reaches back to the concerns of *Dangling Man*, written over forty years before: how to sustain oneself spiritually from within while trying to deal with eroticism, women, history, and the demands of the social world without. Benn Crader is last seen hightailing it for the Pole and his beloved lichens. Kenneth is marrying Dita by default because his beloved mentor has fled and Treckie will not marry him.

With *A Theft*, it appears Bellow is breaking the pattern of the romantic individualist male through his use of Clara as the central protagonist. It is Ithiel Regler, however, whose denial of Clara's romantic idealism dominates the novella and works one more variation on the theme of unattachment and intellectual exceptionality characteristic of Bellow's egocentric male characters. Clara can be seen as one more romantic individualist done in reversed gender, whereas Ithiel, despite numerous marriages and affairs, is essentially preserving himself for his work and the world of male power brokers in Washington, D.C.

The unnamed narrator of *The Bellarosa Connection* must stand back from chaotic and contaminating people and affairs in order to weigh his historical, ethical, and metaphysical import. He, too, is seen primarily alone in his room conjuring up the past through his exceptional memory, as all the significant people in his life are now mostly memories of what his relationships with them might have been. Like all his forebears, he has paid a terrible price for his gifts and his autonomy. He is alone—meditating—the classic stance of the Bellow hero. As for Harry Trellman in *The Actual*, he has stood apart as listener and observer masking his feelings and failing in his attachments. Harry is in recovery from monestic retreat. Ravelstein is mostly connected to his old students via an electronic switchboard, while Chick has lived the solitary emotional life of a writer and scholar. In *Ravelstein*, Chick is accused by Ravelstein of being "inward" (40) and in need of rescue.

In addition to solitariness, there is a marked presence in each of the texts of pairs of competing men engaged in degenerating relationships. This presence is enacted through father-son relationships, the devices of the doppelgänger, blood brotherhood, literal pairs of biological brothers, male boon companionships, male business partnerships, and Platonic dialoguists—nearly all of which fail.

Thinking chronologically, one is put in mind of such obvious pairs as Asa Leventhal and Kirby Allbee, Tommy Wilhelm and Dr. Adler, Tommy Wilhelm and Tamkin, Augie and Simon March, Herzog and his brother Shura, Herzog and Valentine Gersbach, Charlie Citrine and his brother Julius, Charlie Citrine and Von Humboldt Fleisher, Charlie Citrine and Rinaldo Cantabile, Charlie Citrine and Pierre Thaxter, Kenneth Trachtenberg and Benn Crader, Benn Crader and Dr. Layamon, Harry Trellman and Sigmund Adletsky, and Chick and Ravelstein, to mention just a few. Of these only Harry Trellman and Old Adletsky survive as friends, as do Ravelstein and Chick.

Clearly these pairings are indicative of homosocial desire for enduring male companionship and its constant thwarting in the various Bellow texts. Interestingly, despite the fact that these mostly failed male/male relationships cause as much pain as, or more pain than, failed heterosexual relationships, Bellow's protagonists can be far more magnanimous about the failed male/male pairings. Heterosexual failure, in contrast, is likely to produce disproportionately more outrage, monastic withdrawal, and mistrust.

Paranoid fear of persecution by other men also characterizes Bellow's world of men. Joseph feels estranged from his male companions toward whom he projects mistrust and hostility and because of whom he experiences marked paranoia. By the time we see Asa Leventhal and Kirby Allbee, it is clear Bellow is describing developed paranoia. It is not accidental that so many of Bellow's characters display these symptoms, since Bellow demonstrates in *Herzog* that he is quite familiar with the clinical definition of the disease. The classic traits of paranoia, says Herzog, while trying to understand Madeleine, are "Pride, Anger, Excessive 'Rationality,' Homosexual inclinations, Competitiveness, Mistrust of Emotion, Inability to bear criticism, Hostile Projections, [and] Delusions" (*H* 77). Charlie Citrine sees all entrepreneurs and lawyers as the lowest level of society, the very underside of Chicago wolfpack masculinity. Characters such as Tomchek, Srole, Pinsker, Urbanovich, Flonzaley, Koffritz, and Stronson he describes as vultures who are trying to dismember him, heart, soul, and pocket book; he believes that Srole "would willingly chop [him] into bits with his legal cleaver" (*HG* 222) and that Cannibal Pinsker is a pure animal and "gut fighter" (220). Mr. Sammler and the black pickpocket also qualify, as do Harry Fonstein and Billy Rose.

Hypercharged male relationships range from the negative pairings already mentioned to positive ones involving the boon companionship of Henderson and Romilayu, or the serious acolyte-mentor relationship between Henderson and Dahfu. Initially, the relationship between Herzog and Valentine Gersbach is an important one to both men, despite its later collapse. The best example is the excited young Charlie Citrine, who goes to New York to find Von Humboldt Fleisher, a possible mentor. Mr. Sammler's relationship with the admired Arkin causes him to experience jealousy and extreme annoyance when Margotte, Arkin's wife, calls him "my man." Sammler feels that Arkin is *his* man because of their shared intellectual interests. When it is almost too late, Sammler realizes the failings of H. G. Wells, his early mentor, and the depth of the well-placed love he has for Elya Gruner. He rushes to the hospital only to find Elya dead. Kenneth Trachtenberg's whole life has been rearranged around that of his magical uncle, Benn Crader. Hence, his almost hysterical efforts to preserve Benn from women and keep him for himself and the main enterprise—metaphysics. Chick and Ravelstein are Platonic dialoguists, male intellectual companions and team teachers. They are even more intimately connected as biographer and subject. In the latter case the success of the male/male relationship between Chick and Ravelstein and Ravelstein and Nikki is the exception to the rule. However, since Ravelstein dies the relationships are not really tested.

Male bonding over the ruined carcass of a woman occurs with some frequency in these texts. We remember Mr. Sammler's disgust with Margotte's intelligence, which he condemns as ridiculous, "unmasculine," and merely an attempt at impersonating her husband. He admiringly describes Arkin's interruptions of Margotte's opinions as "virile" and delights in remembering the conspiracy of superior male intellect he and Arkin once erected against her. Both deride Margotte's "goodness," and both roar over Arkin's insulting remark that Margotte "was a first-class device as long as someone aimed her in the right direction" (*MSP* 19). He laughs to think that in order to live with Margotte, Arkin must have been "driven to erotic invention" (20). He remembers with pleasure the conversation he and Arkin once had about Arkin's women students at Hunter College: "Charming, idiotic, nonsensical girls. . . . Now and then a powerful female intelligence, but very angry, very complaining, too much sex-ideology, poor things" (16). Sammler adores "splendid" Arkin with his contemptuous indulgence of Margotte and his "half-bald head" with his "good subtle brain" (16).

This tendency to demonize women is most clearly illustrated, however, in Kenneth's cruel and misogynous depictions of crazy, scheming, sexually rapacious women who threaten to destroy his beloved mentor with their emotional difficulties and erotic needs. Kenneth is proud of his spiritual bond with Benn and does not intend to lose his place to a mere woman. "We were doubly, multiply, interlinked. Neither of us by now had other real friends" (*MDH* 15). Like a naughty schoolboy he wonders how Benn made out with Aunt Lena—a typically adolescent attempt at appropriation. He describes Caroline Bunge to Benn as "a big, graceful (old-style) lady, vampy, rich, ornate, slow-moving, a center-stage personality" (75). He describes her heavy use of make-up and writes her off as "a strange siren who took lithium or Elavil" (79). Della Bedell he presents to Benn as a weekend drinker full of belligerence and shrillness. He delights in relating to his audience the story of Benn's first Gogolian bridegroom flight from Della Bedell, which he says caused her to die of a heart attack brought on by sexual deprivation. On the plane trip to Tokyo, Benn's second bridegroom flight, Kenneth eagerly advances his project to secure Benn for himself and deconstruct woman for him once and for all. He explains to Benn that he (Benn) puts out spiritual emanations that attract women who are usually overeducated, girded-up by the expectations of their stage mothers, and living in outer metaphysical darkness. Matilda Layamon, his most recent and powerful rival for Benn's attentions, he calls a Rappaccini's daughter whose hope chest is full of cocaine and will probably bring death to her lover. He imagines her morning moods as ferocious, her teeth as sharp, and her character as bitchy. Kenneth calls Benn the Phoenix who is chased by arsonists. "As Uncle's self-appointed guardian spirit, I, too, had to try to interpret their motives and anticipate their plans" (188), he protests as these various women threaten to steal Benn and contaminate the joint metaphysical quest with their erotic powers.

Exaggerated heterosexual conquest features heavily in Bellow's texts. *The Adventures of Augie March* provides many examples of the role of an exaggerated heterosexuality in the life of the young protagonist. Eugene Henderson's amorous exploits from youth to late middle age are portrayed in *Henderson the Rain King*. First we are treated to the memorable vision of him stripped naked, shaved bald, and tied up as an example to the incoming troops at Palermo. Later we see him with various wives and mistresses and finally in Dahfu's harem. It is the depiction of this harem and Dahfu's explanation that he must perform nightly, or be killed, that provides Bellow's comment on this most extreme anthropological example of exaggerated heterosexuality.

Herzog, with his exotic mistresses, Sono and Ramona, is described as a victim of the droll sexual joke human nature has played on talented men. Then there is Alex Szathmar, who, not content with his own erotic adventures, participates vicariously in the affairs and divorce scandals of his clients. Charlie calls him and Alex "decaying squaw men" (*HG* 209) and sees that Alex is "still smitten with the old West Side sex malaria" of their adolescence (204). Alex, he notes, was capable of "a clumsy but unshakable sexual horsemanship atop pretty ladies" (207). He sums them both up as a pair of "cunt-struck doddering wooers left over from a Goldoni farce" (204). He accuses himself of exaggerated interest in big broads unsuitable for a small, warm-hearted man. Humboldt's exaggerated sexual fantasies are the funniest. Addressing the back street prostitute on the morning he believes he has secured the Princeton chair, he brags, "You don't know what you're missing. I'm a poet. I have a big cock," while the woman behind the door laughs (139). In his possessive jealousy over Kathleen, he follows her to the supermarket, beats her, steals her keys, accuses her of meeting other men, and finally tries running her down in the four holer, all the while engaging in lurid fantasies about her being kidnapped by a Rockefeller.

Myron Swiebel is Charlie, Alex, and George Swiebel's earliest role model in exaggerated heterosexuality. He teaches them as young boys that he owes his sexual vitality to steam baths, bourbon, gambling, and women. Rinaldo Cantabile, with his boots made of unborn calf, minklike furry mustache, and blood red upholstered Thunderbird, seems to be living out an exaggerated heterosexual fantasy by copying his goofy mafioso uncles, patronizing the slightly less swanky male couturiers of the inner city, and modeling his actions on old gangster movies while he courts his graduate student sexual playmate and other women. The ultimate roué, Rudi Trachtenberg, behaves so badly he finally drives his wife into seclusion in Africa. Kenneth describes his father's sexual appeal and exploits with anger. He talks of his classic cast-iron good looks, success with women, and ability to strut (*MDH* 24). He sees his father as a force of nature and is determined to "go beyond him," metaphysically speaking (12).

Mild degrees of sadomasochism, fetishism, acute misogyny, and marked homophobia are also part of Bellow's male homosocial world. His most thorough portrayal of this aspect of men's lives occurs in *Mr. Sammler's Planet*, along with an extended historical explanation of it. There is the portrait of Sammler's early mentor, H. G. Wells, as a "little, lower-class limey" (*MSP* 28) who, despite some admirable liberal views, expressed cruel contempt for women and blasted and cursed everyone. The elderly Sammler is aghast at Wells's disbelief in celibacy and his desire to prolong sexual activity into old age (71-72). He also recalls many of the great men of the Victorian age, who, like Wells, were obsessed with "the breasts, the mouths, and the precious sexual fluids of women" (28). He remembers, "Old Picasso was wildly obsessed by sexual fissures, by phalluses. In the frantic and funny pain of his farewell, creating organs by the thousands, perhaps tens of thousands. Lingam and Yoni" (66). Then he recalls an American president boastfully exposing himself to his cabinet.

Sammler also describes Walter Bruch's uncontrollable sexual fetishism for the arms of young Puerto Rican women as "old-fashioned," "Victorian sex suffering" (*MSP* 60). He discusses the Victorian generation, then and now, as being scarred with sex ideologies due to their entrapment in "a psychiatric standard" (45). He nastily tells Bruch: "Isn't it a comfort that there is no more isolated Victorian sex suffering? Everybody seems to have these vices and tells the whole world about them. By now you are even somewhat old-fashioned. Yes, you have an old nineteenth-century Krafft-Ebing trouble" (60). Sammler decides that "the sexual perplexities of a man like Bruch originated in the repressions of another time, in images of woman and mother that were disappearing. He himself, born in the old century and in the Austro-Hungarian Empire, could discern these changes" (60).

Bellow does not merely subconsciously represent the sexual deviations that were and are inevitably a part of Victorian male homosocialization. Through Mr. Sammler, who is clearly well read in Krafft-Ebing's case histories of Victorian sexual pathology, and

24

sexual fetishism in particular, Bellow establishes a history of the relationship between Victorian taboos and sexual pathology. For Sammler, women are intellectual pygmies, failed mothers, castrators, exotics, or whores, who must be driven out into the wilderness of contemporary Western culture to atone for its sins.

Bellow is very open about the intellectual, political, and cultural roots of misogyny, as well as its sexual and psychocultural manifestations. He deliberately depicts Sammler's social and intellectual acculturation as a classic late-Victorian inheritor of an ancient biblical tradition of misogyny. In short, Bellow is at great pains to provide the reader with a list of Sammler's mentors in misogyny by showing his upbringing as a petted male narcissist in the immediate post-Victorian Age, an era in which British and European nations were still secure in their national patriarchalism as the world's greatest colonizers and still some years away from the fall of Empire and the democratizing changes of World War II. The white, racist, Anglo-European male, elitist social caste systems of Europe still prevailed, and Sammler is described as born into a privileged caste in an age of supreme male triumph and vindication.

Worst in the gallery of misogynists is the appalling Dr. Layamon in *More Die of Heartbreak*, a cruel misogynist-voyeur who drags the horrified Benn through the female surgical ward, displaying to him "the stitched scars, and short thighs, and warm, shiny shins, the mound of Venus and the scanty hair—all those bald mounds" (*MDH* 287). Furthermore, he expounds his daughter's supposed adolescent sexual antics to Benn in such exaggerated detail one can only conclude he has spent a great deal of time fantasizing sexually about her. Jay Wustrin likes sexual arrangements involving threesomes, something Harry Trellman believes he has learned from reading Havelock Ellis.

Male hierarchies are also a feature of the world of American masculinity. They are most explicitly described in *Henderson the Rain King*, *Herzog*, and *Humboldt's Gift*. In *Henderson* we see a scale of Hemingwayesque macho men including Romilayu, Henderson, and Dahfu, as well as the native bearers. At the other end of the machismo scale is the skinny, dope-addicted, milk-drinking, whining Louie Lutz, (*H*) who is finally stripped of his safari gear in a ritual of disgrace and sent home to his mother.

In *Herzog*, Herzog reorders the European academic hierarchy of prestige through his impassioned, humanistic, epistolary critiques.

More explicit is the masculine social hierarchy he constructs after his experiences in court. On the bottom of the scale of depravity is Alex-Alice, the transvestite, who occupies the depths of degeneracy, matched only by the magistrate's abuse of his authority. Then there is the prostitute, Marie Poont, the semiretarded woman who has dashed out the brains of her three-year-old child, and the reclining lover who watched. In a contrasting ordering, Moses Herzog depicts noble old Herzogs in shawls alongside the gibbering hordes as described in Freud and Roheim. On yet another scale are romantic nihilists like Nachman and Laura, and other less dramatic evaders of reality like Tante Taube and Sandor Himmelstein, not to mention delightful Dionysians like Ramona and frightening paranoiacs like Madeleine. On the psychiatric scale are the Protestant Freudian, Dr. Edvig, followed by a descending order of neurotics, maniacs, and perverts.

In *Humboldt's Gift* we see two classes of developers—fat, flashy Ulick and the Hilton at one end, and the Cubans at the other. Fat Ulick is shown in a flaming blue silk shirt, stuffing his face with smoked marlin like a greedy shark and tossing handfuls of peanuts into the back seat of his car. Charlie describes him as a "demonic billionaire clown," a robber baron with a "Business Week Face" (*HG* 391), preoccupied with "capitalistic fugues" (402). The Cuban developers are newer, sleeker, nonwhite Johnny-come-latelys with their golf, racing, twin-engined planes, clothes, and athletic ability. On the bottom end of the legal and financial scale is the legal tribe of Cannibal Pinsker, the very underside of Chicago wolfpack masculinity, featuring such characters as Tomchek, Srole, Pinsker, Urbanovich, Flonzaley, Koffritz, and Stronson. On the Hollywood lineup, John Wayne and his gentlemanly Western glamor contrasts wildly with the foolishly stoic, mean little "Rumpelstiltskin" character Tigler (367), a tough, dishonest, and tantrum-throwing racist bronco-buster who likes "to stick and screw people" (367). Charlie ranks the dozens of men like these whom he has known in a variety of periods in his life. With Humboldt, he remembers a sordid rich elite of his young days comprised of:

> Peaches and Daddy Browning, Harry Thaw, and Evelyn Nesbitt, plus the Jazz Age, Scott Fitzgerald's, and the super-rich. Humboldt who even had the heiresses of Henry James down cold. Capitalists and politicians appear to be ranked

> also, as Charlie describes himself, in his phoniest period,
> in the company of an American power elite, "revolving
> elliptically over the city of New York in that Coast Guard
> Helicopter, with two U.S. Senators and the Mayor and
> officials from Washington and Albany and crack journalists,
> all belted up in puffy life jackets, each jacket with its
> sheath knife." (112)

Jewish old-world gentlemen like his Russian immigrant father, and
now elderly neighborhood men from his childhood like Menasha
and Waldemar, come out on the top of his scale, presumably
because of their *menschlikeit*.

In terms of women, Charlie reverses his recent rankings of tall,
blonde, big-busted *shiksas* in favor of his neighborhood first love,
Naomi Lutz. Among poets and writers he pays tribute to the considerable talents of Humboldt, though he sees that the hierarchies
of hypermasculine capitalist America have done them all in. His
spiritual ranking involves the now fallen poet, against whose initial
promise are ranked divorce lawyers, legal pimps, hucksters, physical
culturists, real estate princes, and mafiosi.

Within the ranks of the mafia, Charlie confesses his admiration
of the elegant, gentlemanly mafia boss, Langobardi, in preference to
the lower echelons occupied by Rinaldo Cantabile and his goofy
mafioso uncles. Langobardi is the princely elegant crook become
gentleman. Charlie admires him for keeping his hands clean and
avoiding rough talk. He notes with awe that Langobardi dresses
better than any board chairman with his ingeniously lined jackets
and paisley waist coats. Charlie is sure he has the "periscope power
of seeing around corners" (*HG* 69). Thinking of the Battaglias and
Murray the Camel of his childhood, Charlie says, "He was manly, he
had power. In his low voice he gave instructions, made rulings, decisions, set penalties, probably" (69). At the other end of this scale are,
of course, uncouth, greedy thugs like Rinaldo Cantabile, who is possessed of a flashy mistress, car, and overcoat. As he loosens his
bowels in the bathhouse in an attempt to humiliate and frighten
Charlie, Charlie wonders if he is having "fantasies of savagery and
monstrosity" (83) and thinks of the pyramids of Egypt and the
Gardens of Ashurbanipal. "It was like water seeking its level, or
like gravitational force," he remarks (84). Despite the unflattering
comparisons, Charlie decides Cantabile can be compared only with

Kohler, Yerkes, and Zuckerman's apes at the London zoo—primitive on the evolutionary scale, comic, and vulgar. Invoking a historical lineage for Cantabile, Charlie says on an evolutionary scale, "He had reached the stage reached by bums, con men, freeloaders, and criminals in France in the eighteenth century, the stage of the intellectual creative man and theorist" (174). Charlie also compares George Swiebel's ancient masculine vitalism, acted out in the Russian bathhouses of his old neighborhood, with the machismo and the contemporary vitalism of the physical culturists of the modern health clubs. Here, Eastern European Jewish immigrants acted out their ancient, barely remembered codes of masculinity. It is a place "where men are as nude as troglodytes of Stone Age Adriatic caverns and sit together dripping and red, like sunset in a mist." The "steam bath was the last refuge in the burning forest where hostile animals observed a truce and the law of fang and claw was suspended" (195). Clearly, Harry Trellman feels both culturally superior to the multitrillionaire, Sigmund Adletsky, and much his junior in a power structure dominated by both money and intellect.

On the cultural index, there is the early Humboldt and his unspoiled acolyte, Charlie, at one end of the scale, and Pierre Thaxter at the other. Unlike Humboldt and Charlie, he is a pseudo-academic, androgynous charlatan who offers himself as an Hegelian Whitmanesque world individual.

On the academic versus capitalistic scale is Charlie's one-time "culture Prince," Durnwald, the professor's professor, his long-time intellectual companion. Charlie has now rejected him and others like him as desiccated academy intellectuals who have not only missed out on poetry, but have done so much less flamboyantly than the racketeers and thieves of the financial and political establishments. On a more positive note there is Chick playing niaf to Ravelstein's basso profundo.

On the scale of physical culturists are the genuine athletes at one end of rankings and the small, sensitive Charlie at the other end, who entertains absurd fantasies about his athletic prowess. Looking back at himself, Charlie cringes at remembrance of his bout with health foods and at his being taken off the racket ball court by the coach and being told to slow down: "Still, night after night, I kept dreaming that I had become the best player in the club, a racquet demon, that my backhand shot skimmed the left wall of the court and fell dead in the corner, it had so much English on it. I dreamed that I was beating all the best players—all those skinny, hairy, speedy fellows who in reality avoided playing with me because I was a dud" (*HG* 109).

The hierarchy of power between poetry and science is also staged in novel after novel. "But a poet can't perform a hysterectomy or send a vehicle out into the solar system. Miracle and power no longer belong to him" (*HG* 118). Masculine hierarchizing tendencies are summed up in the larger politico-social hierarchy that issues forth from the outraged Mr. Sammler:

> The labor of Puritanism now was ending. The dark satanic mills changing into light satanic mills. The reprobates converted into children of joy, the sexual ways of the seraglio and of the Congo bush adopted by the emancipated masses of New York, Amsterdam, London. Old Sammler with his screwy visions! He saw the increasing triumph of Enlightenment—Liberty, Fraternity, Equality, Adultery! Enlightenment, universal education, universal suffrage, the rights of the majority acknowledged by all governments, the rights of women, the rights of children, the rights of criminals, the unity of the different races affirmed, Social Security, public health, the dignity of the person, the right to justice—the struggles of three revolutionary centuries being won while the feudal bonds of Church and Family weakened and the privileges of the aristocracy (without any duties) spread wide, democratized, especially the libidinous privileges, the right to be uninhibited, spontaneous, urinating, defecating, belching, coupling in all positions, tripling, quadrupling, polymorphous, noble in being natural, primitive, combining the leisure and luxurious inventiveness of Versailles with the hibiscus-covered erotic ease of Samoa. (*MSP* 33)

Sammler is chronically elitist in his class consciousness and believes social anarchy will result in dismantling old hierarchies.

Violence and murderous resentment between men is also a part of these homosocial relationships: Asa Leventhal; Tommy Wilhelm and Tamkin; Herzog and Gersbach; Charlie Citrine and Humboldt; Mr. Sammler, Eisen, and the black pickpocket; the Lester murders; the story of Rufus Ridpath; and the Colonel and his violent counterparts in the fascist regime of Eastern Europe. Then there are all of Ravelstein's famously cultivated enemies and Chick's self-confessed thought murders.

Mapping of the feminine or childlike qualities or both onto defeated male opponents or, conversely, much-admired men is another feature of Bellow's homosocial world. Both are equally in evidence in Bellow's novels. Tommy Wilhelm (*SD*) is financially stripped and kept on the short end of the family purse in subjection to his domineering father. Then he is financially stripped by the wily Tamkin and the sickening Rappaport. His responses are to whine, beg, and cry. Louie Lutz is (*HR*) Bellow's depiction of a pathetic second and third generation Jewish-American male who cannot compete with Myron Swiebel or even the Hendersons of the world. Raised in the ethnic neighborhood of his immigrant grandparents, the pathetic Louie has fallen victim to assimilation. He is a skinny dope addict from the Chicago neighborhoods, an arrested, self-indulgent child who is sent by his desperate mother to learn an appropriate masculine role from George Swiebel while on safari in Africa. Unfortunately for Louie, George is an unusable model. Louie cries constantly for milk and fresh fruit, grabs off the best food, pesters Leo (one of the native bearers) to tell him the Swahili for "motherfucker," and entertains lewd notions about supposed black men's secret cults. He is Bellow's version of Portnoy. When George defrocks him of his safari kit and prepares to send him home to his mother, he watches in bewilderment as the mother-hating Louie buys his mother a Masai spear for a gift. Louie is not only feminized but infantilized also.

Rinaldo Cantabile (*HG*) is a feminized Circe who lures swine to their deaths, while Pierre Thaxter *(HG)* is a feminized, flamboyant dandy. He is Bellow's representative—a liberated, modern, pseudopoet, an androgynous parody of Pierre Thaxter, not the Hegelian world individual he would like to be seen as.

Wallace (*MSP*), whom Sammler notes with puzzlement "nearly became a physicist, he nearly became a mathematician, nearly a lawyer . . . nearly an engineer, nearly a Ph.D. in behavioral science. . . . nearly an alcoholic, nearly a homosexual" (*MSP* 88), is a goofy anarchist boy Bakunin in water who floods his father's house looking for mob money. Previously, he has accidentally ended up entering Russia on a horse and is detained by the police in Soviet Armenia. It takes his father five visits to a U.S. Senator to obtain his release. Added to this is the foolish Mason, Corde's nephew (*DD*), whom Corde describes as ungraceful, weak, intellectually confused, unimpressive in argument, and skinny.

On the more positive side, Dean Corde is the admirable male character onto whom are mapped some of Bellow's most positive feminine characteristics. He is depicted as thoughtful and compassionate with Valeria's aging process, genuinely moved by her imminent death and willing to do the nurturing that Minna seems unable to do. Charlie Citrine (*HG*) also ends up with many feminine qualities assigned to him. He nurtures little Roger for several days, cutting up his meat at dinnertime and taking him for walks in the park. He turns back to two elderly men, Waldemar and Menasha, in a warm, nurturing way and lovingly reburies Humboldt. Likewise, Henderson, who has banished Ricey's baby, adopts one of his own in the Persian orphan boy he brings home with him. He learns to place value on the wisdom of women with Willatele and her sister Mtalba. He learns to forgo his wretched "ugly Americanism" over the abortive frog pond episode and becomes much more gentle in his apprenticeship with Dahfu and Atti, the lioness. His abusiveness toward women finally gives way to respect and a relinquishing of macho behaviors.

Homosexual repression as symptom of male homosociality is seen most overtly when Rinaldo Cantabile (*HG*) seeks a homosexual bond with Charlie to cement a proposed business partnership. After forcing Charlie to witness his defecation in a public toilet and beating Charlie's beautiful silver Mercedes supposedly over his refusal to pay off a gambling debt, Rinaldo finds out all about Charlie's divorce miseries and offers to be his manager. Failing this, he offers Charlie his mistress, the voluptuous Polly Palomino. When Charlie fails to take this bait, Rinaldo grabs Charlie's electric razor and shaves himself with it, handing it back to Charlie, warm and uncleaned. He follows Charlie to the bathroom and threatens, "You better not reject me" (*HG* 183). Charlie is horrified at Cantabile's proposal for three-way sexual antics and calls it "a filthy sexual circus." The coordinates of desire here involve sexual connection, male bonding, and financial partnership, which, Charlie says, is the way Chicagoans tell you they love you. This desire is also about Rinaldo's wanting to assimilate class from Charlie. Bellow depicts sexuality and capitalism in the modern age through the metaphor of cannibalism. The only seriously hinted at homosexual relationship in Bellow's novels is that between Nikki and Ravelstein.

Women are clearly functioning here as objects of exchange in these masculine power-bonding transactions.

Alex Szathmar is another dubious male friend, who, while advising Charlie on his divorce, says:

> All your achievements, your knack with words, your luck—because you've been lucky. What I could have done with that! And you had to marry that yenta West Side broad from a family of ward politicians and punchboard gamblers of candy-store kikes and sewer inspectors. That pretentious Vassar girl! Because she talked like a syllabus, and you were dying for understanding and conversation and she had culture. And I who love you, who always loved you, you stupid son of a bitch, I who have had this big glow for you since we were ten years old, and lie awake nights thinking: how do I save Charlie now; how do I protect his dough; find him tax shelters; get him the best legal defense; fix him up with good women. Why you nitwit, you low-grade moron, you don't even know what such love means. (*HG* 208)

Getting Charlie "things," money, and women is how Alex establishes male bonding. The women he procures for Charlie, like the money, function as an exchange that cements the relationship between the two men.

The presence of a shamanistic character who mediates male-female relationships in male homosocial relations is also featured in Bellow's work. There is also the bogus Dr. Edvig (*H*), Herzog's psychiatrist who mediates his relationship with Madeleine, followed by the phony Tamkin (*SD*) with his pagoda-like shoulders and magical powers of deception, who, in solving Tommy's financial problems, will help mediate his relationships with Margaret and Olive. One thinks also of Alex Szathmar (*HG*) and his constant intriguing and pimping in the name of divorce lawyering. It is Valentine Gersbach, appropriately named, who attempts, through cuckoldry, to mediate the relationship between Herzog and Madeleine. The Senora is one of the funniest intermediaries, with her foreignness and unclear origins. Sammler, the prophet, attempts to mediate the romance between Angela and Horicker. The goofiest parody of a shamanistic intermediary with women, however, has to be Kenneth Trachtenberg (*MDH*) in his attempt to mediate all of Benn's relationships with women. Sorella Fonstein (*BR*) is a shamanistic character with mysterious spiritual powers and serious emanations who mediates the relationship between Harry Fonstein and Billy Rose, while the decidedly nonmystical Sigmund Adletsky plays cupid to Harry and Amy. Significantly it is Ravelstein who is the intermediary between Chick and Rosamund *(R)*.

Creation of a pseudopatriarchal family out of leftovers and remnants of solitary males is also characteristic of the male homosociality Bellow describes. This is seen in Charlie's reconnection with Menasha, Waldemar Wald, and Humboldt. Clearly, his girlfriend, Renata, has no place in this old circle of male friends and relatives, including friends like George Swiebel and the neighborhood immigrant fathers Waldemar, Menasha, and even Humboldt (*HG*).

The bisexual designation of the poetic imaginary is also demonstrated in *Humboldt's Gift* and in *More Die of Heartbreak*. This orphic, romantic readiness and sensibility are gendered feminine in Bellow's texts. Charlie Citrine, older and more chastened after his meditations on Humboldt's loss of poetic powers and his own failure to keep his, now comes to understand that it is a Protestantized hypermasculine American capitalism that has all but blasted the poetic realm. Through his rich taxonomy of destructive American alter egos, Charlie is able to see that such a culture has gendered the poetic imaginary as outside its definitions of masculinity. Therefore, men like Poe, Humboldt, and Charlie must rediscover their animas, the female realm within themselves, in order to preserve their powers. The synthesis of capitalism and poetry has not worked in Humboldt's case: "He intended to be a divine artist, a man of visionary states and enchantments, Platonic possession. He got a Rationalistic, Naturalistic education at CCNY. This was not easily reconciled with the Orphic. . . . He wanted . . . to prove that the imagination was just as potent as machinery, to free and to bless humankind. But he was out also to be rich and famous" (*HG* 119).

More dramatically, Charlie observes that Humboldt wanted to bring "Coney Island into the Aegean and [unite] Buffalo Bill with Rasputin. He was going to join-together the Art sacrament and the Industrial USA as equal powers" (*HG* 119). As Charlie sees it, the failure was in trying to join outer America with inner America, action with contemplation, or, symbolically speaking, the hypermasculine world with its estranged feminine counterpart. Yet mired as he is in typically Chicago "sex malaria," thuggery, threats, scams, divorce lawyers, legal pimps, physical culturists, and real estate princes, Charlie realizes that America has overcome that which signifies the feminine—a "school thing, a skirt thing, a church thing," called poetry (118). Against a model of the Jungian animus in harmony with the anima, Charlie Citrine tells a cautionary tale about an advanced industrial nation that has destroyed the feminine side of its national psyche—the side that Bellow defines as nature, art, contemplation, imagination, music, family feeling, fatherly love, and true brotherhood.

It naturally follows that, given these dynamics of male homosociality, a thwarted desire for enduring male friendship will ensue. One only has to think of Joseph's (*DM*) failed relationships with both his wife and all of the men with whom he comes in contact. In his case, there is a failure of homosociality. Asa (*TV*) fails also in learning the rules of homosociality but nevertheless absorbs its values. Most of his relationships with men cause him paranoia and prevent masculine bonding. His gratitude at his wife's return may suggest more about his failure in the world of men than it does any particular marital success. It would seem that Asa's desire is for a world of men, better even than his friend Harkavy, with whom he can enjoy trust and bonding. Symbolic of this thwarted desire is his failed relationship with his much more adept brother, Max. Augie (*AM*) ends up successfully negotiating the masculine world but resolved to maintain his autonomy.

Henderson (*HRK*) is only too successful within the masculine world, for he is the character through whom it is parodied so brilliantly. He fails with women, however, and is likely to go on failing because his greatest desire has been focused on Dahfu, whose friendship and love he has prized above that of any woman. In his case, death produces this thwarted desire for male friendship. Herzog (*H*) cannot find his way in the world of men and retreats from it, shocked at its violence. Neither is he reconciled to a feminine world. We finally see him in retreat from both. Charlie Citrine (*HG*) never has relationships that come close to supplanting that unfinished, unreconciled relationship with Humboldt. He casts off all his erotic entanglements in order to repossess himself and, by extension, Humboldt. Charlie's desire at the end of the novel is to symbolically re-create his ruptured blood brotherhood with Humboldt and to reclaim Waldemar, Humboldt's uncle, and Menasha, the old neighborhood friend of his boyhood, as an all-male pseudofamily. He even moves Humboldt's dead body back to the old neighborhood. Humboldt might be physically absent in that death, but at least his grave can be moved.

Mr. Sammler has never remarried and clearly has never learned to take seriously either his dead wife or his disturbed daughter. He prefers male intellectuals (many of whom are long dead) and the manly Arkin. At the end of this novel, his desire is toward acknowledging his love and admiration for Elya Gruner. His living daughter inspires more unfatherly sexual speculation and patriarchal disapproval than the type of deep love and affection Sammler directs toward Elya. His desire for Elya, however, is defeated by death. Dean Corde (*DD*) is surrounded by fascists of all sorts with whom it is impossible to form any enduring male friendship. Rufus Ridpath is black and in a different line of business. Dewey Spangler has sold out on unmediated truth, his nephew Mason is a washout, and there is really no one else. Neither is he really connected with his childlike, preoccupied wife, or the community of women who have surrounded Valeria. His vision through the Mount Palomar telescope suggests that his final desire is toward some unknown God. But he sees only reflections of entities refracted across thousands of light years.

Kenneth's (*MDH*) homosocial desire, first for his father, Rudi Trachtenberg, and then for Benn Crader, is thwarted at the end of this novel. So, too, are the relationships he still cherishes with the intellectuals of his father's circle, people now all dead. He will marry Dita Schultz out of pity and admiration for her sadic face sanding and because Benn, who has long been the object of his personal and metaphysical desire, is gone for an indefinite period.

Bellow's most detailed account of failed male friendship has to be that of Harry Fonstein and Billy Rose (*BC*), a failure that not even the resourceful and mysterious Sorella can mediate. The pattern is only broken slightly in the focus the anonymous male narrator places on the lost possibility of a relationship with Sorella Fonstein, whom he finally realizes to be more metaphysically valuable than any of his male acquaintances. Chick's desire for a Platonic intellectual companionship with Ravelstein must finally be satisfied through Ravelstein's student, Rosamund, and the writing of his biography after his death.

The textual production of female sexuality as punishing and destructive is one of the final characteristics of male homosociality. It is a particularly interesting dynamic because it is clear that there are ample failed male bondings to account for the majority of grief Bellow's protagonists feel. Ironically, however, it is in the realm of female betrayal that they project most of their anger. Joseph is less than enthusiastic about either his wife or his mistress. Augie March suffers at the hands of Thea Fenchel, who wants to train a hunting falcon to be vicious and rejects him when he fails the test. Tommy Wilhelm's wife, Margaret, is the precipitating factor in his dismemberment. We see her acting only in her role as "bitch" trying to bully and extract money from him. Herzog's ex-wife Madeleine is described as a murderous paranoiac. She has colluded with Valentine Gersbach to cuckold him. Ramona is a deathly sexual priestess from whom he runs away. Charlie Citrine is nearly derailed by another equally deathly priestess, Renata. Mr. Sammler feels surrounded by dirty whores. He hates Margotte for her sexuality, condemns his niece Angela for her erotic adventures, and fantasizes about his wavering-witted daughter's supposed sexual liaisons. He even thinks unkindly about his long-dead wife's socioerotic responses. Dean Corde's wife, Minna, withdraws from him at crucial soul-searching moments, leaving him feeling lonely, misunderstood, and even parental. *More Die of Heartbreak* is full of destructive, shrewish, and erotically deadly females such as Caroline Bunge, Della Bedell, Treckie, and Matilda Layamon. Also featured are the self-destructive women like Dita and like Mrs. Rudi Trachtenberg, who renounces sexuality and her responsibilities as a mother and takes the drastic measure of entering an order of nuns in Africa.

It appears that Bellow has produced mostly androcentric, single-voiced texts that silence and exclude the voices of femininity. Alone in their various rooms, these male monologists hold up their respective mirrors in which to examine the object, only to be taken in by their own pretense of autosufficiency. Monastic by instinct, unable to sustain permanent relationships with women and children, they speak themselves into endless monologues, thus foreclosing the very thing they most desire—their feminine other—as they pursue male homosociality.

3

THOSE DREADFUL
MOTHERS

If a writer has to rob his mother, he will not hesitate: the "Ode on
a Grecian Urn" is worth any number of old ladies.
                                    —William Faulkner, *Lion in the Garden*

The androcentric text, by its very nature, is rarely able to see the
feminine. In Bellow's middle to later novels in particular,
however, even his most narcissistic monologists experience a melancholic absence, a place of emptiness, or an abyss that draws them to
seek that missing element of the feminine which is symbolized in
the Bellow text as the soul, the anima, the spirit of being, poetry,
genuine feeling, the transcendental, or a literal woman.

Yet for all their yearning, these protagonists both seek and evade
literal women who, as they are represented to us, quickly become
only the women of androcentric representation. The maternal,
mother matter, or maternal ground of the male protagonists'
masculine physical and spiritual existence is erased or hidden from
view, its only trace a nostalgically constructed sense of absence or
lack in the Bellow text, a lack that then animates the comic quest
of the Bellow protagonists.

Ironically, then, it is the Bellow monologist's narcissistic representation of his own masculine subjectivity that inevitably results in
the erasure of the feminine in these mostly male-voiced monoglossias. As the male monologist fills the narrative with a constant
recounting of his impressions, his remembered events, or his
historical experience, he is able only to delineate who he is, where he

is, and what he is talking about. Others whose presence is necessary to him he locates according to his own need. Through such an apparently seamless staging of the male subjectivity, all other voices are virtually preempted. Thus he creates the feminine absence he can rarely name, but almost always mourns because women in Bellow's novels are severely tailored to the androcentric desire and are contained almost entirely within the masculine gaze of the protagonist.[1]

It is this policing, egocentric voice engaged in self-representation (and much feminine misrepresentation) in Bellow's novels that constructs the patterns of masculinity and femininity these books simultaneously reveal and suppress. More specifically, it is the textual or semiotic apparatus of tripled masculine "looks" of the protagonist, the narratee, and the sympathetic reader that enable the kind of readerly voyeurism which feeds on the stereotypical women that recur in Bellow's novels. For some readers there is the ego ideal represented by the narrator or monologist with whom he or she identifies. Readerly desire, then, contributes to the doubling, if not tripling, of its effects. The alternative is a resisting reading, producing a rupture within the reading subject and the text that can be produced either by the inability of some readers to make this ego ideal identification or their deliberate choice not to.

Bellow's novels, however, are more complex and self-aware in their understanding of gender than are many androcentric novels. Bellow and several of his monologists seem to sense the nature of the melancholic absence that haunts them, even to the extent of locating the problem within their own masculine subjectivity. And even though they control the narrative gaze, traces of the feminine inevitably erupt. Sometimes the male protagonists actually recognize it, and sometimes they barely apprehend its possibility. Regardless, their common search for this elusive feminine is usually foreclosed by their joint failures to unthink their own imprisoning masculinities. For these same reasons, it could be said that masculinity in the Bellow text is also imagined poorly by the egocentric monologist. For all that he speaks, he rarely speaks himself. Rather, he speaks incessantly *about* himself according to the cultural pattern of the sequestered romantic individualist-dreamer who longs for solitude, autosufficiency, and mystical powers. Enclosed within such a social construction, as well as within the typically worldly masculinity he also inhabits, he frequently succeeds in erasing an undiscovered part of his own masculinity as well as much of femininity in what amounts to a double movement of human loss. Throughout every novel, from *Dangling Man* to *The Bellarosa Connection*, *The Actual*, and *Ravelstein*, the male protagonist attempts to untangle his own social construction by trying to reclaim the lost feminine within himself.[2] In *Ravelstein's* case it is his significant other, Nikki.

Such storytelling as Bellow's produces the figure of woman cut mainly to the dimensions of the masculine symbolic. Just as in narrative cinema, woman in the Bellow novel is very often framed by the look of the male protagonist as an icon, a cut-out, the object of the male gaze, and even as a spectacle. It is an image made by a male writer and a male narratee mostly for the consumption of a male spectator/reader. The male protagonist, the bearer of the spectator's look, empowered by both a male narratee and a complicitous male reader, controls the events of the narrative by passing this look back and forth between men in a collusive trafficking in woman. This effectively triples the scopic drive of the novels in its textual and readerly production of woman as object.[3]

But phallocentric representations of woman in the Bellow text have a habit of breaking down. Despite the protective policing of representation within the masculine symbolic economy, she always threatens to escape from the protagonist's look and become real outside of an isomorphic male imaginary. Hence, the elaborate narrative strategies employed by the androcentric text for her containment, concealment, or complete erasure. In order to find the displaced or relegated feminine in the margins of the Bellow texts, we must look elsewhere and differently, there where there is no spectacle, as Cixous suggests.[4] It is behind the spectacle produced by phallocentric representation of woman, somewhere in that elsewhere in the shadows and margins of the texts, that her traces may occasionally be seen.

A relatively large number of women are present in Bellow's texts. They are, however, built around a few disappointingly familiar stereotypes. The majority of them function as silent bit players or as prisoners on the scene of representation. Though many of them are as brilliantly imagined as any characters created by Hogarth or Dickens, and often much funnier, few of them are heard speaking in their own voices. More important, none, not even Clara Velde, speaks herself into an equivalent female subjectivity. Despite a few spectacular voicings here and there, they remain more spoken about than speaking, despite their sharp tongues, keen minds, impressive educations, distinctive personalities, and saving insights. Such remarkable creations as Grandma Lausch, Charlotte Magnus, Anna Coblin, Thea Fenchel, Madeleine Pontritter, Tante Taube, Renata Koffritz, Matilda Layamon, Treckie, Clara Velde, and Sorella Fonstein are unforgettable. Nevertheless, these women characters are mostly variations on the recurring images found in the traditional masculine representational economy. It is not that women are more negatively portrayed than the male characters. When men are negatively portrayed in the Bellow novel, however, the actual portrayals are not usually built on a narrow series of stereotypes as are the portrayals of women. Neither are they portrayed as disempowered or emptied of metaphysical content as are the stereotypical women. When Bellow's men fall from grace, they do not fall out of his sympathy or tolerance.

Furthermore, the male monologist exercises a very different kind of representational power when he creates negative stereotypes of women than when he creates a broad variety of negative representations of men. The difference lies in power relations between the genders, the larger historical representation of gender in Western culture, and the relationship between representation and social structures that these texts circulate and reinscribe.

Mothers, wives, mistresses, elderly women, sisters-in-law, and sexual consorts comprise the majority of Bellow's female characters, and only rarely do we see them outside of the emotional economy of the male protagonists' needs. There are, however, those female characters whose outlines do not fit within this bankrupt representational economy and, conversely, those who suggest the excess, multiplicity, and trace of a femininity. Their presence, sometimes literal and sometimes only a melancholic absence, always hovers around edges of Bellow's texts, suggesting that not all can be contained and controlled within the androcentric text.

The male protagonists' mothers include their biological mothers (living and dead), mothers-in-law, stepmothers, and surrogate mothers. One is immediately struck by the male protagonists' ambivalence toward these women. The feelings range everywhere from severe pity to contempt, hostility, revulsion, mistrust, great good humor, and love. As a group, however, the previously mentioned women are generally mentally inadequate, emotionally unstable, cunning, untrustworthy, scheming, coarse, physically grotesque, whorish, or decaying. Ultimately, they are repulsive or pitiable in the eyes of these fastidious, narcissistic protagonists. These women constitute that rejected mother, mother matter, or maternal ground and have been relegated to the realm of nature, whose rot and chaos threaten to contaminate the male protagonists' attempts to transcend it. They are typically of nature—gross, malformed, poorly socialized, mentally and spiritually inadequate, neurotic, decaying, dirty, irrational, promiscuous, loud, vengeful, destructive, and subversive. They are that untrustworthy maternal ground that always threatens to engulf the protagonist's body, strip him of higher resolves, overwhelm him with its erotic powers, undermine his aesthetic sensibilities, make inordinate demands on his material and emotional resources, strip him of his illusions of self-sufficiency, and threaten him with bodily decay. The male protagonist blames them for bestowing upon him an inadequate genetic endowment, or even for their absence. Above all, they threaten to fetter him in his quest for metaphysical abstractions.

We do not hear about Joseph's (*DM*) own mother, but we do see his revulsion and resentment of his mother-in-law, Mrs. Almstadt. He says he has always disliked her because she is foolish and unknowing (*DM* 19), not to mention babbling, tedious, oblivious, and ugly. He hates her thick face powder, her wrinkles, and her bathroom full of face packs and lotions (20). He is appalled by her constant talking on the phone and asks his father-in-law how he has ever managed to stick with her. He cannot tell whether she is malicious or merely guileless.

Asa Leventhal's (*TV*) dead mother arouses fear, hatred, and mistrust in him. With narcissistic anger he remembers her face as distracted and mad-looking, with nothing in it that is directed toward him. Her absence is coupled with a sense of his own erasure and is linked in the reader's mind with his condition of paranoia, "He dreaded [her face]; he dreaded the manifestation of anything resembling it in himself" (*TV* 46). Neither has he "forgotten his mother's screaming" (*TV* 47). Later he will project this instability and madness onto his sister-in-law, Elena, and her mother.

Augie (*AM*) loves his mother, Rebecca, but knows she has been morally compromised since he and his brother seem to be the random by-blows of a passing salesman. She is simple minded, meek, easily commanded, and gentle. He also remembers her as round-eyed, tall, and toothless. She wears circular glasses, ravelly coat sweaters, and men's shoes without strings on her large feet (*AM* 4). She is virtually a servant to Grandma Lausch, is bullied terribly by Simon, and is only intermittently attended to by Augie (3–4). Not even Grandma Lausch's dog treats her with respect.

Augie, however, has two more surrogate mothers, Grandma Lausch and Anna Coblin. Despite his obvious love for them both and the welter of comic detail with which he describes them, his misogynous gaze is not lost. He calls Grandma a Machiavelli of neighborhood politics, a plotter, a despot, a fierce contestant, who commands, governs, schemes, advises, and intrigues in all languages (*AM* 5). He describes her playing cards with "palatal catty harshness and sharp gold in her eyes" (5). His funniest terms for her include "Eastern Great Llama" and "pouncy old hawk of a Bolshevik" (10–12). He is highly amused by her masculine smoking, her autocratic manner, and her fascinating combination of guile and malice (10–12), and he laughs at her self-designation as "intelligentsia." When she dies, he sees her as a pitiful fallen Pharaoh or Caesar and notes how old, powerless, and pathetic she has become. Although his heart goes out to her, realizing what she has meant to them in former years and how much they took her for granted, he can see her only as a pathetic old woman.

Periodically, Augie is sent to stay with Anna Coblin, his mother's cousin. She is one of nature's gross aberrations, according to his depiction of her. Although he has great affection for her, he is repelled by her physicality. She has, coupled with great size and energy, moles, blebs, hairs, and bumps of all kinds. She has a burning, morose face and a voice crippled by weeping and asthma. He describes her lying in bed with compresses, towels, and rags, cursing her enemies extravagantly, swollen, fire-eyed, her face framed in a "terrific" halo of red hair (*AM* 16–19). Augie remembers with great irony "she had the will of a martyr to carry a mangled head in paradise until doomsday, in the suffering mothers band led by Eve and Hannah" (16–17). In his eyes "she is in a desert pastoral condition of development and not up to the fancy stage of Belshazzar's feasts of barbaric later days" (22). He comments on her religious excesses and remembers that she was "a strong believer in eating" (21). She is also a filthy housekeeper who spends much of the day "shouting incomprehensibly on the telephone" (19). Her kitchen religion and hilariously distorted renderings of biblical stories amuse him, as does her strong grasp of her husband's business affairs.

Augie's description of Mrs. Renling is worse. He describes her as a lustful old woman who bribes him with elegant clothes while he squires her around. Augie thinks she is "dotty," a false "flatterer" with "ungentle eyes" and "a smarting, all-interfering face" (*AM* 135). He despises her for her grievances, antipathies, doomedness, and nasty mouth.

Tommy Wilhelm (*SD*), like Asa Leventhal, has a deep-seated ambivalence toward his dead mother. In his moment of crisis and failure, he remembers her opposing his plans for an acting career. Though he loved her and feels badly about having disappointed her, he remembers that she denied him her blessing and instead bequeathed him her sensitive feelings, soft heart, brooding nature, and tendency to be confused under pressure. In short, he believes she has endowed him with his weaknesses. And though he laments that he can do nothing for her (*SD* 94), we wonder if he is really lamenting that in death she can do nothing for him.

Herzog's (*H*) mother is also dead, but we do see his stepmother, Tante Taube, and his sometime surrogate mother, Aunt Zipporah. Tante Taube, now in extreme old age, has a face "grooved with woe and age" (*H* 244). She has thin gray hair, no eyebrows, luminous, tame, protuberant eyes, a steady, slow, shrewd gaze, a pleated mouth, poorly made dental plates, a pendulous lip, an accent, a thickening neck, loose skin, and an arthritic body. Herzog thinks she looks like a woodchuck but remembers with boyish narcissism that she was an excellent cook who made strudel like a jeweler's work (243). Despite his grudging admission, given at her request, that she was a good stepmother to him, he can only associate her with food and with the collapse of nature.

Aunt Zipporah fares less well. Herzog is clearly in awe of her strong grudging character, flushed thin face, large hips, heavy steps, wit, terrible denunciations, harsh affection, malicious mouthy tongue, antagonistic nature, and powerful curses. He recalls her "nervous, critical awkward feet" and calls her "a stormy woman, a daughter of Fate," whose visits to his childhood home "were like a military inspection" (*H* 147). To the adult Herzog she is funny because she is ugly, terrifying, and masculine.

Charlie glimpses Humboldt's mother (*HG*) only once and

briefly. He watches her staring out of a dim doorway "with some powerful female grievance" (5).

Mr. Sammler's mother (*MSP*) is mentioned only briefly as a culturally privileged, beautiful young woman, a freethinker whom Sammler blames for giving him his education in male privilege. He recalls her giving him a copy of a work by the notoriously misogynist and anti-Semitic Artur Schopenhauer on his sixteenth birthday, just as earlier she had named him for the philosopher. Sammler recalls how she herself brought "the nervous young Sammler his chocolate and croissants as he sat in his room reading Trollope and Bagehot, and making an 'Englishman' out of himself" (*MSP* 59). The adult Sammler blames her for this petted upbringing, which has made him "pleased," "haughty," "eccentric," "irritable," and worse still, "without compassion" (59).

Dean Corde's mother-in-law (*DD*), Dr. Valeria Raresh constitutes a special case. (And so does Dean Corde.) She is one of the rare women who escapes the fixed scene of masculine representation. Though she is first seen in an intensive care unit, half-paralyzed, and clearly dying, hooked into respirator, scanner and monitor, Corde never allows us to think of her as weak and helpless. Through Dean Corde's recollections of her emerges the picture of a powerful and heroic political figure. Corde describes her face as "criss-crossed every way with tapes, like the Union Jack. Or like windowpanes in cities under bombardment" (*DD* 4). He looks at her loose, long, fine white hair and wonders what it was once like. Then he is moved to pity by the big belly and thin legs, genuinely moved, but with a kind of get-it-over-with eager violence, and concludes that part of him is monster (5). He also concludes that she was a great woman (7). His picture of her is respectful, kindly, involved, and compassionate. Both Dean Corde and Valeria Raresh represent a better imagined masculinity and femininity, a difference that marks them off sharply from all the other pairs of sons and mothers. As he examines her bookshelves in the favorite room where she sewed, trying to know something of her and of her daughter to whom he is married, Corde remembers that she has always been fair and tactful with him, even when he was uncomfortable under her scrutiny. He remembers her in London, shopping at Harrods, and being undemonstratively accommodating. It is Albert, not Minna, who notices the pills in her pocketbook, her tripping, listing, and increasing lack of coordination. It is he and not Minna who monitors her exhaustion.

Mrs. Layamon (*MDH*) is only eight years Benn Crader's senior and is not a well-developed character. Benn suggests, however, that she is rather cold, extremely polite, and given to an unwelcoming kind of privacy. He is shocked when she lets it be known that she reserves her little office exclusively for herself. It is this office which contains the artificial azalea that tricks the botanist, Benn, into thinking it is real and thus demonstrates to him how badly his powers have been blasted by association with these money-hungry Layamons (*MDH* 180). Ravelstein's mother is described as a power-house, but not in any positive sense. She fails to protect him from his abusive father.

With the notable exception of Valeria Raresh, all of these mothers are depicted by the male protagonists as metaphysically inadequate, socially pitiable, and constituted of a myriad of short-comings. Generally speaking, the portraits are remarkably consistent in their portrayals of women as loony, ugly, silent, powerless, powerful, scheming, vindictive, full of guile, decaying, or ineffectual. They are noticeably lacking in integrity, nobility, and intellectual horsepower. For the most part, they are regarded with ambivalence or hostility or both by their untrusting sons, regardless of whether they are loved.

Mothers not in maternal relation to the male protagonists fair badly also. Mimi Villars (*AM*) aborts her child. Simon March's mother-in-law is depicted as the willing victim of Simon's cruel, rejecting behavior, which she mistakenly interprets as humorous acceptance. Margaret Wilhelm (*SD*) is seen by Tommy as a castrating bitch; Ricey (*HRK*) is an unwed teenage mother; Madeleine (*H*) is an enraged manic depressive; Renata (*HG*) appears to be an unsuitable mother; the wily Señora (*HG*) is a scheming, batty stage mother. Kenneth Trachtenberg's would-be mother-in-law (*MDH*) establishes new standards of disappointment in the mother depart-ment. Sensing that her daughter, Treckie, has made a mistake in passing Kenneth up as a husband, she decides to have him for her-self. Acknowledging that she is ten years his senior (he thinks it is more like twenty), she suggests that a quiet marriage of pleasant nights would suit both their needs. Kenneth, however, comments nastily: "What stunning offers you get from the insane" (*MDH* 282).

He notes her winsome teeth, which contrast dramatically with the sheer preposterousness of her "violent-bluish raccoonlike mask" (274). He thinks her eyebrows are made-up with a magic marker, and despises her Arabian musk perfume. She is full of charm signals, he reports, and has "a calculating manner like General Patton, who sat deciding from which side to hit you next" (277). He condemns her morally by concluding that like Uncle's friend, Caroline Bunge, she had probably seen more naked men than the surgeon general. Old Adletsky describes Frances Jellicoe as "built like a brick shithouse," a woman whose cortisone swellings make her "look like Babe Ruth" (*TA* 10). Jay describes Amy Wustrin, the love of his life, as a "gray-faced maid-of-all-work—an overworked mother" who is almost unidentifiable under the black girders of the el tracks (19). Madge Heisinger fairs even worse. She is notorious, provocative, and murderous.

Jay Wustrin's mother is a great embarrassment to him. She would shake her "big brainless head" possessed of rich stupid black eyes. Furthermore, she seemed to be "sexually arrested" and in the final analysis strikes Harry as "an old country village woman" (41).

As a group, these women seem callous, destructive, mentally unstable, careless, ill-prepared, hysterical, wily, abandoning, sexually rapacious, castrating, and generally wacky. Nowhere in either group is there anything approaching a normal, adequate mother.

With few exceptions Bellow's mistresses are also loony and destructive. Aged women, however, bear the brunt of the most graphic and perhaps unkind representations. They seem to have all the fascination of reptiles for the male protagonists, who usually admire and love them inordinately. They are present from the earliest to the latest work, occurring in the single largest number in *The Adventures of Augie March*. Some are minor and others major presences in the life of the male protagonist, but none escapes his eye for the physically grotesque, not even the most loved, such as Mother March, Grandma Lausch, Anna Coblin, and Tante Taube. From the earliest to the latest novels, there is no softening of the grotesque detail with which these women are described. There is, however, a hardening of the gaze of the male protagonists of middle and later works with regard to the perceived erotic and passive-aggressive female scheming capacities of these old women. Each is ultimately viewed with disgust and in large part dismissed as metaphysically unusable, along with mothers, wives, and mistresses, sisters-in-law, and women friends. In nearly all cases, however, something of personal need and something of metaphysical endeavor draws the male protagonist to these women as powerfully as he is repelled by even the most loved of them. In these characters, as much as in any of the others, lies the clue to the real quest of the male protagonist for that elusive feminine he subconsciously senses, pursues, and fails to "see." The category is large and includes Mrs. Almstadt, Joseph's mother-in-law, Asa's sister-in-law, Elena, and her mother, Mrs. Nunez, Asa's neighbor, Grandma Lausch, Anna Coblin, Mrs. Renling, Mrs. Lennox, Willatele, Wanda, Tennie, Zinka, Zelda, Zipporah, Tante Taube, Humboldt's unnamed mother, Margotte Arkin, the old Señora, Rebecca Volstad, Valeria Raresh the anonymous aging women of Dr. Layamon's female surgical wards, Della Bedell, Caroline Bunge, Sorella Fonstein, Amy Wustrin, and Madge Heisinger. And despite their old age and grotesquerie, they are still subjected to the searching, voyeuristic gaze of a male who loves some of them and fears and ridicules all of them for their apparently still dangerous and even more corrupt sexuality, that same erotic power manifested by younger women.

Asa (*TV*) decides Elena's mother is an ignorant, superstitious, ugly old immigrant woman who is using her daughter against his own brother Max, whom she blames for the death of her grandson. He looks fearfully at her "grizzled temples, thin straight line of her nose, the severity of her head pressed back on her shoulders, the baring of her teeth as she opened her lips to make a remark to her daughter" (*TV*). Asa is still convinced she is mad, vindictive, and crazy. Her smiling he interprets as "frightful glances of spite and exultation, as though he were the devil" (159). When he attempts to gain Max's complicity in this viewpoint, Max identifies his paranoia, "Well you've sure turned out to be a suspicious person" (216).

Aunt Zipporah fares less well. Herzog is clearly in awe of this "stormy woman, a daughter of Fate" (*H* 147) but mainly because she is ugly, terrifying, and masculine. Then there is the "fat-assed 200 pound" Auntie Rae, who appalls the young Herzog, who is forced to speculate upon her enormous rear end.

He describes Tennie (*H*), Simkin's wife, as a kindly elderly sister woman with bad legs, stiff, dyed hair, abstract jewelry, and butterfly-shaped eyeglasses. She is diabetic, and Herzog accuses her of wickedness, hypocrisy, and cunning. Aunt Zelda seems to Herzog

47

the epitome of "female deceit" and a woman "lying from an over-flowing heart" (*H* 41). He thinks of her kitchen of enamel and copper and can only see the molded female forms bulging from all sides and Aunt Zelda's face full of mistrust. After she has accused him of shouting at Madeleine and the baby, bullying, being sexually selfish, and burying Madeleine alive in the Berkshires, the resentful Herzog says: "I will never understand what women want. What do they want? They eat green salad and drink human blood" (41–42).

Mrs. Lennox (*HRK*), Henderson's housekeeper, is a batty old neighbor with a toothless old face who, like a seventeenth-century witch, lives in a tree with her cats. Her tree is hung with a myriad of mirrors and old bicycle lights, while her yard is strewn with junk. She is a dirty derelict, and, in the finish, Henderson literally shouts her to death in his kitchen, leaving a "don't disturb" note pinned to her clothing.

Humboldt's mother is a madwoman in the attic of her husband's nineteenth-century masculine world of capitalistic endeavor. Charlie is particularly hard on the old Señora. He says that there is a "serpentine dryness" about her eyes (*HG* 410), and that she is probably bananas. His pity is completely aroused the morning he sees her sans eyebrows and makeup on her way to the bathroom. To him she is the ultimate stage mother and schemer responsible for her daughter's "sexual monkeyshines." He cruelly describes her unassailable, furious rationality, her whiskery lips, operatic nostrils, and chicken luster eyeballs (410).

Rebecca Volstad, the Danish lady whom Charlie meets while parenting the abandoned Roger, he describes as a haggard elderly lady with a bad hip who is desperate to find a husband.

Miss Porson (*DD*), secretary to Dean Corde, is described as an old gossip, a "gabby old bag, not worth a damn" (41). "In her late sixties, she was fleshy, but her bearing was jaunty. Her plump face, heavily made up, was whitish pink, as if washed in calamine lotion, and on some days she painted a racoon band across her face in blue eye shadow—the mask of a burglar or a Venetian reveler. She kept her pants up with heavy silver and turquoise belts. . . . Her erotic confidences and boasts set his teeth on edge" (143–44). He admits the only reason he keeps her on is that she has him hostage because of his hatred of administrative detail.

Della Bedell is passed around the listening circle of Kenneth, Uncle Benn, and the implied listener, as an excessive weekend drinker who is inappropriately forward with Uncle Benn. She is, according to these two, full of sexual predatoriness, belligerence, and shrillness. He delights in recounting to his audience how Benn has hightailed it to Brazil, causing Della Bedell to die of a heart attack brought on by sexual deprivation. Kenneth laughingly sums her up as "a fat little lady who hit the bottle" (*MDH* 88).

Kenneth talks of Caroline Bunge as "a big graceful (old style) lady, vampy, rich, ornate, slow-moving, a center-stage personality. Middle-aged, she still stood out like a goddess from a Zeigfield extravaganza, the Venus de Oro type" (*MDH* 75). He laughs at the way she speaks through her nose, uses mood pills, and wears heavy makeup. She is "détraquée" (76), and her general air "somnambulistic." Because he cannot share the surrogate father, Kenneth signifies this rival for Uncle's affections as "a strange siren who took lithium or Elavil" (79). Harry Trellman and Sigmund Adletsky are another pair of classic misogynists sitting together and gossiping about various women, most of whom fall victim to their critical gaze as they are passed back and forth as barter-goods in the formation of this "intellectual" partnership.

"Good sports" and other men's mistresses and wives are frequently reduced to stereotypes of "good lay," despite the fact that some of them are quite liked and quite complexly drawn. Mimi Villars (*AM*), Polly Palomino (*HG*), the woman designated only as the lover of the "tuxedo man" (*HG*), and Angela Horicker (*MSP*) offer themselves as obvious examples.

Sisters-in-law are represented with similar hostility and suspicion tempered only occasionally with grudging admiration. They seem to be strong-willed, heavy, spoiled, materialistic, compromising, unattractive, powerful, and often hostile toward their cerebral and sentimental brothers-in-law. Most stand condemned for their power and their lack of sexual or intellectual appeal for him. Some stand condemned for their husband's lack of spiritual peace, even when they are grudgingly admired. They include Elena Leventhal (*TV*), Charlotte Magnus (*AM*), and Hortense (*HG*).

The pattern is that of the classic witch, crone, sexual predator, mad woman, deceiver, mantrap, and siren. Not even old women are sexually neutral or innocent of wicked designs upon men. None of these women presents a pleasant picture, and in nearly every depiction, the text makes it clear that the problem is the flawed, misogynistic, male protagonist through whose eyes she is viewed.

4

DESTRUCTIVE WIVES AND LOVERS

Woman may be monstrous, unclean, mad, oriental, profane, or improper, yet she is that which is necessary to the completion of misguided male desire.

—Jacques Derrida, *Of Grammatology*

Wives in the novels occupy a continuum that ranges from passive to destructive to muselike. Earlier in the novels we see Iva (*DM*), Joseph's wife; Mary Leventhal (*TV*); Henderson's three wives, Margaret, Francis, and Lily (*HRK*); Daisy (*HG*); the deceased Antonina Sammler (*MSP*); Minna Corde (*DD*); and Kenneth Trachtenberg's mother (*MDH*). The later group seem castrating unstable man-eaters like Madeleine Pontritter (*H*), Denise (*HG*), Matilda Layamon (*MDH*), and Madge Heisinger (*TA*). With the exception of Minna Raresh Corde, however, it is the later wives who engender the most hatred and fear in their men. In the middle and later Bellow novels, the gaze of the various male protagonists has hardened, become more invasive, even enraged. In the most recent novel, *Ravelstein*, we get a bad wife and a saintly helpmeet.

Joseph (*DM*) describes his wife, Iva, as "a quiet girl. She has about her that which discourages talk. We no longer confide in each other; in fact, there are many things I could not mention to her" (*DM* 12). Iva has had to forgo luxuries like clothes and entertainment to support Joseph, who does not wish to work. She is the maternal ground or support for his intellectual and metaphysical ambitions. Joseph blithely describes her as only too willing to serve this function: "She claims that it is no burden and that she wants me to enjoy this liberty, to read and to do all the delightful things I will be unable to do in the army" (11). Yet he is unfaithful to her with Kitty Daumler, for whom he barely cares, insulting to their friends and relatives, and irritated with Iva for not allowing him to shape her. He concludes that Iva's light-minded enjoyment of clothes, mysteries, entertainment, and fashion magazines is "because women . . . were not equipped by training to resist such things" (98). He gets angry at her for disobeying him at the Servatious party by getting slightly drunk. When he views her unconscious and naked on the bed later that night, however, he wonders if, in his voyeurism and desire for control of her, he is as bad as Albert, who has hypnotized Minna and treated her spitefully. Minna seems to be boring, silent, aloof, and somewhat unsympathetic. For all her generosity, Iva has failed to please Joseph by "keeping" him and by failing to be his Pygmalion or hypnotized subject.

Mary Leventhal is absent from the scene of *The Victim*, and the only account of her we get is that Asa misses her terribly, has a satisfying intimate relationship with her, and lapses into paranoia during her absence. She functions as an absent presence of the feminine— perhaps only one of two or three wives in these novels who is not alienated come the end of the narrative.

Margaret Wilhelm (*SD*) is seen only through Tommy's accounts of her. She sends letters of protest about unpaid child support and alimony, accusing him of gross immaturity, and tells him that he deserves his misery. He believes she is strangling him and will smash him with her quiet, fair, rising voice, and sundry accusations. He characterizes her as a sort of shark or barracuda, for being fierce in her demands for child support.

Henderson describes Frances, his first wife, as withdrawn, "like Shelly's moon, wandering companionless" (*HRK* 5). He calls her an intense letter writer and deep reader who is on a philosophy kick. So much for the female intellect. Lily, his second wife, is a classic case of the verbally battered wife. He raves at her in public, swears at her in private, and embarrasses her when her "ladies" come to visit by pretending not to remember who she is. He also fires his guns in the house to frighten and embarrass her. He describes her as a large, lively woman with a sweet face and temperament who is intelligent, moralizing, and often crying (6). He also accuses her of mumbling, having dirty underwear, making him suffer, and having a crazy face.

Charlie's wife, Denise (*HG*), is one of the most fully delineated of the destructive wives, and the descriptions of her are full of ambivalence. Charlie decides her paternal inheritance is stronger than her maternal inheritance and notes: "On days when she was curt and tough, in her high tense, voice you heard that old precinct captain and bagman, her grandfather" (*HG* 41). He thinks her wit is cruel and clever and is furious with her for not valuing his lifelong friend, the déclassé George Swiebel. She says with fierce hate, "Don't bring him to this house. I can't bear to see his ass on my sofa, his feet on my rug. You're like one of those overbred race horses that must have a goat in his stall to calm his nerves. George Swiebel is your billy goat" (41). Charlie notes that she "was warlike and shrill . . . her voice clear, thrilling, and minutely articulate—the rising arpeggios of hysteria" (42). She hates his immigrant history, his attachments to old friends, his sentiment for the old neighborhood, his attachment to Humboldt, his love of gritty Chicago, and his attachment to the Jewish fathers buried there. Charlie concludes that abuse does Denise "more good than vitamins" (44).

Neither does Charlie respect Denise's intellect. He remembers that when he first met her she kept earnest school girlish notes for the actor Verviger. Charlie says he can always tell when Denise has been speed-reading the news magazines at the hairdressers because she comes home brimming with conversation about weighty world affairs. He is amused when she corners the president while visiting the White House and begins just such a conversation. Charlie believes she cannot distinguish her own anxieties from those induced by world crisis and jokingly observes that, because Kennedy also gleans his news from the same sources, she would probably have made him a good Secretary of State (*HG* 57). He also sneers at her for bringing "superior persons" to his Kenwood home and recalls with amusement her annoyance over his rudeness and indifference to them. Although she is stripped naked on the bed, brushing her hair, and ready dutifully to ease Charlie's morbid aberrations about grief and his recent encounter of the down-and-out Humboldt, Charlie is ungrateful. He depicts her failure of sympathy with his attachment to the dead. "Oh, you're on *that* kick again. You must quit all this operatic bullshit. Talk to a psychiatrist. Why are you hung up on the past and always lamenting some dead party or other" (115). Clearly, Charlie is pointing to his own inadequacies, but the brunt of the criticism falls on the frustrated Denise for being cruel, insensitive, and mocking. In short, while Charlie acknowledges his own excessive demands on her and his own neuroses, he depicts himself as deep and his wife as vulgar and shallow, wanting in the finer sensibilities, basically uncompassionate, and making very little effort to understand him. In court, he complains she is trying to destroy him. He calls her "nutty" and observes that today she is being friendly because beating him like a dog "released her affections" (224). He jokingly notes how, in contrast, just getting out of bed to make breakfast was a challenge to her and that for special effect she is wearing stockings with holes to court (224). In other words she is basically incompetent, except when fired up by hatred and full of guile about how to make her case for the judge.

Conversely, Charlie does see in Kathleen a sympathetic light and seems drawn to her in friendship, as few of Bellow's male characters ever are. "She loved a poet-king and allowed him to hold her captive in the country" (*HG* 25), he realizes. Charlie, saddened and amused by Humboldt's paranoid possessiveness, understands the meaning of Humboldt's fantasy about Kathleen's father having sold her to a Rockefeller. He is shocked when Humboldt tries to run her down in the car in Princeton (143). Later that evening, at the Littlewood's party, when Humboldt begins to criticize her, Charlie recalls how Humboldt "clutched her with sensational violence" (145), punched her in the stomach, hauled her out into the yard, pulled her by the hair into the Buick, and drove the car over the lawn in his wild departure. Charlie likens him to a raging King Leontes, whose behavior is learned from the books he has read. He also laments both her disappearance from Rocco's restaurant and Humboldt's lunatic attempts at violence on Magnasco. Charlie comments, "I think he wanted Kathleen to protect him when he entered the states a poet needed to be in. These high dreaming states, always being punctured and torn by American flak, were what he wanted Kathleen to preserve for him. She did her best to help him with the enchantment. But he could never come up with enough dream material to sheath himself in. It would not cover. However, I saw what Kathleen had to do and admired her for it" (240).

Sammler blames Antonina for having done the unwomanly thing, causing her own death by having gone to Europe to liquidate her father's estate on the eve of the Nazi invasion. She has inappropriately entered the world of the fathers and thus brought on her own Holocaust death. He blames Shula-Slawa's craziness not on the Nazis and nuns who made her a Roman Catholic, but on her "hysterical" mother. When he recalls Antonina, Sammler does so philosophically and critically. He is snidely amused to remember her as having been socioerotically aroused by their association with the famous members of the Bloomsbury set, H. G. Wells in particular. Such behavior by Antonina has unhinged Shula-Slawa, he concludes, as he thinks on his daughter's theft of the Lal manuscript. Again, a woman, and not Nazis, is to blame for his daughter's wavering wittedness. He is even able to able to deny his onetime sexual attraction to Antonina with no remorse at all:

> Old Sammler thinking of his wife in prewar Bloomsbury days interpreted a certain quiet, bosomful way she had of conveying with a downward stroke of the hand, so delicate you had to know her well to identify it as a vaunting gesture: we have the most distinguished intimacy with the finest people in Britain. A small vice, almost nutritive, digestive— which gave Antonina softer cheeks, smoother hair, deeper color. . . . And the little girl may actually have observed that the very mention of Wells had a combined social-erotic influence on her mother. (*MSP* 28)

Corde fails also for her lack of empathy, though she does not arouse the kind of ire other wives do. Albert Corde, the compassionate, feminized male, describes Minna the way a wife would describe a career-oriented, abstracted scientist-child genius. Her scientific genius seems to make her unfit for wifely, warm, and human interaction. Corde feels alone and parental toward her. He observes that she is unable see her mother's failing health and seems to misinterpret her apparent selflessness for lack of personal desire (*DD* 12). She has been shielded from political realities by her family and has lived in a world of science. Try as she might, she cannot grasp the human and moral impact of Corde's writings. It is enough for her that an important scientist is impressed by them. Corde criticizes her for being the "gold star pupil," whom he describes as "a beautiful and elegant woman" who like a school girl sets out each day "with a satchel and pencil box," never missing any professional obligation at the university and "rehearsing her tutorials far into the night" until "they must have been like concerts" (*DD* 253). He sees her as orderly and ritualistic, even magical, but totally unprepared for the world of human feeling and psychology Valeria has lived in. It is Dean Albert Corde who must explain her fear, grief, anger, and depression to her. "What an innocent person! She did stars; human matters were her husband's field. Some division of labor!" (*DD* 256). Minna is devastated by Valeria's not keeping her promise to live to be ninety. "Mature, highly serious women entering into such an agreement. And it had twelve more years to run. During this time Minna was to get on with her astronomy, equally safe from the decadent West and the Decadent East," says Dean Corde (*DD* 258). Later when they are preparing for the funeral, she gives her husband the only offering of support she can, having ignored his crises throughout the entire episode: "She trusted you. . . . What you told her last of all was what she wanted most of all to hear" (*DD* 308). Our last view of Minna is of her seated at the viewing end of the Mt. Palomar telescope as the vast curved surface of the dome opens above them both. We are left to assume Minna's observations are purely scientific because we are given Albert Corde's human, poetic, and religious impressions in great detail. The teller of the tale has construed himself in feminine fashion, nurturing, tuned in to human suffering and feeling, whereas Corde has construed his wife in a masculine fashion, describing her as unable to communicate very much in the way of human feeling, politically oblivious, and possessed of a host of school-girlish habits and emotional responses.

Mrs. Rudi Trachtenberg is depicted as a much put-upon French matron who has tried to turn a blind eye to her husband's philandering, all the while being fobbed off with fancy silk dresses from the finest Parisian couturieres. Kenneth personally feels abandoned when she immolates herself in Djibouti with a group of medical volunteers, where famine victims are dying by the thousands. He resentfully describes her cheap skirts, "as close to sackcloth as she could get. No more high-fashion cashmeres, and silks, no more couturieres, an end to tea dates, according to the Paris convention, with Papa's girlfriends" (*MDH* 29). He grudgingly acknowledges that she wore these clothes elegantly but condemns her for being a Mother Theresa in cheap cotton twill and entirely fails to understand her perspective as the wife of a notorious adulterer. He sees no altruism or spiritual worth in her final choice of lifestyle, condemning her for running away from him and for merely aping Mother Theresa.

Matilda Layamon fares worse than almost any of them. Her father calls her "a mastermind" fit only for the "War College" (*MDH* 168) or a rich bitch with bohemian sexual tastes who is moody, scheming, pot-smoking, greedy, shallow, tormenting, too sexually adept, too beautiful, too educated. Benn turns on her so violently that Kenneth calls him a "negative fetishist" (264). Suddenly, Matilda's teeth and shoulders are unsatisfactory. During a performance of Tony Perkin's *Psycho*, he imaginatively transforms her from desirable female to perverted transvestite, bearing first Perkin's shoulders and then her dreadful father's. Shoulder by tooth by widely spaced breasts, Benn deconstructs his Helen until she is transformed from classic, mythical beauty to vulgar rich bitch and finally to demiurge.

Clara Velde is the chief protagonist in *A Theft*, but it is not her sensibility or subjectivity that is staged in the novel. The point-of-view, the narratorial voice of the novel, is that of a male speaker. Once again a woman is perceived through male eyes, even when she is the principal character. She is portrayed as a flighty fashion maven who was once a hick from the sticks with a history of moral and emotional instability. She is a snob, a racist, who has made it to the Protestant managerial world. With her "ancestrally North Sea nose" (*AT* 1), big bones, Illinois farming background, and old time religion, she is no Naomi Lutz, Valeria, or great beauty. "In her you might see suddenly a girl from a remote town, from the vestigial America of one-room schoolhouses. Constables, covered dish suppers, one of those communities bypassed by technology and urban development" (39). From this advantaged position she can afford to slum with Clifford, who ends up in the Attica jail, and designate Hamilton the jeweler as one who "might have been an Armenian, passing" (17). This is the woman who has had intimate association with Spontini and Giancomo, mafia crooks and billionaire revolutionists, and who, all by herself, has stolen a large sum of money from the insurance company. In her peculiar accounting, these colorful global thieves fare better than a petty thief like Frederic, or a thief of the human heart like Ithiel, or her own thieving, "utilizing" self. Then there are the four utility husbands, the most recent of whom she designates as "big, and handsome, indolent, defiantly incompetent" (3). In short, she is a woman who has had a spotted sexual career, four utility husbands, a suicide attempt, inappropriate lovers, and four divorces.

Sorella Fonstein, like Valeria, constitutes a unique case. She does not escape the misogynous male gaze but she does become a mysterious woman of moral and metaphysical stature. The narrator admits, "My pictures of them are probably too clear and pleasing to be true," and the difference between "literal and affective recollection" (*BC* 3). Initially he describes her as a "New Jersey girl—correction lady. She was very heavy and she wore make-up. Her cheeks were downy. Her hair was done up in a beehive. A pince-nez, highly unusual, a deliberate disguise, gave her a theatrical air. Her aim was to achieve an authoritative, declarative manner. However, she was no fool" (6). But immediately he admits his imagination fails when he tries to understand what Sorella and Fonstein saw in each other:

> When she crossed her legs and he noted the volume of her underthighs, an American observer like me could, and would, picture the entire woman unclothed, and depending on his experience of life and his acquaintance with art, he might attribute her type to an appropriate painter. In my mental picture of Sorella, I chose Rembrandt's Saskia over the nudes of Rubens. . . . Sorella's obesity, her beehive coif, the preposterous pince-nez—a "lady" put-on—made me wonder: What is it with such people? Are they female impersonators, drag queens? (19–20)

The narrator realizes, looking back, that Sorella "was a tiger wife" without whom Fonstein's business would have gone broke (*BC* 21). Despite his continuing obsession with "the mad overflow of her behind," he notes, "She proved quite a talker, this Sorella. I began to look forward to our conversations as much for what came out of her as for the intrinsic interest of the subject" (26). And "it was no negligible person who had patented Fonstein's thermostat and rounded up the money for his little factory (it was little at first), meanwhile raising a boy who was a mathematical genius. She was a spirited woman, at home with ideas. This heavy tailored lady was extremely well informed" (27).

> Then there was Sorella. No ordinary woman, she broke with every sign of ordinariness. Her obesity, assuming she had some psychic choice in the matter, was a sign of this. She might have willed herself to be thinner, for she had the strength of character to do it. Instead she accepted the challenge of size as a Houdini might have asked for tighter knots, more locks on the trunk, deeper rivers to escape from. She

was as people nowadays say, "off the continuum"—her graph went beyond the chart and filled up the whole wall. (32)

Later, when he becomes aware of her scheme to blackmail Billy Rose with Mrs. Hamet's record, the narrator is quick to vindicate her character.

> Sorella was a proper person. She was not suggesting that I share any lewdness with her. Nothing was farther from her than evil communications. She had never in her life seduced anyone—I'd bet a year's income on that. She was as stable in character as she was immense in her person. The square on the bosom of her dress, with its scalloped design, was like a repudiation of all trivial mischief. The scallops themselves seemed to me to be a kind of message in cursive characters, warning against kinky interpretations, perverse attributions. (*BC* 39)

He attributes to her a heart that beats "with the persistence of fidelity, a faith in the necessary continuation of radical mystery—don't ask me to spell it out" and, again, "Sorella was too big a person to play any kind of troublemaking games or to create a minor mischief. Her eyes were like vents of atmospheric blue, and their backing (the camera obscura) referred you to the black of universal space, where there is no object to reflect the flow of invisible light" (40). The matter of size, however, continues to amaze him. "Sorella . . . was so much bigger than the bride I had first met in Lakewood that I could not keep from speculating on her expansion. . . . All I can say is that it (whatever it was at bottom [awful pun]) was accomplished with some class or style. Exquisite singers can make you forget what hillocks of suet their backsides are. Besides, Sorella did dead sober what delirious sopranos put over on us in a state of false Wagnerian intoxication" (48-49).

Sorella both is and is not a Bellow stereotype, and his narrator both is and is not the typical Bellow male monologist. Sorella's fatness and sexual appeal remain a constant fascination and grotesquerie with him, despite his recognitions of her intellectual and spiritual worth. She is and is not the diva of his spiritual stage. He is not faithful to his intuitions of her value. Furthermore, he even doubts his own earlier perceptions and remains fixated on the immensity of her personage, the grand presence notwithstanding.

He is in the finish able to admit his callow Americanness and own his gender values. He is even able, finally, to realize his earlier more patronizing ascriptions of genuineness and intellect to her and his immature sexual curiosity about her mountainous body. In this last novel, the unnamed protagonist actually finds his sought-after feminine, admits it, and then illustrates how he has lost her. For it is Sorella and the feminine she represents that he has lost, and it means that almost everything he has lived for is negated. The recognition of this discovery, neglect, and therefore loss, brings him to admit that the realization under the reading lamp was not less shocking than Moses' burning bush and the ram in the thicket. It is an ironic image for what is lost and what is left. The illumination has come too late, and it is a picture of a certain kind of ram-like American masculine self that he is left staring at in the thickets of clouding memory. This time the text reveals most clearly the self-conscious narrator's awareness of what is contained within his American masculinity and what inevitably escapes him. His final admission is that Sorella is one of his dead whom he will ask God not to forget. "Yiskor Elohim" (*BC* 102).

Madge Heisinger seems to be the most destructive wife of all, a throwback to an earlier period in Bellow's work. She has actually hired a killer to dispose of her husband, Bodo, and has gone to prison for it. She also pours hot tea in her guest's lap and then invades the victim's privacy in the bathroom. Amy Wustrin describes her as a "wild bitch" (53) who has picked up some appalling habits in prison, including blackmail. Like Sorella Fonstein, however, Frances Jellicoe is another aging, heavy woman with some admirable qualities who used to be "a slim gentle creature, once . . . " (9). Likewise, Amy, for all her wear and tear, is still pleasing to Harry. In *Ravelstein* there is the extremely aloof Vela and the benevolent Rosamund.

Mistresses and lovers tend to fall into the same passive and aggressive groupings as the wives. The first group tends to be the early period mistresses, whereas the latter evokes the most dramatic erotic responses from various men and is also the most feared and resented.

Kitty Daumler (*DM*) has picked up the bored Joseph when he is a customer in her travel agency. The affair is a desultory one with almost no enthusiasm on Joseph's part. He indicates he begins it because Iva won't bend so easily to his control and because he is flattered that the handsome Kitty Daumler has made a pass at him. He never really describes her attractions, except her availability, seems only mildly interested sexually, and soon tires of her. His final picture of her is revealing of him. Never once feeling guilty for living off his wife while being unfaithful to her, Joseph is disgusted to turn up at Kitty's one night to reclaim a loaned book, only to realize he has been replaced. "I passed into the outer hall thinking, as I did so, that by this time Kitty had slipped back into bed and that she and her companion had (I sought a way to say it) fallen together again, his appetite increased by the intrusion. And, while I could objectively find no reason why she should not do as she pleased, I found myself nevertheless ambiguously resentful and insulted" (*DM* 105).

Thea Fenchel (*AM*) is the first real mistress and femme fatale in the novels. In many ways, she provides the model for several subsequent mistresses and wives. It is Thea Fenchel who rescues Augie from Mrs. Renling and initiates him sexually. She is rich, estranged from her family, independent, transient, careless with money, lavish, slightly disheveled, disorganized, involuntarily shrewd, slightly crazy, erotically inclined, jealous, frequently crude, sometimes barbarous looking, given to taking toy-boy lovers, prone to passionate excitement, and inclined to sadomasochism. She is also flighty, nervous, contradictory, and unstable. Her worst revelation of character comes when her trained eagle, Caligula, refuses to attack and eat his prey. At this point she tries to stone him for his lack of brute instinct and cries tears of frustrated disappointment and sheer wrath at the bird. What kind of woman has built her entire life around training a vicious animal to kill on command? She is the first of Bellow's deathly erotics. In an interesting reversal of male-female stereotypes, it is she who teaches Augie to hunt and shoot. She is a controlling, destructive, sadistic, erotic bitch. She is one of the most hostile portraits of a woman anywhere in the novels, Madeleine and Denise notwithstanding.

Sono (*H*), the perfect Oriental lover, tells Herzog he should come to a woman with the "pride of the peacock, the lust of the goat, the wrath of the lion and the wisdom of God" (*H* 188). She is usually depicted bathing Herzog, soaping his feet, massaging his body, and singing to him. She keeps the best of everything on hand for him and fries, bakes, and brews to please him. What she offers is oriental luxury aimed to please the ultimate narcissist. Herzog recalls that she is a war refugee, has a graveyard sense of humor, is greedy for intrigue, imitates fat ladies, grows little gingko trees, and keeps a dirty cat pan. He remembers also that she has a lovely body, smells of musk, and wears elaborate makeup. She is an avid bargain hunter and tells him no lies (167). Though he cannot remember when she went back to Japan, he remembers her with no remorse and no rancor. She is one of the few mistresses who has left no wounds and, ironically, is the only Oriental among many American mistresses. More to the point, she is the only mistress who has absolutely no expectations of her lover.

Ramona (*H*), on the other hand, is an American business-woman, slightly foreign, well educated, a fine cook, and an experienced lover. In summing up her impact on men, Herzog says she is "full of erotic monkeyshines" (*H* 17). He describes her as a classic Castilian courtesan with her international background; her short, full, substantial figure; her walking in guarded Castilian style, her way of entering a room provocatively, swaggering slightly, play-ing out the role of the tough Spanish broad, wearing an extravagant, strapless merry widow, and as the "true sack artist" (17). His chief appreciation is of her body and her erotic talents and little else. He is hypnotized by her shrewd, erotic, calculating eyes, warm sexual odors, downy arms, slightly bowed legs, and short, deep, white thighs. Even as he admires her sexual talents, he sees her merely as a talented lay who knows it. Since she is an orphic type, Herzog knows she is death to his spiritual powers. In many ways, she is descended from Thea Fenchel and the forerunner to Renata. Ramona's sexual powers must ultimately be evaded, for she is the incarnation of the deathly erotic. With her wine, flowers, Egyptian music, and undressing rituals (157), she is highly experienced at entertaining gentleman. Herzog notes her "intoxicating eyes," "robust breasts," "Carmen airs," and her "thievishly seductive" ways (151). He notes her "female passion for secrecy and double games" and likens her to a "wily serpent" (153).

Charlie describes Naomi Lutz, his first adolescent love, as "the most beautiful and perfect young girl I have ever seen, I adored her, and love brought out my deepest peculiarities" (*HG* 76). "When I loved Naomi Lutz I was safely within life. Its phenomena added up, they made sense. . . . Even in winter Naomi petted behind the rose garden with me. Among the frozen twigs I made myself warm inside her raccoon coat. There was a delicious mixture of coonskin and maiden fragrance" (76). Now in late middle age, as he watches her in her garrison cap and Sam Browne belt directing the crosswalk at Marquette Park, he notices her obliterated figure and the damage life has done to her breasts and thighs. "That was all right for her friend Hank—Hank and Naomi had grown old together—but not for me, who knew her way-back-when. There was no prospect of this" (297). And later, "I couldn't help thinking what a blessed life I might have led with Naomi Lutz. Fifteen thousand nights embracing Naomi and I would have smiled at solitude and boredom of the grave. I would have needed no bibliography, no stock portfolios, no medal from the Legion of Honor" (77). When he meets her again, she is fifty-three, married for a second time and dealing with a dead-beat son. Charlie again acknowledges his affinity for her.

> How comfortable she looked in slippers, smiling in the kitchen, her fat arms crossed. I kept repeating that it would have been bliss to sleep with her for forty years, that it would have defeated death, and so on. But could I have really borne it? The fact was that I became more and more fastidious as I grew older. So now I was honor bound to answer the question: could I have really loved her to the end? She really didn't look good. She had been beaten about by biological storms (the mineral body is worn out by the developing spirit). But this was a challenge I could have met. Yes, I could have done it. Yes, it would have worked. Molecule for molecule she was still Naomi. Each cell of those stout arms was still a Naomi cell. The charm of those short teeth still went to my heart. Her drawl was as effective as ever. The spirits of Personality had done a real job on her. For me the Anima, as C. G. Jung called it, was still there. The counterpart soul, the missing half described by Aristophanes in the *Symposium*. (304)

Though Charlie has glimpsed some kind of feminine in Naomi, then and now, his own masculine erotic preferences have precluded his capturing it. Naomi recognizes this when she warns Charlie to steer clear of "big broads." Later it is clear she pities Charlie for all his high-flown intellectual talk and chides him for his going away to Europe with a "big broad." After telling him he is a crackpot, but one with a genuine soul, she says, "Don't wear yourself out proving something with these giant broads. Remember, your great love for me, just five feet tall" (308).

Charlie's description of Demmie Vonghel is brilliant, funny, loving, and detailed. It invokes an amazing array of stereotypes and negatives, however. He describes Demmie as a messed up little rich girl who, despite her expensive finishing school education at Bryn Mawr, has belonged to a gang of car thieves. She tells Charlie, "I have a record—hubcap-stealing, marijuana, sex offenses, hot cars, chased by cops, crashing, hospital, probation officers, the whole works. But I know about three thousand Bible verses. Brought up on hellfire and damnation" (*HG* 19). Charlie, after generally placing her in the category of "religiously, morally, and socially damaged goods," describes her beautiful but defective legs with their knock-knees and turned-out feet, and then as a conscience-stricken sleeper who dreamt of hell fires and is possessed by unclean spirits, but who looks like a country girl in her nightgown (20). He also describes her as an "unauthorized pill-taker" who dreads sleep and plays solitaire late into the night in order to avoid her demons (21). Charlie notes, "Demmie cried passionately, as only a woman who believes in sin can cry. When she cried you not only pitied her, you respected her strength of soul" (29). We don't believe Charlie, however. He does not find her metaphysically important, but rather a silly girl from the sticks whose fundamentalist religion has ruined her.

The transformation he describes in her on the night of the Littlewood's party is revealing. One moment Demmie is dressed in a black chiffon dress looking the picture of Mainline class and sophistication. The next minute she is described as a tormented primordial soul speaking broken words in her sleep.

> The voice expressed her terror of this strange place, the earth, and of this strange state, being. Laboring and groan-ing she tried to get out of it. This was the primordial Demmie beneath the farmer's daughter beneath the teacher, beneath the elegant Mainline horsewoman, Latinist, accom-plished cocktail sipper in black chiffon, with the upturned nose. I let her go on a while, trying to comprehend. I pitied her, I loved her. But then I put an end to it. I kissed her. She knew who it was. She pressed her toes to my shins and held me in powerful female arms. She cried "I love you" in the same deep voice but her eyes were still shut blind. I think she never actually woke up. (*HG* 147)

His solution: sex. He describes her as an obese child who was treated with hormones and thyroxin to slim her down, causing her breasts to retain permanent wrinkles. For Charlie, she is one day a child, the next "a van der Weyden beauty," "sometimes Mortimer Snerd," and sometimes "a Zeigfield girl" (*HG* 153). Sometimes she is a good girl, preparing a whole term's worth of Latin lessons, and sometimes a bad one, consuming large amounts of whiskey, having hysterics, and taking up with "desperadoes" (153). Charlie tells us that sometimes "she stroked him like a fairy princess or punched [him] in the ribs like a cow hand" (153). The bottom line (pun intended), however, is sexual intoxication. His most voyeuristic picture of her: "In hot weather she stripped herself naked to wax the floors on her knees. Then there appeared big tendons, lanky arms, laboring feet. And when it was seen from behind the organ I adored in a different context as small, fine, intricate, rich in delightful difficulties of access, stood out like a primitive limb" (154). Her contraries never cease to amaze him—the hockey field star, the breaker of Western horses, the society girl who writes charming bread-and-butter notes on Tiffany paper (153–54). She is the ideal woman for him since he tells how she has "steered me now, acting as my trainer, my manager, my cook, my lover, and my strawboss. She had her work cut out for her and was terribly busy" (163). His final description of her before he tells of her death in the South American jungle is how she was "strongly drawn to sickbeds, hospitals, terminal cancers, and funerals" (166). He also describes her as unable to do arithmetic, but able to fix a cranky radio. He remembers with fondness her screaming at him like a barroom brawler as she cleans him out at cards, while sitting on the bed with her legs spread. Charlie says, "It's the open view of Shangri-La that takes my mind off these cards, Demmie" (166). Angel or whore, sane or crazy, humanly valuable or not, we ask? We see all her physical imperfections, psychological hangups, and traumas. She is an interestingly complex and lovingly drawn picture. But for all her uniqueness and his love for her, she is a cleverer than usual composite of stereotypes—rich bitch, farm girl, mannish card player, erotic tease, neurotic drug-taker, emotionally unstable religious nut, Latin teacher, accomplished mainliner, and tormented, abused child.

Renata is an even more developed version of the deathly erotic woman. Charlie laughingly describes himself embracing the busty Renata, the most voluptuous of all the mistresses, on a posturpedic mattress while looking into her love pious eyes and enjoying her delicious dampness. He fears the effects of her slow glance, which takes men in whole, and the effect her florid, fragrant, and large self has on him. She is a "gypsy," and he cools her lust. Renata knows exactly how she affects him and in what kind of esteem he holds her when she says, "To you I'm a big, beautiful palooka, a dumb broad. You'd like me to be your Kama-Sutra dream-girl" (*HG* 191). Charlie inadvertently concurs when he calls her perfect like a leopard or race horse, a noble animal (192). He sees her as Goya's Maja smoking a cigar or Wallace Stevens' Fretful Concubine (401).

Angela Gruner seems a step down from Thea, Ramona, or Renata. She is seen entirely through the eyes of Mr. Sammler, Bellow's quintessential misogynist. With Angela, he explains, "You confronted sensual womanhood without remission. You smelled it, too. She wore the odd stylish things which Sammler noted with detached and purified dryness, as if from a different part of the universe. What were those, white-kid buskins? What were those tights—sheer, opaque? Where did they lead? That effect of the hair called frosting, that color under the lioness's muzzle, that swagger to enhance the natural power of the bust" (*MSP* 36). Like any Old Testament prophet, Sammler equates whoring with the collapse of civilized order. Angela's supposed nymphomania becomes a metaphor for a modern American Babylon and the general decline of human values. While thinking of Angela, Sammler comments, "Great cities are whores. Doesn't everyone know? Babylon was a whore" (163). Angela accurately senses his mind-set when she complains, "All of the oldest, deepest, worst sexual prejudices are mobilized against me" (163). He tells her that she "represents the realism of the race, which is always pointing out that wisdom, beauty, glory, courage in men are just vanities and her business is to beat down man's legend about himself" (187). The elderly Sammler makes his ultimate pathological denunciation of women generally: "Females were naturally more prone to grossness, had more smells, needed more washing, clipping, binding, pruning, grooming, perfuming, and training" (37). She has become for him a fearful archetypal mother-devourer, scapegoat, bitch-goddess, castrator, and whore. Like any scapegoat she must be driven out into the urban wilderness to where she can practice her pagan sexuality, her ingratitude and failure of filial piety, and wear her green, "sexual kindergarten" minidress away from the purer realms of male endeavor (300–301).

Treckie (*MDH*) is a far more trivialized mistress than these former "sack artists." She qualifies as sexually attractive but on an entirely new model. She is short, tough, and apparently proud of the bruises she has received from other lovers. But Kenneth immediately labels himself serious and Treckie as not serious because she will not marry him. "Affinity" for Kenneth means seeing what can be "put together of a permanent nature" (*MDH* 63). This affinity he describes as two people having matching particles and counterbalancing each other's somatic types. He admits that, like Poe, he is probably fixated on child-woman types; and although, unlike Poe, he is not attached to a retarded girl, he gives the impression he regards her as morally retarded for choosing single parenthood over his offer of marriage. Talk about affinity and celltypes, however, soon becomes submerged in a catalogue of Kenneth's erotic tastes.

> The fashion word *petite*, referring to height only, is inadequate since it doesn't tell you whether the figure is flat or full. Treckie has exactly the bosom—top of its class—that I prefer. From the first, I especially resonated to the swell of her shape because of what seemed to me its connection with the physical . . . and by physical I mean planetary or, more broadly, gravitational forces—strength for strength. . . . This sexual kid, I went for her, her small face and miniature smiles together with the full figure, her well-developed bosom. She was like a pale girl-aborigine. (63)

The racial qualifier also suggests some additional racial ideologies governing his sexual interests. Note also his self-deception in attempting to turn this all into some higher planetary affair. It is as if Kenneth cannot abide the immediate implications of his own sexual immaturities and has to ascribe them to astral sources, a move that is typical of his capacity for avoiding the physical and leaping into ether and abstractions. Discussing Treckie with his more sexually experienced father, he gets the following male assessment: "What we have here: grown women in the child class? He understood immediately. Girls of this type, tiny creatures, got a special kick out of showing that they were sexually full women. They could make bruisers and giants obey them. Afraid of no man, as hot-blooded and capable as any six-foot Swede of African. 'Domineering diminutives,' Dad called them. 'Let's see who's boss here'" (65). He fails to tell his father he adores Treckie for fear his father would take him out of it by calling him a masochist. That of course makes Treckie, at least in Rudi's eyes, a manipulative, domineering sadist, another ball breaker of a slightly more contemporary type than most of the other mistresses. He further damns her morally by telling of her stock portfolio gift from a dead grandfather and her attitude that, if people in the power structure in Washington, D.C., were making themselves personal gifts of millions, why should people like her work. Treckie, however, also has some unflattering but true things to say to Kenneth that demonstrate some very good reasons why she will not marry him. "You're a very self-sufficient person, with a life plan of his own." By this, Kenneth understands her to be calling him arrogant when he interprets, "There she was right on the nail. Particularly in this day and age, you have no reason to exist unless you believe you can make your life a turning point. A turning point for everybody—for humankind. This takes a certain amount of gall" (68). Treckie is accusing him of not really having room for her or Nancy and of wishing to assume a metaphysically important position vis-à-vis the life of humankind. She rightly calls this arrogant and dismisses Kenneth from further consideration as a marriage mate. No doubt this seems bossy and domineering to her, diminishing her intentionality to say the very least. She knows she is less metaphysically important to him than Uncle Benn himself. He is right to believe that all this repels her and even admits he can see why it would (70). Finally admitting his error, he says, "What should she care—and why should she care?—for the imaginations, the sexual pictures I carried in my head of her female wealth, the fallopian tubes like the twin serpents of Caduceus; or like the ornate clips for sheet music springing up on trombones and cornets of marching bands" (71). He writes her off as totally irresponsible when she leaves her VA job and decides to head for snowmobile country in Puget Sound with Ronald. He nastily pictures her living on the trailer court circuit like "gypsies, tinkers, hoboes," engaging in flea market trade. Interestingly, she is heading in the same general direction as Uncle Benn, toward lichens and the polar ice cap.

Clara Velde (*AT*), Bellow's one major female protagonist, is also presented through a male narrator. He portrays her as a four times married woman who has had a long-time relationship as the mistress of Ithiel Regler. It is this latter relationship from which she takes her primary identity. Her romantic ideologies and her gender assessments seem those of a typical male protagonist. Like them, she is a somewhat obtuse protagonist who cannot resolve the dichotomy between desire for the ultimate heterosexual union and desire for the rational. Clara and Ithiel alternately embrace and flee, seek higher consciousness, and become mired in temporal mundanity and experience the demythologization of love in "Gogmagogsville." Like the female lovers of the male protagonists, Ithiel cannot bear the weight of Clara's expectations. Clara, like the male protagonists, never really sees through the causes of her romantic failure with Ithiel. "We have this total, delicious connection, which is also a disaster" (*AT* 9). Instead of loving Ithiel for his own soul's sake, Clara loves him in large part because he is "flying high as a wunderkind in nuclear strategy, and he might have gone all the way to the top, to the negotiating table in Geneva, facing Russians, if he had been less quirky" (17). She calls him analytically deep and comments on his breadth of knowledge, his fantastic reports, and his reputation. Yet the narrator steadily reveals him as a Washington careerist who places his career above personal commitment. Ironically, the one moment Clara feels they have achieved the status of the perfectly synchronized human heterosexual pair, they are geographically separated and communicating by transatlantic phone, while she, student-wife fashion, organizes and edits his notes "in a style resembling his own. . . . She could do any amount of labor—long dizzy days at the tinny Olivetti—to link herself to him" (20). Equally ironic is the picture of Clara naked, wearing only clogs in the kitchen preparing Ithiel's food, while he, seemingly oblivious, is stretched on the bed, "studying his dangerous documents (all those forbidden facts) . . . not that the deadly information affected Ithiel enough to change the expression of his straight profile" (23). At every turn the text undercuts Clara's generous views on Ithiel Regler's geopolitical and interpersonal skills. In fact, it reveals her as a rather stereotypical racist, classist, Wasp snob attracted sexually to the politically powerful man of geopolitical affairs. The qualities of masculine rationality and restraint she admires in him are the very qualities that prevent him from completing the ultimate human pair she imagines them to be. Without quite realizing the implications of what she is saying, Clara notes of Ithiel:

> He could be as remote about such judgements as if his soul were one of a dozen similar souls in a jury box, hearing

evidence: to find us innocent would be nice, but guilty couldn't shock him much. She decided he was in a dangerous moral state and that it was up to her to rescue him from it. . . . You couldn't separate love from being. You could Be, even though you were alone. But in that case you loved only yourself. If so, everybody else was a phantom, and then world politics was a shadow play. Therefore, she, Clara, was the only key to politics that Ithiel was likely to find. Otherwise he might as well stop bothering his head about his grotesque game theories, ideologies, treaties, and the rest of it. (30–31)

This is as close as any Bellow protagonist gets to admitting the consequences of the colonized feminine—nothing short of geo-political disaster—the ultimate incompletion of the human pair described literally as global catastrophe. Though Clara fails to confront the classic contradiction inherent in her own version of the male mystique, she finally does accuse Ithiel of being "as frozen as his pledge" (43) and of crawling off "to [his] office hideaway" to do his "thing about Russia or Iran" (55). The implied author comments, "She might as well have been talking to one of those Minoans dug up by Evans or Schlieman or whoever, characters like those in the silent films, painted with eye-lengthening makeup" (55). When she makes him her last offer, the implied narrator reports, "Teddy [Ithiel Regler] was stirred, and looked aside. He wasn't ready, and perhaps never would be ready to go farther. No, they never would be man and wife. When they stood up to go, they kissed like friends" (80). Even after the season of tears, Clara believes that Ithiel is the one with the "big, big picture," and could have provided her with a clue to her authentic self. In effect, she has abdicated feminine self-knowledge about identity to the empowered, intellectual male and put him in charge of finding out who she might really be—a classic move by a male-identified female. By now, because Ithiel's character has been seriously undercut by the text itself, the reader doubts that Ithiel has the big picture on anything. Clara, in overvaluing Ithiel in all the stereotypical ways, has undersold herself, and other women in the text, including her Chinese friend, Ms. Wong, Gina Wegman, and her daughter. Ithiel Regler is as archaic a male type as a Minoan with eye make-up, and Clara is true to type with her "ancestrally North Sea nose," "big bones," hailing "from the sticks" from

"Indiana and Illinois farmers and small town businessmen who were very religious" and reared on "old-time religion" (1). The narrator tells us, "In her you might see suddenly a girl from a remote town, from the vestigial America of one-room schoolhouses. Constables, covered dish suppers, one of those communities bypassed by technology and urban development" (39).

The rest of the detail with which Clara is described puts her in the same category, as morally and emotionally unstable, into which most of the women previously discussed have fallen. She has slummed with Clifford, who is now in the Attica jail; had a nervous breakdown; enjoyed an intimate association with Spontini and Giancomo, mafia crooks and billionaire revolutionists; stolen a large sum from an insurance company; had a long affair with Ithiel and married four "utility" husbands; and made racist remarks about Frederic. Empowered as a white, Protestant, executive-level professional woman reared on fundamental Christianity and a white middle-class work and racial ethic, Clara is immersed in the values of her class and type. The pattern is the same for all these groups of representations of women cut to male desire within the masculine symbolic which devalues women in stereotypical ways. More precisely, they are cut to the personality types, emotional hangups, and acculturation of Bellow's male monologists and implied listeners.

There are some women not entirely contained by the protagonist's erotic gaze, women who somehow escape into the texts to wander its margins with different spiritual powers and values attached to them, despite the brevity and ultimate inconsequentiality of their appearances and their ultimate abandonment or loss to the world of male homosociality. They are often, however, much less certainly and skillfully drawn. Amy Wustrin in *AT* and Rosamund in *R* fit into this category.

Ultimately, the Bellow protagonist constructs use-value hierarchies from these many women, based on the libidinal economy of the male homosocial identity, hierarchies that he will ultimately reject as he dimly realizes the gender dynamics and masculine erotic codes by which he has been operating and failing for most of his life. The conflicts and contradictions he will only partly perceive, however, and mostly fail to rectify, in some cases expanding the use-value of some women or, conversely, becoming even more virulently gynophobic and misogynistic, depending on his degree of self-awareness and ability to move beyond his own narcissism.

The classic male gaze of the androcentric text using the narrative apparatus previously described easily accumulates enough power to draw us into its misogynistic designs. The egocentric and misogynist gaze of the Bellow monologist is nearly always split between a passive female who is gazed at and a male who does the gazing. To this extent woman, not women, becomes the object of the combined triple gaze of the author, narratee, and actual male reader. She always ends up relegated to the margins by the male protagonist, who is the only figure in the landscape of the novel free to command the stage of narrative illusion. On that stage, or page, which he fills with his thoughts, the account of his masculine subjectivity, he and he alone articulates the look and creates the hermeneutic machinery in which this symbolic figure of woman is manipulated.

But what of this look, which is capable, for the most part, only of staging a traditional masculine desire? In the Bellow novel, an image of woman is projected onto the fictional screen to be looked on, desired, shunned, hated, investigated, pursued, controlled, gossiped about, and ultimately possessed or vanquished from sight by a male viewing subject in whom is vested the desiring of the male author, male protagonist, sympathetic male narratee, and the male reader. Only briefly do we catch glimpses of some surplus or excess of femininity not contained by this dominant visual economy. Only in a few instances are there women in the picture who threaten to disrupt masculinity and the fixity of the misogynist gaze. When this happens, the Bellow protagonists almost catch a glimpse of that elusive feminine that symbolizes their respective metaphysical quests.

In the meantime we must ask, if this is how such a text functions for the male reader, how does it function for the female reader? Being tied up in just this way, says Irigaray, is what happens to women within this male economy of desiring, where the devaluation or erasure of the feminine, her relegation to the margins, if not her total eclipse, is a perpetual erasure that always forestalls the representation of the feminine. This erasure in turn creates a reification of the male/male relationship, causing the subordinate, utilitarian figure of a woman to function as a bodily conduit through which the male protagonist will triangulate his desire for masculine filiation.

Ultimately, then, it is Bellow's repeated choice of masculine monologue that attributes the power of the gaze and the voice to the male narrator. Bellow's choice of male monologue accounts for the repeated patterns of male homosocial desire in each Bellow novel, which in turn produces the endless male (not female) "fantasy of pursuit, capture, distance, desire, memory, and loss."[1] Such androcentric narrative machinery ties up not only female seeing, but male seeing as well. The consequences for Bellow's protagonists are profound and constitute the central issues of metaphysical awareness and human happiness every text explores. For the brief period of the reading, male readers identify with the male monologist in experiencing a comic fantasy of love, hate, possession, loss, and mourning. What results is "a gaze, a world, an object . . . cut to the measure of [masculine] desire as it is to any 'reality.'"[2] The Bellow novel, by this means, offers an image of reality, not immediate or neutral, but posed, framed, and centered. The spectator/reader is stitched into place by the sense of the image as he completes the image as its subject. This literally engages the male spectator in the process of that reproduction, as one more articulator of the text's coherence. The spectator is then held somewhat immobile, controlled, for the duration of the novel, as if he were in front of a screen. Bellow's use of the male protagonist allows him absolute control of the construction of male desire in the text. In Stephen Heath's words, it enables him "to regulate that movement of the individual subject, beheld and beholder, in a shifting and placing of desire, energy, contradiction, in perpetual retotalization of the imaginary."[3]

It is at the cost of serious conflicts within himself, however, that Bellow's protagonist does so. This kind of masculine structuring of desire produces within him that very dichotomy of selfhood represented by that polarity of the masculine figured forth in the types of Don Juan (Humboldt, Charlie, and Herzog) and the priestly celibate (Mr. Sammler, Benn Crader). It is also this mechanism that constructs his misogyny and thus blinds him from finding the elusive feminine. The problem lies in the lenses of his own eyes, in that flat mirror of the masculine selfsame he holds up to himself that produces self but not "not self."

Inevitably we must ask "what of the female reader?" Mary Ann Caws raises complex moral and metaphysical issues with regard to both the male writer and the female reader of the androcentric text: "Are we to refuse looking as part of being looked at? The whole issue of looking at ourselves as looked at calls into question how and where we may be thought to possess ourselves within this fiction of painless consuming of images-as-other. They are not, in this case, entirely other, nor can we pretend to see them as such. We are folded up in and into— implicated—even tied up in our seeing."[4]

But it is not just women characters and women readers who are tied up in their seeing. The Bellow protagonist is also tied up in his own seeing, to his serious spiritual and social detriment. To fail to see the feminine in the flat mirror of the masculine selfsame is also to lose himself in the very specular apparatus in which he loses sight of her.

5

THE LAND ELSEWHERE

It is not the life of sexuality that literature cannot capture; it is literature that inhabits the very heart of what makes sexuality problematic.

—Barbara Johnson, *The Critical Difference: Essays in the Contemporary Rhetoric of Reading*

From *Dangling Man* to *Humboldt's Gift*, there is a steady attempt by the transgressive male protagonist to elude, modify, and transcend the masculinities he inherits in his search for a space that does not seem to exist. For this space I have borrowed the term "the land elsewhere" from Hélène Cixous to refer to the rejected element of the feminine that haunts Bellow's protagonists and which exists mostly outside of these traditional masculinities. It would appear to be an intuitive, visionary, dreaming, orphic, or yet-to-be imagined feminine self. It eludes Joseph and appears only when Asa's wife returns to him. Augie can never realize it, while Tommy Wilhelm can only register its absence. Henderson briefly apprehends it in a mythical Africa of the mind, in a lioness's den, and ultimately with an orphan child. Herzog briefly finds it in the final tranquility of his ruined Ludeyville estate. Humboldt briefly has it as a very young poet and then loses it. Charlie must start from the beginning to find where he went wrong. Mr. Sammler finally understands how his masculine acculturation in misogyny has failed to prepare him for the feminine. He at least senses he must opt for life on this planet, acknowledge his love for Elya Gruner, and take responsibility for his daughter, Shula-Slawa. Corde maps the distractions within and without that make it so hard for him to apprehend the "*mysterium tremendum*" and realizes the presence of the true feminine in his alter ego self, Valeria Raresh, and her community of women. More than most of Bellow's men, he can begin to imagine the feminine. Kenneth Trachtenberg and Benn Crader, that pair-bonded couple of would-be comic metaphysical questers, also seek and lose both the literal and the metaphoric feminine. Ithiel Regler chooses the masculine power games of Washington, D.C., instead of Clara's genuine tenth-century soul. The unnamed protagonist of *The Bellarosa Connection*, despite his phenomenal memory, leaves it too late to pursue his mysterious connection with the remarkable Sorella Fonstein, the closest embodiment of the missing feminine within himself. Harry Trellman captures a renewed glimpse of it in the memory of his first love, Amy Wustrin. Ravelstein and Chick are only uncoupled through death and are the most complete soulmates, whereupon Rosamund becomes the only wife in whom resides the potential for a new feminine.

Having immersed themselves in masculine narcissism, antisocial romantic individualism, American capitalism, and the whole American masculine experience from Columbus to the Cold War, these men have so rejected, repressed, and relegated the literal feminine that they have all but lost it. Here lies much of their disease with their lives and times.

Though many able critics have successfully mapped the eclipse of the transcendental by the capitalist, rationalist, American experiences of the Bellow hero, the eclipse of this feminine, orphic realm of experience has everything to do with how the men both seek and alienate the feminine within themselves, as well as with literal women. The self-destructive codes of masculinity that drive these male characters cause the very scotomas or blind spots they are afflicted with as they gaze into that narcissistic mirror and fail to glimpse traces of that fuller masculinity, that surplus, which remains always just behind the mirror of that imprisoning masculine self-same. Driven and haunted by this absent presence, they repeatedly seek and reject actual women, never really able to grasp femininity. Having colonized the feminine as other and constructed their masculine sense of self against it, they are at a loss as to how to accommodate the absence that now haunts them.[1]

Bellow usually develops his gendered cultural critique by juxtaposing two symbolic and mutually exclusive masculine gender constructs—an overweening hypermasculinity[2] on the one hand,

and an all but culturally eclipsed feminine on the other. The hyper-masculine and other masculinities are usually elaborated through a rich taxonomy of destructive American male alter egos. The feminine construct is metaphorized often in terms close to Jung's anima. Bellow uses the paradigm to suggest Cixous's metaphysical concept of "the land elsewhere," the possibility or even the neces-sity of a new history of man that would reclaim its lost feminine by creating a more spiritually productive circuit of gender exchanges.

As we have already seen, however, the principal masculine construct Bellow is working with is an ironic version of the self-absorbed male romantic individualist developed from an American version of nineteenth-century individualism. This recent American historical model with its narcissism and its scotomas is best under-stood in its original nonironic forms as it appears in Cooper, Emerson, Thoreau, and Melville. Bellow makes it very clear that this tradition is his symbolic referent. Writing in his notebooks, Emerson inadvertently states the very problem that lies at the heart of the masculine selfsame: "I am always environed by myself: what I am all things reflect to me."[3] Typically, this is the stance and the method by which the Bellow male protagonist characterizes his world. He, too, is typically American white, bourgeois, sometimes Jewish, and sometimes Gentile. Furthermore, he is Bellow's ironic late-twenti-eth-century manifestation through which the author is at pains to demonstrate a variety of culturally differentiated masculinities.

Bellow's men mostly occupy stereotypical, historical, masculine subjectivities, but they also reveal split and contradictory masculinities better described as masculine difference. Some openly rebel at the masculine roles imposed on them and seek kinds of new spaces for men like themselves. They intuitively seek what Clément and Cixous describe as "a repressed enigmatic hieroglyph of an absence striving to become a presence."[4] As artists, intellectuals, and sometimes hermetical personalities, Bellow's male protagonists are transgressive figures. They demonstrate American masculinities in disarray. Some are even feminine hysterics,[5] while others demonstrate intense hypermasculinities, enact transgressive or revisionist masculinities, or wander between multiple masculinities.

The contradictory and oppositional discourses at play within these male subjects make them historically transitional figures as masculine subjects implicated in the legacy of American individualism, romanticism, frontier ethics, capitalist paradigms, iconoclastic narcissism, manifest destiny, notions of whiteness and blackness, and various ethnic heritages. Their intuitive, poetic, meditative, dreaming impulses often run counter to their social acculturation. Frequently, femininity is seen as a utopian possibility they do glimpse. Thus, the Bellow protagonist registers historically the end of one kind of manhood and the beginning of another. To borrow Maurice Blanchot's paradigm once more, they are the "last men" of a certain historical type.[6] In Michel Foucault's words: "As the archaeology of our thought easily shows, man is an invention of recent date. And one perhaps nearing its end . . . if some event of which we can at the moment do no more than sense the possibility—without knowing either what its form will be or what it promises—were to cause them to crumble . . . then one can certainly wager that man would be erased, like a face drawn in sand at the edge of the sea."[7] At the very moment Bellow's texts seem to be reifying old codes of masculinity, they are already creating spaces for thinking new ones.

Despite the striving for masculine difference within the Bellow text, however, there is no denying the fact that these are still androcentric novels that, like so many of their type, end up being gynophobic boys' books. Constance Rourke has observed that so many American heroes were solitary male figures without wife, family, or any other human relationship: they appeared always as single figures, or merely doubled and multiplied, never as one of a natural group, never as part of the complex human situation, always nomadic. These legendary figures became emblems of national life.[8] The "American Narcissus," says Joyce Warren, looked at himself in this unreal, inflated, isolated figure and saw what he wanted to see—an ideal picture of himself. The narcissism of the American Dreamer lies in his acceptance of this mammoth image of himself. The persona that he creates for himself enables him to reconcile his personal shortcomings with the myth of American Individualism: he sees himself as all-powerful and all-encompassing.[9]

Leslie Fiedler, in *Love and Death in the American Novel* (1966), argues that there is the strong presence of the masculine adolescence in the American novel and a subsequent failure of American novelists (unlike nineteenth-century European writers) to portray adult heterosexual relationships and fully drawn women.[10] Although his observations on male homosociality look dated now, Fiedler was the first to suggest that the male pair bonding which characterized the lives of the fictional heroes of the classic American androcentric novel had gynophobic, misogynistic, and even homosexual implications. Implicit in his critique, of course, is the failure of the American novel to represent femininity. Both Rourke and Fiedler were describing the aftermath of a nineteenth-century cult of masculine individualism that had stressed self-assertion and material progress for the white male bourgeoisie, and that inevitably tended to eclipse women, Indians, Blacks, and immigrant populations. "Like the legendary Narcissus, the American individualist focused on his own image to such an extent that he could grant little reality to others."[11]

Warren, in *The American Narcissus*, asserts that this masculine conditioning to accept unreal myths about masculine power and autonomy has proved to be a snare and a delusion for many American men in the nineteenth and twentieth centuries. Finding failure, she argues, many men, instead of jettisoning the myth, create false images of themselves, a persona who possesses all of the qualities of greatness that the myth of the individual tells him he should possess. She also notes that the woman reader must identify with the male protagonist in order to find a role model that encourages the development of her individuality. Because most American literature is written from a masculine perspective in which man acts out his destiny apart from society and from women, however, such texts portray women as "associated with the pressures of society and . . . as entrappers, unattractive adversaries of the American [masculine] experience" (2–3). She notes also that "a corollary of manifest destiny is, of course, the belief that the other guy, the victim of your destiny, does not count." This is the other side of American individualism, the side that is visible only if we look at individualism not from the point of view of the individual but from the point of view of the other—the person or persons whom the individual sees either as useful to or standing in the way of his expansion (14). "However illusory the promise of America may have proved to be for many men, the dominant image for the white American male was that of a larger-than-life superhero whose world was wrought for himself and by himself" (17). Hence, the dilemma of Bellow's protagonists who cannot quite reconcile this masculinity with their sense of the absurd and the ironic.

James Fenimore Cooper was obviously the original literary architect of the Solitary Man and Superfluous Woman gender paradigm in American literature. His fictional world is a man's world and includes heroines only to satisfy an almost all-female reading audience. His women have no existence in his novels except in relation to men because his novels stand squarely in the androcentric tradition of male adventure narratives. Cooper, like his creation, Natty Bumppo, saw others as shadowy nonpersons not important in the life of a manly hero. More specifically, he saw no active role for women in the world of the American frontier dreamer.

The tradition of masculine solitude begun by Cooper finds its fullest expression in Emerson, Thoreau, and Melville. Ralph Waldo Emerson, speaking of friendship and marriage, asserted that other people can be regarded only as "feeders and coadjutors" of the self.[12]

Philip Slater provides a contemporary commentary on the consequences of such masculine egotism:

> By raising the spectre of immersion in group life—of losing one's narcissistic consciousness—[male individualists] were frightened and shamed people into an ever more frantic pursuit of autonomy and self-sufficiency. . . . Ripped out of their social fabric, their social responses are constantly seeking a stimulus to which they can attach themselves. . . . By heaping scorn on social responses fundamental to humankind, they helped further the process of disconnection in the society. . . . The ideology of freedom and individualism [produces]—desperate and shame-faced efforts to fill the hole left by the every-man-should-strive-to-be-a-lonely-genius-head-and-shoulders-above-the-worthless-gregarious-dependent-masses guilt trip.[13]

Slater's commentary describes so well the plight of the Bellow protagonist torn between head and heart, solitude and society, sex and celibacy, family and self, the mundane and the mystical, art and popular culture, seriousness and self-irony. So many of Bellow's novels tell the tragicomic story of a capitalist American culture in which hypermasculine striving for power and self-aggrandizement has all but excluded love, the soul, beauty, poetry, and visionary states, that is, the feminine. American poets and men of feeling such as Edgar Allen Poe, Isaac Rosenfeld, Delmore Schwartz, Augie March (*AM*), Eugene Henderson (*HRK*), Moses Herzog (*H*), Mr. Sammler (*MSP*), Dean Corde (*DD*), Uncle Benn Crader (*MDH*), Ithiel Regler (*AT*), the unnamed founder of the Mnemosyne Institute (*BC*), Harry Trellman (*TA*), and Chick *(R)* register the

79

tensions wrought upon men by the American historical experience. They find their personal lives impoverished by the seeming impossibility of combining capitalism and poetry, self and other, heterosexual union and individualism. Hence, the familiar pattern that governs Bellow's representation of masculinity: narcissism, misogyny, alienation, protagonists separated from their children, the sense of damaged poetic powers, regression into the community of one, flight from women, the seeking of a special destiny, and the comic collapse back into a modern world. For each protagonist, there is also the grief about how women have treated him, the flight from traditional masculinity, the immersion in male homosocial values, and, increasingly, the search for the absent feminine.

Dangling Man

Joseph (*DM*), Bellow's first protagonist, represents an unsettling of received codes of white bourgeois masculinity within American culture of the 1940s.[14] He is the first of Bellow's transgressive male protagonists for whom the prevailing masculine codes of World War II white culture are destructive of the feminine. Already in the Bellow text, masculine difference is being posited. Clément and Cixous express well what Joseph senses and does not have the words to describe:

> There has to be somewhere else, I tell myself. And everyone knows that to go somewhere else there are routes, signs, "maps"—for an exploration, a trip. That's what books are. Everyone knows that a place exists which is not economically or politically indebted to all the vileness and compromise. That is not obliged to reproduce the system. That is writing. If there is a somewhere else that can escape the infernal repetition, it lies in that direction, where *it* writes itself, where *it* dreams, where *it* invents new worlds.[15]

The "infernal" repetition is of course the continuing drama of the masculine selfsame (*Propre*). The dreaming and inventing of new worlds through the rethinking of masculinity is Joseph's taste. A different thematics of desire propels him to write himself (in a journal) out of one gender impasse into a new space where the "repressed enigmatic hieroglyphs of an absence striving to become a presence" can become real. In Clément's and Cixous's language,

80

what he and so many other Bellow protagonists seem to want is passage "[i]nto elsewheres opened by men who are capable of becoming woman. For the huge machine [the masculine symbolic economy] that ticks and repeats its 'truth' for all these centuries has had failures. . . . There have been poets who let something different from tradition get through at any price—men able to love love; therefore to love others, to want them" (98).

Joseph understands this dimly. But, ironically, he is a man trying to create a new space by trying to reoccupy an old one—romantic individualism and the community of one. He is living in a historio-cultural transition, World War II America, in which for a long time it has been "impossible. . . . to think or even imagine an elsewhere" (*DM* 83). He is the first of several Bellow male protagonists trying to escape a certain history of man by attempting to reclaim the poetic impulse, spiritual and metaphysical yearning, meditation, thinking, and high dreaming. Although he is not the repressed "hysteric" and poet later Bellow protagonists seem to be, he is the first man Bellow presents us with in whom we see the spiritual stress and rupture that precedes the attempt to liberate masculinity. He represents that moment in American history when things seem to be astir.

It is highly significant that the first speech any Bellow protagonist makes on the first page of the very first novel is about the historical problematics of American masculinity in the latter half of the twentieth century:

> There was a time when people [men] were in the habit of addressing themselves frequently and felt no shame at making a record of their inward transactions. But to keep a journal nowadays is considered a kind of self-indulgence, a weakness, and in poor taste. For this is an era of hard-boiled-dom. Today, the code of the athlete, of the tough-boy—an American inheritance, I believe, from the English gentleman—that curious mixture of striving, asceticism, and rigor, the origins of which trace back to Alexander The Great—is stronger than ever. Do you have feelings? There are correct and incorrect ways of indicating them. Do you have an inner life? It is nobody's business but your own. Do you have emotions? Strangle them. To a degree, everyone obeys this code. And it does admit a limited kind of candor, a closemouthed straight forwardness. But on the truest candor it has an inhibitory effect. Most serious

matters are closed to the hard-boiled. They are unpracticed in introspection, and therefore badly equipped to deal with opponents whom they cannot shoot like big game or outdo in daring.

If you have difficulties, grapple with them silently, goes one of their commandments. To hell with that! I intend to talk about mine, and if I had as many mouths as Siva has arms and kept them going all the time, I still could not do myself justice. In my present state of demoralization, it has become necessary for me to keep a journal—that is to talk to myself—I do not feel guilty of self-indulgence in the least. The hard-boiled are compensated for their silence: they fly planes or fight bulls or catch tarpon, whereas I rarely leave my room.

In a city where one has lived nearly all his life, it is not likely that he will ever be solitary; and yet, in a very real sense, I am just that. I am alone ten hours a day in a single room. . . . I am well supplied with books. My wife is always bringing new ones in the hope that I will use them. I only wish I could. In the old days, when we had a flat of our own, I read constantly. I was forever buying new books, faster, admittedly, than I could read them. But as long as they surrounded me they stood as guarantors of an extended life, far more precious and necessary than the one I was forced to lead daily. If it was impossible to sustain this superior life at all times, I could at least keep its signs within reach. When it became tenuous I could see them and touch them. Now, however, now that I have the leisure and should be able to devote myself to the studies I once began, I find myself unable to read. Books do not hold me. After two or three pages or, as it sometimes happens, paragraphs, I simply cannot go on. (*DM* 9–10)

Behind Joseph's refusal of Hemingwayesque stoicism is his refusal of an ancient code of masculine adventure. The generations of writers who, having written masculinity in terms of the code of adventure, have produced a generation of men who are now compelled to imagine themselves in these terms. Joseph, Augie, and Simon's generation has inherited a textual tradition of masculine adventure created by such writers as James Fenimore Cooper, J. M. Barrie, Sir Henry Newboldt, Jules Verne, Alexandre Dumas, Stanley Weyman, H. G. Wells, Edgar Allen Poe, Sir Arthur Conan Doyle,

Mark Twain, John Buchan, Evelyn Waugh, Graham Greene, Joseph Conrad, Henry Stanley, François Le Vaillant, Peter Knox-Shaw, Richard Burton, Alan Moorehead, Charles Gordon, Samuel Baker, Blaise Cendrars, Rudyard Kipling, and Ernest Hemingway.

Even the modernist metaphysical tradition Joseph inherits has been influenced by this ideology of masculine adventure. Nietzsche, for instance, was opposed to "The Christian Virtues"—pity, humility, meekness—because they were the moral antidotes to adventure. It has been suggested by Antonio Gramsci that Nietzsche's notion of the superman was not entirely uninfluenced by the cult of adventure in French serial novels popular among intellectuals at least until the 1870s.[16] He cites Alexandre Dumas's *Count of Monte Cristo* as particularly influential. Nietzsche, after all, contrasted adventurous man with "the priestly Jewish forms" of humankind.[17] He favored the knightly caste with its origins in tribal man and primitive man and praised Napoleon as the greatest of adventurers.[18] The narrator locates Joseph on the feminine side of this equation:

> In things of this sort his friends sometimes find him ridiculous. And, yes, he says, he admits he is on "the funny side" in many ways. But that can't be helped. The appearance and behavior of reflective men is seldom comparable to that of the less reflective, who unhesitatingly entrust all they stand for to their looks and gestures. What he is trying to do is not easy, and it is not unlikely that the more he succeeds, the more odd he may seem. Besides, he says, there is an element of the comic or fantastic in everyone. You can never bring that altogether under control. . . . Joseph since leaving school, has not stopped thinking of himself as a scholar, and he surrounds himself with books. Before he interested himself in the Enlightenment he made a study of the early ascetics and, earlier, of Romanticism and the child prodigy. (*DM* 28)

The masculine models Joseph has examined—asceticism, Romanticism, and the Enlightenment—are all solitary, meditative models that are bound ideologically to a certain kind of male subjectivity. Emersonian romantic individualism and Enlightenment thinking are only late historical manifestations of the masculine search for truth through a masculine self-examination reproducing only masculine subjectivity. No wonder Joseph is forced to admit in the end: "I had not done well alone. I doubted whether anyone could. To be pushed upon oneself entirely put the very facts of simple existence in doubt. Perhaps the war could teach me, by violence, what I had been unable to learn during those months in the room. Perhaps I could sound creation through other means. Perhaps. But things were now out of my hands. The next move was the world's. I could not bring myself to regret it" (*DM* 190–91).

Joseph has resisted the patriotic fervor of a world at war, and conscription, resisted being solely defined by the workplace, and alienated most of his friends. In the middle of a world war he has tried to find Walden Pond in a cheap boarding house in New York where he alienates himself from family, friends, and old acquaintances and writes the journal of the Self in which the only Beloved who appears is himself. But it is too late in the century. The narcissism of the model defeats him, as do the times. He finds that he does not "contain multitudes." He simply cannot sing a tuneful "song of myself." As he slowly turns in upon himself, he becomes quarrelsome and even slightly paranoid. Likewise, he becomes morbid about physical decay, death, and persecution as the great suck of self engulfs him.

In evading the Hemingwayesque codes of masculinity and Wasp restraint by voicing his feminine self in a journal, he still fails to encounter those high dreaming states that lure him. His energies begin to break down and he becomes bossy and domineering. He tries to shape his wife's artistic tastes and moral values and despairs when she rebels. He cuts her off from dinners, movies, clothes, magazines, and serene family interactions by trying to make her over in his own pattern. At no time does he accord her equal social or metaphysical value. She is the maternal ground on which he erects much more important desires. The ironic voice of the narrator comments on his narcissism and foolishness: "He is a person greatly concerned with keeping intact and free from encumbrance a sense of his own being, its importance. Yet he is not abnormally cold, nor is he egotistical. He keeps a tight hold because, as he himself explains, he is keenly intent on knowing what is happening to him. He wants to miss nothing" (*DM* 27). Ultimately, his experiment has been conducted at the expense of a subordinated wife whom he doubly insults by having a desultory affair with a woman he doesn't even care about.

I quote at length from *Dangling Man* because in all of these passages we have all the basic patterns of the masculine values, paradigms, and dilemmas of the Bellow protagonist, from *Dangling Man* to *The Bellarosa Connection*, *The Actual*, and *Ravelstein*. This is the rupture with a historical masculinity whose lineage Joseph is quite explicit about—American WASP culture, Hemingwayesque sto-icism, Enlightenment romantic individualism, English codes of striving, asceticism, and rigor stemming back to Alexander the Great. It is the warrior code of classic Western masculinity he protests, in its cross-cultural and American manifestations. Can I say it any more strongly? The first Bellow protagonist's first lament is about prevailing codes of masculinity, and so are the laments of all subsequent protagonists. Joseph knows that one of the manifesta-tions of masculine narcissism is misogyny. As he views Abt's revolting "spite" and "rage" directed at the helpless, hypnotized Minna, Joseph wonders to what extent he is just as guilty. Later that night as he stares at the helpless naked body of his wife, he wonders if his attempts to erase her and make her over in the pattern of his own masculine desiring are not doing exactly the same thing. His final comment as he falls asleep is

> But I already knew that I had hit upon the truth and that I could not easily dispel it tomorrow or any other day. I had an uneasy dream-ridden night.
> This was only the beginning. In the months that followed I began to discover one weakness after another in all I had built up around me. I saw what Jack Brill had seen, but, knowing it better, saw it more keenly and severely. (*DM* 57)

Joseph's experiment at discovering a higher destiny, an expanded masculinity, is aborted as he waits in line at the field house with all the other recruits who are all told to strip naked. As he stands there with the old conscripts, "examining their scars and blemishes as they did mine," he is felt in the groin by an aging doctor with a cigar who administers a blood test and then dismisses him (*DM* 188). So much for a higher masculine destiny.

As he takes his leave of the boardinghouse room he has shared with Minna, he revisits the room in which he spent his childhood. It is here the whole problem with the "room of his own," the "community of one," and the bankruptcy of romantic individualism strikes him:

> It was suddenly given me to experience one of those consummating glimpses that come to all of us periodically. The room, delusively, dwindled and became a tiny square, swiftly drawn back, myself and all the objects in it growing smaller. This was not a mere visual trick. I understood it to be a revelation of the ephemeral agreements by which we live and pace ourselves. I looked around at the restored walls. This place which I avoided ordinarily, had great personal significance for me. But it was not here thirty years ago. Birds flew through this space. It may be gone fifty years hence. Such reality, I thought, is actually very dangerous, very treacherous. It should not be trusted. And I rose rather unsteadily from the rocker, feeling that there was an element of treason to common sense in the very objects of common sense. (*DM* 190)

Danahay's "community of one" is a masculine formula he rejects, quickly, finding of this spiritual insight: "[It] is not achieved in a vacuum, but in the company of other men, attended by love. I, in this room, separate, alienated, distrustful, find in my purpose not an open world, but a closed hopeless jail. My perspectives end in the walls. Nothing of the future comes to me. Only the past, in its shabbiness and innocence. Some men seem to know exactly where their opportunities lie; they break prisons and cross whole Siberias to pursue them. One room holds me" (*DM* 92).

Furthermore, he senses the end of a certain history of man in his rejection of legendary historical male archetypes:

> Of course, we suffer from bottomless avidity. Our lives are so precious to us, we are so watchful of waste. Or perhaps a better name for it would be the Sense of Personal Destiny. Yes, I think that is better than avidity. . . . And then there are our plans, idealizations. These are dangerous too. They can consume us like parasites, eat us, drink us, and leave us lifelessly prostrate. And yet we are always inviting the parasite, as if we were eager to be drained and eaten.
>
> It is because we have been taught there is no limit to what a man can be. Six hundred years ago, a man was what he was born to be. Satan and the Church, representing God, did

battle over him. He, by reason of his choice, partially decided the outcome. But whether, after life, he went to hell or to heaven, his place among other men was given. It could not be contested. But, since, the stage has been reset and human beings only walk on it, and, under this revision, we have, instead, history to answer to. We were important enough then for our souls to be fought over. Now each of us is responsible for his own salvation, which is in his greatness. And that, that greatness, is the rock our hearts are abraded on. Great minds, great beauties, great lovers and criminals surround us. From the great sadness and desperation of Werthers and Don Juans we went to the great ruling images of Napoleons; from these to murderers who had that right over victims because they were greater than the victims; to men who felt privileged to approach others with a whip; to schoolboys and clerks who roared like revolutionary lions; to those pimps and subway creatures, debaters in midnight cafeterias who believed they could be great in treachery and catch the throats of those they felt were sound and well in the lassos of their morbidity; to dreams of greatly beautiful shadows embracing on a flawless screen. Because of these things we hate immoderately and punish one another immoderately. The fear of lagging pursues and maddens us. The fear lies in us like a cloud. It makes an inner climate of darkness. And occasionally there is a storm and hate and wounding rain out of us. (*DM* 88–89)

Here is the long history of a troubled masculinity laid out and lamented. And here are the roots of the dream of an "elsewhere" for masculinity and the sense that neither romantic introspection nor romantic adventure is capable of defining it.

The Victim

In his second novel, *The Victim*, Bellow seems to focus on some of the psychological particulars that prevent that "elsewhere" from being realized. Asa Leventhal, literally a victim of his own masculine insecurities and misogyny, suffers greatly from a kind of male cultural paranoia that is not relieved until he has dealt with his contempt for his own brother and with his nemesis, that gentile doppelgänger, Kirby Allbee. Both are very different men competing for survival in a workplace arena. This novel offers an examination of masculine identity within the social class and Jewish-Gentile paradigms.

The son of a small Jewish dry goods merchant from Hartford, Asa seems unable to feel for or feel empowered by his now-deceased father. Neither can he get past the haunting memory of the screaming madness of his mother. He has gone to New York after high school to work for Harkavy, a friend of his Uncle Schacter. He has been a poor prelegal student, and when the son, Daniel Harkavy, arrives to take over after the death of his father, Asa is too mistrustful and dispirited to stay on. From the beginning he is solitary, having only really had Harkavy senior as a friend. He endures unemployment, during which he stays in the awful hotel on lower Broadway, where he is still haunted by feeling "the lost, the outcast, the overcome, the effaced, the ruined" (*TV* 16). But on top of all this, he is a Jew living through a period of penultimate global antisemitism, as news of the Holocaust becomes known. He has grown up during the 1920s, a moment of antisemitic paranoia and backlash against Jewish immigration, followed by increased feeling against Jews in the workplace during the Depression. His is not of the privileged Wasp New England heritage the gentile Allbee enjoys. They are natural enemies, and the class hubris and decadence of the one undermines the cultural inferiority complex of the other. These are the two masculinities that now comprise white American masculinity, in addition to all the other historical models that have already laid the foundations of American manhood. *The Victim*, among other things, explores the great spiritual question of Judeo-Christian masculine identity—the responsibility of self for other. What is the moral responsibility of one man for the random suffering that befalls another? Bellow's exploration, however, adds the dimension of the dilemma of the modern post-Holocaust secular Jew for his white masculine oppressor and the atmosphere of paranoia which infects them both.

What Leventhal must do is what Joseph finally has to do— emerge from his room and deal with unjust accusations, the madness of everyday life, and a deepening paranoia. The paranoia we see in Joseph has deepened in Leventhal, but the problem is the same—to emerge from the narcissistic masculine formulas he has inherited, to avoid and deny, or to eternally complain and be afraid. It is not clear how successful Leventhal is at emerging from his crises and dealing with social complicity, but since the novel ends with the return of his wife and the upcoming birth of a child, we assume that for now Leventhal is learning to confront life and be happy. His rescue, however, has consisted of the embrace of the literally feminine. It is Mary's love, her conception, and the prospect of a baby that enables Asa to enter a renewed relationship with himself and his social world. Without his wife, Mary, as the literal conduit, we sense he would not have survived his crisis with his alter ego and nemesis, Allbee. It is Mary who creates the space for Leventhal to claim his fuller masculine self, even though the first manifestations of this are his bonding with his nephew Philip and a lessening of the strain in his relationship with his brother, Max.

The Adventures of Augie March

In *The Adventures of Augie March*, Bellow provides new hope for American masculinity. It is a book Irving Howe has called "a paen to the idea of personal freedom in hostile circumstances."[19] It is also Bellow's continuing exploration of male escape from prevailing codes of American masculinity. Through the use of the picaresque novel form wedded to the psychological complexities of the *bildungsroman*, Bellow is able to track a psychologically complex character through a significant transitional period in the expression of American manhood, the Great Depression and its aftermath.

In the comically mixed voices of the eighteenth-century gentleman and the lower-middle-class Yiddish picaro, Bellow sets out to compile a history of masculine types. Much parodied and alluded to are literally dozens of texts and male characters belonging to the heroic traditions of masculine adventure in classical literature. This forms the subtext and context of Augie's life. The point of view, however, is that of an older, wiser, middle-aged, and more philosophical Augie looking back at the younger man he was.

In this novel Bellow begins to develop a wide range of masculinities that Augie rejects and Simon espouses. As Robert Crozier has stated, Augie, along with Holden Caulfield in *The Catcher in the Rye*, inaugurates a significant reaction to the formulas of power, love, money, and urbanization that drive previous heroes of American literature. Its time is the liberal revisionist 1950s. Augie is a direct revision of the nineteenth-century American masculinity established in the texts of Cooper, Emerson, Thoreau, and Whitman. He is Bellow's deliberate transformation of the adventurous male in the middle of the twentieth century. Augie begins in freedom and in the end relapses into the old romantic solipsism that never works for the Bellow hero. Augie and Simon are also parodies on rags-to-riches Horatio Alger models of American masculinity.[20] Others have called Augie a typically nineteenth-century explorer-discoverer, somewhat removed from the civil state and resembling Melville's Pierre.[21] Another critic correctly likens Augie to Whitman in his refusal of definition, which is to say the romantic individualist choice of self-definition, meaning masculine self-definition.[22] While he tries to picture Augie surrounded by masculine models he cannot identify with permanently, he leaves us with a male character for whom old and current definitions of masculinity are problematic. Simply put, neither Emerson's romanticism nor Simon's capitalism will do.

Augie and Simon have been reared by a Russian matriarch. It is also significant that Simon's first assertion of his masculinity involves deposing the old woman and putting her into a rest home. Augie describes him as "a blond boy with big cheekbones and wide gray eyes" who has "the arms of a cricketer" (*AM* 4) and sports a "British style": "School absorbed him more, and he had his sentiments anyway, a mixed extract from Natty Bumppo, Quentin Durward, Tom Brown, Clark at Kaskaskia, the messenger who brought the good news from Ratisbon, and so on" (12).

Simon puts in hours with a Sandor muscle builder (*AM* 11) and adopts "an Iroquois posture and eagle bearing, the lithe step that didn't crack a twig, the grace of Chevalier Bayard and the hand of Cincinnatus at the plow, the industry of a Nassau Street match-boy who became the king of corporations" (29). Furthermore, Simon stands out at the "head of the school police patrol, in starched linen Sam Browne belt ironed the night before and serge cap. He had a handsome, bold, blond face; even the short scar on his brow was handsome and assertive. . . . Simon had a distinguished record here, President of the Royal League, he wore a shield on his sweater, and was valedictorian" (29). Augie also notes that he had "an oriental bestowing temperament" (32). To the middle-aged Augie, Simon had always had

> a governor's clear-eyed gaze like that of John Sevier, or of Jackson . . . a lifted look of unforgiving, cosmological captaincy; that look where honesty had the strength

of prejudice, and foresight appeared as the noble cramp of impersonal worry in the forehead. My opinion is that at one time it was genuine in Simon. And if it was once genuine, how could you say definitely that the genuineness was ever all gone. But he used these things. He employed them, I know damned well. (110)

He is firmly located in the textual tradition of male adventure. With his dancing, letter writing, restaurant etiquette, fancy clothes, and courtship skills, Simon lays siege to the affections of the daughter of a wealthy family purely for the purpose of acquiring social, political, and monetary capital. He says of marriage, "I'll never again go for all that nonsense. . . . Do you see anything so exceptional or wonderful about it that makes it such a big deal? . . . What's it going to save you from? Has it saved anybody—the jerks, the fools, the morons, the *schleppers*, the jag-offs, the monkeys, the rats, rabbits, or the decent unhappy people who are what you call nice people?" (198).

The day Simon turns up in the coal yard for his wedding, Augie notes how earnest he is about money because it was now "proved by the mental wounds of his face, the death of its color, and the near insanity of his behavior. The misery of his look at this black Sargasso of a yard in its summer stagnation and stifling would sometimes make my blood crawl in me with horror" (*AM* 226). One day after Simon's honeymoon and on subsequent days, Augie remembers Simon as haggard, desperately unhappy, violent, erratic, harsh, gross, suicidal, and sickeningly flamboyant by turns. He is appalled at the violence of Simon's treatment of women, from his mother to his mother-in-law, not to mention his cruelty and unfaithfulness to his wife. The cars, the clothes, the drink, the fast women, and the fancy restaurants Augie describes as Simon's near-suicidal attempt to make the masculine formulas he is following work. The most moving of Augie's memories is that of Simon weeping in the car.

In Augie's mind Simon combined all the noble models of American masculinity and has ended up in hell. Simon is the representation of the failures of the historical composite masculine model offered by the self-made American capitalist and the American Dream. But he is also a composite of several other more romantic models of masculinity whose textual roots Bellow has delineated very clearly.

For Augie's part, the Emersonian model of masculinity he tries intermittently to follow fails also. History has already intervened, and social complicity is too powerful a Jewish counterethic to Emerson's social withdrawal. As Steven Gerson has pointed out, Augie, Bellow's American Adam, is left defeated and pessimistic, traits that are anathema to early American Adamism.[23] Augie is a transformed Adam who is left dangling just as helplessly as Joseph because he cannot find the lost northwest passage between these two quintessentially American masculine idealities. But clearly he seeks that space for the creation of a more viable masculine elsewhere. While Simon earnestly, and later desperately, follows his all-American boy identity, Augie says: "I was too larky and boisterous" to take things like his Jewishness and social status to heart (*AM* 12). He refuses to take the antisemitism of the street gangs seriously and to make an all-American boy out of himself with the Sandor muscle builder (12). Neither will he give over his less-than-socially-acceptable street friends in Simon's kind of attempt at upward social mobility. "I didn't have his singleness of purpose, but was more diffuse, and anybody who offered entertainment could get me to skip and do the alleys for junk, or prowl in the boathouse. . . . My marks showed it" (29).

Yet it is Augie who is the true romantic idealist:

> Unless you want to say that we're at the dwarf-end of all times and mere children whose only share in grandeur is like a boy's share in fairy-tale kings, beings of a different kind from times better and stronger than ours. But if we're comparing men and men, not men and children or men and demigods, which is just what would please Caesar among us teeming democrats, and if we don't have any special wish to abdicate into some different, lower form of existence out of shame for our defects before the golden faces of these and other old-time men, then I have the right to praise Einhorn . . . (*AM* 60)

He cannot accept that the chivalric models of masculinity from the textual heritage of Western literature will not work. Thinking one quiet, sunny afternoon in Einhorn's back study, he realizes:

> If you want to pick your own ideal creature in the mirror coastal air and sharp leaves of ancient perfections and be at home where a great mankind was at home, I've never seen

any reason why not. Though unable to go along one hundred percent with a man like the Reverend Beecher telling his congregations, "Ye are Gods, you are crystalline, your faces are radiant!" I'm not an optimist of that degree, from the actual faces, congregated or separate, that I've seen; always admitting that the true vision of things is a gift, particularly in times of special disfigurement and world-wide Babylonishness, when plug-ugly macadam and volcanic peperino look commoner than crystal—to eyes with an ordinary amount of grace—anyhow and when it appears like a good sensible policy to settle for medium-grade quartz. (76)

Augie's association with Einhorn, Dingbat, Kreindl, Five Properties, Jimmy Kline, and Clem Tambow enables him to say he has been around men of many kinds, including "a few who read whopping books in German or French and knew their physics and botany manuals backwards, readers of Nietzsche and Spengler" (*AM* 113).

When Einhorn tells him, "You've got *opposition* in you. You don't slide through everything. You just make it look so" (*AM* 117), Augie realizes he is looking for some absent presence outside of these masculine models. In accounting for this one recognizably true trait in himself, he realizes he is the product of entirely new social forces that have forged a different kind of American masculinity than that anticipated in the elitist formulas of romantic individualism.

And the students were children of immigrants from all parts, coming up from Hell's kitchen, Little Sicily, the Black Belt, the mass of Polonia, the Jewish streets of Humboldt Park, put through the course sifters of curriculum, and also bringing wisdom of their own with them. They filled the factory-length corridors and giant classrooms with every human character and germ, to undergo consolidation and become, the idea was, American. In the mixture there was beauty—a good proportion—pimple-insolence, and parri-cide faces, gum-chew innocence, labor fodder and secretarial forces, Danish stability, Dago inspiration, catarrh-hampered mathematical genius; there were waxed-eared shovelers' chil-dren, sex-promising businessmen's daughters—an immense sampling of a tremendous host, the multitudes of holy writ, begotten by West-moving, factor-shoved parents. Or me, the by-blow of a traveling man. (125)

This is the Chicagoan immigrant male as symbol of a new American masculine identity. Small wonder that Augie and Simon have separate fates. Augie is Mrs. Renling's toy boy, Simon's general factotum, footman to the Magnuses, ladies' man to Lucy Magnus, and gigolo to Thea Fenchel. He knows he is lost in unpraiseworthy old masculinities and unable to find his way out. "It was not only for me that being moored wasn't permitted; there was general motion, as of people driven from angles and corners into the open, by places being valueless and inhospitable to them. In the example of the Son of Man having no place to lay His head; or belonging in the world in general; except that the illuminated understanding of this was absent, nobody much guessing what was up on the face of the earth" (160). Finally, it is the notion of eternally becoming, not yet arrived, or arriving and leaving again that enables him to fix on the unfixedness of his own American masculine identity. At the end of his American picaresque youth, and well into his more learned and mature years, Augie sums up the nature of the masculine dilemma: "Look at me, going everywhere! Why, I am a sort of Columbus of those near-at-hand and believe you can come to them in this immediate *terra incognita* that spreads out in every gaze. I may well be a flop at this line of endeavor. Columbus too thought he was a flop, probably, when they sent him back in chains. Which didn't prove there was no America" (536). That "elsewhere" Columbus sought was actually found, and Augie still hopes to find his masculine American identity outside of that exhibited by nearly every other male in the book. It is the very presence of multiple emerging American masculinities beyond all the historical types of masculinity alluded to in the book which affords him hope of an "elsewhere" or feminine. It lies partially in the myriad classical models Augie alludes to, partially in the more recent American historical models, and partially in the emerging masculinities of the immigrant experience.

Seize the Day

Tommy Wilhelm in *Seize the Day* represents another attempt by a Bellow protagonist to extricate himself from damaging Jewish-American masculinities. His first attempt has been to refuse or fail at the roles of the stereotypical Jewish son, medical student, and actor. His second attempt is to become a Willy Loman, the archetypal American salesman who loses his job. Central to this text is the assemblage of sinister fathers among the sinister museum collection of masculine types gathered in the ironically named Hotel Gloriana. Worse still, he is afflicted with a German immigrant father who is powerful and without love or respect for the failed Tommy. Clearly, the measure of American manhood in this museum of aged American masculine types is corporate power and money. No other talents, sensibilities, or models of masculinity can dislodge the fixed masculine image of a corporate man espoused by this elderly generation. Tommy is the all-but-destroyed feminine soul of corporate America—pitied, derided, henpecked, conned, outcast, and left for dead. His father calls him a loser and a slob and makes him beg for help. Tamkin, the false priest, false psychiatrist, false poet, and false modernist philosopher, tries to strip him of his romantic hope in humankind. Then he strips him of his money. *Seize the Day* would seem to be the lament of the metaphorical feminine or Jewish soul in face of an overwhelmingly destructive American capitalist masculinity, which destroys even the dream of a masculine elsewhere.

Tommy, for all his anguish, senses otherwise. By every measure of American masculinity Tommy has fallen outside the system. He has no relationship with his father, has failed to maintain his own family, and is estranged from his sons. His mistress has left him, and he has lost his corporate identity, gets conned by Tamkin, and fails at the stock market. Furthermore, he rejects the masculinity suggested by a stoic, skeptical existentialism preached by the bogus Tamkin. Yet these realizations are actually the beginnings of his move toward a new space.

> And was everybody crazy here? What sort of people did you see? Every other man spoke a language entirely his own, which he had figured out by private thinking; he had his own ideas and peculiar ways. If you wanted to talk about a glass of water, you had to start back with God creating the heavens and earth; the apple; Abraham; Moses and Jesus; Rome; the Middle Ages; gunpowder; the Revolution; back to Newton; up to Einstein; then war and Lenin and Hitler. After reviewing all this and getting it all straight again you could proceed to talk about a glass of water. (*SD* 83)

The spiritual failures of the Willy Loman capitalist from rags-to-riches American fathers are symbolized in the eerie, sepulchral Hotel Gloriana, a faded monument to a fading era of masculine triumph, a spiritual desert in which only similarly successful sons are admitted to the club. More than anything, *Seize the Day* is a lament about the complete rejection of the feminine by modernism and a late capitalist construction of masculinity imaged in the bizarre persons of Dr. Adler, Dr. Tamkin, Mr. Rappaport, and Mr. Perls.

The space elsewhere Tommy seeks can be discovered only once he is completely outside the entrapping masculinity of men like these. Away from the Hotel Gloriana and its larger representation, New York, and the whirring numbers and flickering lights of the quasi-magical stock exchange, Tommy seeks the consummation of his heart's desire in the outpouring of repressed feeling for the sea of disfigured anonymous humanity he encounters in the New York subway and for a dead man he does not know. This transgressive feminine, with its discovery of love, feeling, and mystical identification with other, emerges in direct contrast to the stoic, competitive, and destructive Darwinian masculinity of the national culture. This is a book about the historical emergence of a kind of masculinity that has nearly destroyed American fathers and sons.

Henderson the Rain King

Henderson the Rain King continues the Bellovian deconstruction of American masculine codes of capitalism, adventure, and conquest. Through his parodic exposé of the masculine myths of primitivism, the exotic pleasures of dark-skinned women, the mystery of darkest Africa, male boon companionship, masculine technological triumph over nature, masculine identification with wild animals, and the pursuit of visionary states, the various sicknesses of American masculinity are comically revealed. Initially, we see Eugene Henderson dressed in hunting cap, using a .357 magnum rifle, raising pigs, alienating wives, shooting his rifle off in the house to terrify Lily, giving away his grandchild, and shouting his housekeeper to death. He is a crude, noisy, oafish, wealthy, misogynous, Hemingwayesque character who is eaten up by a great lack he cannot satisfy or name. All he knows is the tormenting inner voice: "I want. I want" (*AM* 12).

A giant gentile American masculine imago of sorts, he is the parodic representation of a system gone mad. David Anderson has ably connected Bellow and this book to the Hemingwayesque traditions of masculinity.[24] To his detailed study, I will simply add mention of the rich adventure novel tradition in Western literature already detailed in my remarks on *The Adventures of Augie March*.

96

Clearly, as Joni Adamson Clarke mentions in her article "A Negation Offering Possibility: *Henderson the Rain King* and the Paradox of Gender,"[25] Henderson is a transgressive figure who explodes that masculine mythos with its incessant "I want, I want" and, in so doing, opens up new spaces within which to reclaim the feminine. Once Henderson has escaped for Africa, Bellow shows the amalgam of masculinities he represents. Henderson is a fallen Adam, Don Quixote, Natty Bumppo, Dr. Livingstone, Mungo Park, Robinson Crusoe, Henry Stanley, and Richard Burton, and a host of other imperialistic adventurers. He is also an aging Huckleberry Finn, a comic Ishmael, and a nutty Marlowe all rolled into one. But more recently, he is Bellow's ugly American in the form of the myth of Ernest Hemingway now thoroughly demythologized and reduced to size. Invading, breaking, destroying, technologizing, blundering, and trying to possess by main force, Henderson is that great masculine disruption into nature and the feminine, which is trying to complete itself through taking by force that which it thinks it lacks. Comically sinking his face into Willatele's navel and, later, seizing the Mummah around its middle, Henderson wishes to immerse himself in this exotic feminine. Only after he has ceased striving and seizing, learned to purge himself of piggishness, and found his ability to love an other in the form of a little Persian orphan boy, however, does he begin to heal.

But the journey is ambiguous; Dahfu's transcendentalism fails. He dies a violent death in a violent system which says that as soon as he loses masculine skill and potency he must die in order that the new life might spring forth for the tribe. This central mythos of the king sacrifice mentioned all throughout James George Frazer's *The Golden Bough*[26] seems to function as a cautionary tale and a lament for the destructive masculine mythos that lies at the heart of the historic construction of both ancient and modern masculinity. And, ironically, it is through the gorgeous, feminized Dahfu and Atti the lioness that Henderson begins to learn how to quell the wanting.

Yet out of this very destructive paradigm springs forth the new spirit in the form of the tiny, woolly-haired, Persian orphan boy Henderson is last seen dancing with on the polar ice cap. It is perhaps symbolic of pristine surroundings, the repossession of childlike innocence, and the presence of the lamb as traditional feminine symbol of renewal and spiritual healing. But it is not in the form of a literal female. It is in the form of an orphaned male child.

97

Herzog

The beginning pages of *Herzog*, which represent him at the end of his marathon of letter writing and heartbreak, are indicative of his slipping out of a traditional masculine space into a new/old one. He is Bellow's version of the feminine hysteric. He wonders if he is out of his mind and feels odd, but cheerful and clairvoyant. He picks raspberries in his overgrown garden, snacks out of cans and paper packages, and shares his food willingly with mice, owls, and rats. At night he sleeps outdoors in a hammock among tall, bearded grasses and maple seedlings:

> When he opened his eyes in the night, the stars were near like spiritual bodies. Fires, of course, gases—minerals, heat, atoms, but eloquent at five in the morning to a man lying in a hammock, wrapped in his overcoat. . . . He looked keenly at everything but he felt half blind. . . . He was taking a turn around the empty house and saw the shadow of his face in a gray, webby window. He looked weirdly tranquil. A radiant line went from mid-forehead over his straight nose and full, silent lips. (*H* 1–2)

What he has jettisoned of traditional masculinity in order to find this feminine orphic, tranquility, and spiritual apprehension is not less than everything: the masculine intellectual tradition, masculine erotic arrangements, masculine expectations of marriage, and immersion in the many other traditional American masculinities. It is a massive mea culpa on the failure of the masculine traditions. By his own admission, Herzog has been a bad husband and a loving but bad father. He has not been much of a patriot, even though he has been an affectionate but remote sibling. To his parents he has been an ungrateful and unloving child. In friendship he has been egotistical, and with his lovers, selfish, narcissistic, and uncommitted. His conclusion as his marriage breaks down and the long personal crisis is precipitated is that he and Madeleine are guilty of two kinds of egoism, hers that of domination and his of passivity. "What he was about to suffer, he deserved; he had sinned long and hard; he had earned it. This was it" (*H* 8–9). In short, Herzog realizes that this masculine self was a destructive and selfish one. "There is someone inside me. I am in his grip. When I speak of him I feel him in my head, pounding for order. He will ruin me" (11).

The quarrel with the male-authored metaphysical tradition of Western culture, however, is the primary focus of *Herzog*. It is about Herzog's rejection of the great fathers of the metaphysical tradition who have constructed masculine subjectivity and therefore modern manhood itself. This jettisoning of erroneous ideas, a ruined career, a bad marriage, and archaic heterosexual relations is done like the Baconian grand synthesis in reverse. Late one spring, during the course of five days, he undoes the historical accumulation of the modernist synthesis and falls out of the old masculine life he has led into the half-ruined Ludeyville estate. It is a great purgation of the unusable elements of an unacceptable masculinity.

His primary task has been to abandon his project on "The Roots of Romanticism" and contest the continental philosophers through his compulsive and near-manic letter writing, as he attempts "to explain, have it out, to make amends" (*H* 2). He seeks an aboriginal self not tainted with the masculine narcissism of the modern age and the other degenerate masculinities that surround him. These inherited philosophical notions and agreed upon estimates he must escape in order to find that elsewhere or beyond. It is a Herculean sifting, resulting in dozens of mental letters written "endlessly, fanatically, to the newspapers, to people in public life, to friends and relatives, and at the last to the dead, his own obscure dead, and finally the famous dead" (1).

The surface texture reflects Herzog's disintegrating masculinity in its wild punctuation, italics, parentheses, switches in point-of-view, quotations, ellipses, salutations, letters, debates, reminiscences, social portraits, mental asides, impromptu lectures, lyric descriptions, prayers, wry humor, and moments of explosive invective. This is a man in total upheaval. Bellow himself said in a series of interviews that it was an attempt to test "Heraclitan fashion" his sense of life, "that he might dismiss a great mass of irrelevancy and nonsense in order to survive."[27] His other intention was to "in part . . . bring to an end, under blinding light, a certain course of development. . . . He comes to realize at last that what he considers 'intellectual privilege' has proved to be another form of bondage. . . . Any man who has rid himself of superfluous ideas in order to take that first step has done something significant."[28]

His first quarrel, having just gone through Freudian analysis with the duplicitous Dr. Edvig, is with Protestant-Freudian estimates of human love as "hysterical dependence," narcissism, masochism, and anachronism. Herzog bursts out in a tirade against "the creeping psychoanalysis of everyday life" (*H* 99). He condemns Shapiro and Banowitch for accepting these psychoanalytical premises, which see all political power struggle in terms of "paranoid mentality," the conviction that "madness always rules the world," and that humankind resembles "a lot of cannibals running around in packs, gibbering, bewailing its own murders, pressing out the living world as dead excrement" (77). It is Freud's primal horde theory; he resents being put at the base of social and cultural histories. Seeing Calvin's influence behind Freud, he protests in a poison pen mental letter to Edvig, "I've read your stuff about the psychological realism of Calvin. I hope you don't mind my saying but it reveals a lousy, cringing, grudging conception of human nature" (58).

Dewey, Whitehead, and Nietzsche he accuses of coming to the damaging conclusion that "mankind distrusts its own nature and tries to find stability beyond or above, in religion or philosophy" (*H* 51). He hates their descriptions of an ever-present impulse to masculine power. Nietzsche he particularly resents because in masculinist fashion he has juxtaposed his all-powerful Superman against a feminized group of priestly Jews infected with a slave mentality, and for conceiving of man as a "thieving, stinking, unilluminated, sodden rabble" (388). After telling Nietzsche that we have seen enough of destruction and evil, Herzog, the Holocaust era Jew, says he thinks we have had enough of Dionysiac destruction and that it all has a very "Germanic ring" (319). Clearly, he locates Nietzsche's thought as a product of a high imperialist German culture of the late nineteenth century, the worst kind of masculinism.

Oswald Spengler is also guilty of having masculinized non-Jews and feminized Jews in the manner of Nietzsche. Herzog recalls reading Spengler as a young Jewish boy and discovering that "I, as a Jew, was a born Magian and that we Magians had already had our great age, forever past. No matter how hard I tried, I would never grasp the Christian and Faustian world idea, forever alien to me . . . a Jew, a relic as lizards are relics of the great age of reptiles" (*H* 234).

Heidegger he blames for the ultimate masculine power construct, that the common, ordinary existence of the race is an imprisoning humiliation. In his most scathing letter he argues for eliminating the now "feminized" and subjugated ordinary man whose only accomplishment or possession is his private life, not his domination of continents or capital. "Dear Doktor Professor Heidegger, I should like to know what you mean by the expression 'the fall into the quotidian.' When did this fall occur? Where were we standing when it happened?" (*H* 49). Existentialist death theory he decries not as a manly and stoic acceptance of the inevitable, but merely a new wrinkle of *memento mori*, the monk's skull on the table, morbidity against human feeling (270).

Continuing with his thesis about the relationship between masculine power and contemporary Continental philosophy, he argues that not all the traditions and beliefs have dried up, neither are we at the moment when moral conscience dies. The world is not merely a Wasteland, and we are not suffering an irreversible alienation. The void does not exist, except as a philosophical concept. Partially due to such destructive ideas generated by male philosophers, however, Herzog realizes:

> We are survivors, in this age, so theories of progress ill become us, because we are intimately acquainted with the costs. To realize you are a survivor is a shock. At the realization of such election, you feel like bursting into tears. As the dead go their way, you want to call to them, but they depart in a black cloud of faces, souls. They flow out in smoke from the extermination chimneys, and leave you in the clear light of historical success—the technical success of the West. Then you know with a crash of blood that mankind is making it—making it in glory though deafened by the explosions of blood. Unified by horrible wars, instructed in our brutal stupidity by revolutions, by engineered famines directed by "ideologists" (heirs of Marx and Hegel and trained in the cunning of reason). . . . No, the analogy of the decline and fall of the classical world will not hold for us. (*H* 75)

This destructive form of masculine thinking, says Herzog, infects modern physics as well as the entropic notion of a dissolving universe, involving biological phenomena and the gradual degeneration of chemical wastes. Likewise, the followers of T. E. Hulme have gone to the other masculine extremes with their "clear, dry, spare, pure, cool and hard" estimates of man. They made "sterility their truth, [thereby] confessing their impotence" (*H* 129).

In the fields of genetics, demography, evolution, and statistics, with their notions of biological or genetic predestination, "survival of the fittest" ideas are not scientific absolutes and are in fact suspect because of their ill reasoning.

On the other side of the nihilistic and pessimistic male critiques of human life and nature are those attributable to romantic individualists. "Shall we concede the [feminine] idea of transcendence in face of these overwhelmingly masculine assaults on the life and worth of the human soul," says Herzog (*H* 163). Masculine philosophical and scientific derision, with its depictions of human beings as monsters, calls for a "total reconsideration of human [masculine and feminine] qualities. Or perhaps even the discovery of qualities. I am certain that there are human qualities still to be discovered. Such discovery is only hampered by definitions" (164).

Herzog attempts to think himself out of this set of destructive, masculine paradigms, with their violent and extreme conceptions of power and destruction. What kind of an American man is he if he does not believe in paranoid power paradigms of human existence but in the truth of his own feelings and personal history? What if his memory of the warmth of his family of childhood, the feelings of safety and peace experienced there, and the life of the intellect are more valuable than Shura's life buried in "the heart of Leviathan?" (*H* 78). Are those feminized Jews of Spengler's account still extant and still valuable ways of being masculine human? Edvig, after all, has told him that his Jewish upbringing has produced humane feelings which are childish, that he resembles in adulthood the silly goose who has not yet experienced the axe. "Simkin seemed to see him as he saw that sickly, innocent girl, the epileptic cousin" (231). Herzog himself wonders if "young Jews [were] brought up on moral principles as Victorian ladies were on pianoforte and needlepoint" (231). In Herzog's thinking, destructive nihilism is a masculine set of constructs, while old-fashioned religious traditions, intuition as opposed to rationality, feeling as opposed to facts, and morality as opposed to cynicism are feminine traits. He is desperately trying to restore to value the feminine. He seeks the lost feminine within himself, which is in danger of being eclipsed by the philosophical hypermasculinity of modernism. The deconstruction and chastising of Calvin, Kant, Freud, Hegel, Heidegger, Nietzsche, Hobbes, Darwin, Marx, Fichte, Joachin de Floris, Comte,

Proudhon, Kierkegaard, Berdyaev, Sartre, Camus, Rousseau, Emerson, Schopenhauer, Dewey, Whitehead, Arendt, and Buber are a rejection of what contemporary intellectual historians of modernism now call the core of the masculinism at the heart of modernism.

While Herzog is slipping backwards out of the destructiveness and despair of masculine metaphysical traditions of the modernist thinkers, he contemplates the cost of becoming a contemporary American male immersed in capitalism. The image of his assimilated American brother Shura is daunting, with his expensive suits, "vicuña coat," Italian hats, many rings, limousines, and "princely hauteur" (*H* 78). Herzog sees him as the worst masculine type, an embodiment of Thomas Hobbes's estimate of life, one for whom "universal concerns were idiocy" (78). Shura, he notes, "asked for nothing better than to prosper in the belly of Leviathan and set a hedonistic example to the community" (78). He is another version of Simon March and Ulick Citrine. Each of these pairs of brothers are either capitalists or thinkers, visionaries, dreamers, or optimists. As the feminine half of the family equation, they are sentimental about their families of childhood, burdened with "potato love," repulsed by violence, skeptical of rags-to-riches ideologies, and given to the Dionysiac excesses of sexuality and sensuality. Accordingly, Herzog, the old-world Jewish man of feeling, is designated feminine in his recovery of his ability to lament his life, repent of it, seclude himself in nature, eschew concern for money, and attain religious states of contemplation and tranquility. It is a fight to reverse sensibility, the feminine part of his soul. Sandor tells him, "All he wants is everybody should love him," and labels this desire a feminine trait. "Well, when you suffer you really suffer. You're a real, genuine old Jewish type that digs the emotions. I'll give you that. I understand it. I grew up on Sangamon Street" (83–84). Later, when Sandor gives him a kiss, we are reminded of Alex Szathmar's love for Charlie Citrine: "He gave Moses a kiss. Moses felt the potato love. Amorphous, swelling, hungry, indiscriminate, cowardly potato love" (91). It is immediately after this that he sees the purity of the air around him, the bright reflections of sunlight on water and is moved to say, "Praise God—praise God." "His breathing had become freer. His heart was greatly stirred by the opening horizon; the deep colors; the faint iodine pungency of the Atlantic rising from the weeds and mollusks; the white, fine, heavy sand; but principally by the green transparency as he looked down to the stony bottom webbed with golden lines" (91).

Later, while reading Pratt on the Civil War and Kierkegaard's essays, he concludes that the sickness unto death Kierkegaard is talking about "is that a man refuses to be what he is" (*H* 105), a creature with poetic, feminine, and orphic powers, not just a creature overdetermined by modern philosophy and other unhelpful concocted descriptions of himself that destroy this residual feminine. Reading *The Phenomenology of Mind*, he determines to reemphasize the importance of the human heart in Western tradition, "to pull the carpet from under all other scholars . . . expose their triviality once and for all" (199). "Then after many billions of years, light-years, this childlike but far from innocent creature, a straw hat on his head, and a heart in his breast, part pure, part wicked, . . . would try to form his own shaky picture of this magnificent [intellectual] web" (47–48). The feminine within him admits its lack of perfect masculine control: "I ran to fight in Thy holy cause, but kept tripping, never reached the scene of the struggle" (128). Contrasted with this humility is the picture of T. E. Hulme, that ultimate masculine modernist who wanted "things to be clear, dry, spare, pure, cool, and hard" (160). He accuses Hulme and his followers of having ironically "made sterility their truth" (129).

Far from embracing masculine emotional sterility, Herzog recalls the emotional memories of his mother struggling through an icy January, sacrificing her strength to pull the young Herzog, or fainting from the rinsing and washing and wringing involved in getting out the family wash (*H* 139). The roots of this reservoir of feminine feeling are all contained in his memories of Napoleon Street, where he realizes there "was a wider range of human feelings than he had ever again been able to find. . . . All he ever wanted was there. . . . He fought the insidious blight of nostalgia in New York—softening heart-rotting emotions" (140–41). He remembers that his father, the bootlegger, admitted he could not use the big pistol to shoot thieves and knows that neither could he (Herzog) use it to shoot Gersbach. "Whom did I ever love as I loved them?" he asks (147). It is the "great schooling in grief" that he shares with his father, who shares it with Jewish antiquity, which he realizes has humanized them all. He laments the more modern, masculine standard, which is "terminal" and "indifferent" (148).

Thinking later of the historical origins of masculine emotional stoicism, he notes, "A good subject: the history of composure in Calvinistic societies. When each man, feeling fearful damnation, had to behave as one of the elect. All such historic terrors—every agony of the spirit— must at last be released" (*H* 179). Basically the feminine hysteric, in whom alternative truth and feeling will break out, Herzog knows: "When he talked like this he was again in the grip of that eccentric, dangerous force that had been capturing him. It was at work now, and he felt himself bending" (216). He concludes that his emotional type is "*archaic. Belongs to the cultural or pastoral stages*" (265).

As Herzog speaks to Lucas Asphalter, who expresses his love for Herzog, "His eyes filled up. The potato love, he announced to himself. It's here. To advert to his temperament, call things by the correct name, restored his control" (*H* 267). He worries that Junie will "inherit this world of great instruments, the principles of physics and applied science," but never know her emotional heritage (338). He calls it a "European pollution" of "Old World feelings" like "Love—Filial Emotion. Old Stuporous Dreams" (281). He knows of his brother Will: "[He] sees me spluttering fire in the wilderness of this world and pities me no doubt for my temperament. Under the old dispensation, as the stumbling, ingenuous, burlap Moses, a heart without guile, in need of protections, a morbid phenomenon." Will, instead, is "a quiet man of duty and routine . . . and is just as glad to be rid of his private or personal side (307). His final conclusion is that the human soul is "*an Amphibian, and I have touched its sides*. . . . It lives in more elements than I will ever know; and I assume that in those remote stars matter is in the making which will create stranger beings yet" (257–58).

Herzog has reclaimed that amphibian feminine, that maternal ground of selfhood within the hostile circumstances of that most masculine of all conditions, modern philosophy and modern American and international history. He knows he is much more than the sum of his American masculinities and realizes that in this process he has learned "what it means to be a man. In a city. In a century. In transition. In a mass. Transformed by science. Under organized power. Subject to tremendous controls" (*H* 201). He senses he is Blanchot's "last man" and has just begun to rediscover the feminine through which he can be healed. He walks between rotted stumps, moss, fungi, and leaves following a deer trail, like Natty Bumppo of old, and is sustained by silence and calm.

Unlike Natty Bumppo, he frames a prayer from "within the hollowness of God, deaf to the final multiplicity of facts" and says: "*How my mind has struggled to make coherent sense. I have not been too good at it. But have desired to do your unknowable will, taking it, and you, without symbols*" (324–25). He has escaped the destructive masculinity of Western metaphysics and the resultant modern life and slipped into an expanded masculine subjectivity now reunited with the relegated feminine.

What must be purged, however, are all those masculinities that threaten to engulf him. He recalls his earliest memories of his old neighborhood.

> Napoleon Street, rotten, toylike, crazy and filthy, riddled, flogged with harsh weather—the bootlegger's boys reciting ancient prayers. To this Moses' heart was attached with great power. Here was a wider range of human feelings than he had ever again been able to find. The children of the race, by a never-failing miracle, opened their eyes on one strange world after another, age after age, and uttered the same prayer in each, eagerly loving what they found. What was wrong with Napoleon Street? All he ever wanted was there. (*H* 140)

Against Ramona's masculine traits of pride, anger, excessive rationality, competitiveness, mistrust of emotion, scheming, power plays, tongue-lashings, savagery, and icy rages, Herzog sees himself as feminized, passive, sexually damaged, and the recipient of a great violence.

In the scenes in the courtroom with Alex-Alice, Marie Poont, and the semiretarded woman who has dashed her child's brains out, he finds that nothing he has read and nothing he has felt help him to understand this lack of feeling. Physically he feels "something terrible, inflammatory, bitter, had been grated into his bloodstream and stung and burned his veins, his face, his heart" (*H* 294). Next day, while walking with June, he notes that he is that paradoxical creature, the technological American who carries "European pollution" and is infected by the "Old World with feelings like Love—Filial emotion. Old Stuporous dreams" (281). By the fourth day, he has rid himself of violent thoughts about shooting Gersbach and then confronts Madeleine at the police station, only to discover she no longer has any power over him. Returning to Ludeyville on the fifth day, he feels an extraordinary sense of peace and contentment.

His final letters reflect the recovery of a firm sense of the feminine. To Ramona, his onetime sexual priestess, he writes: *"The light of truth is never far away, and no human being is too negligible or corrupt to come into it"* (*H* 314).

To his son Marco, he offers a feminine model of male power rather than a Darwinian or modernist one in the account of the man in Scott's expedition who walked off into the snow to allow the others to go on unimpeded by him and of the dogs who would not eat one of their own until its distinctive smell was removed through skinning. To Rozanov he eschews the futility of masculine rationalism and intellectual synthesis in favor of the fortuitousness of Providence. To Professor Mermelstein he denounces Banowitch's book filled with male paranoia, violence, and vile notions of tyrants, power, and apocalypse. Instead he offers his reclaimed vision of the land elsewhere and the powers of the feminine.

> The advocacy and praise of suffering take us in the wrong direction and those of us who remain loyal to civilization must not go for it. You have to have the power to employ pain, to repent, to be illuminated, you must have the opportunity and even the time. With the religious, the love of suffering is a form of gratitude to experience or an opportunity to experience evil and change it into good. They believe the spiritual cycle can and will be completed in a man's existence and he will somehow make use of his suffering . . . when the mercy of God will reward him with a vision of truth, and he will die transfigured. But this is a special exercise . . . I am willing without further exercise in pain to open my heart. And this needs no doctrine or theology of suffering. We love apocalypses too much, and crisis ethics and florid extremism with its thrilling language. Excuse me, no. I have had all the monstrosity I want. (*H* 317)

Finally, he says, "I want to send you, and others, the most loving wish I have in my heart. This is the only way I have to reach out—out where it is incomprehensible. I can only pray toward it. So . . . Peace!" (*H* 396–98). Forsaking the masculine rationality of philosophical and scientific explanation, he changes to "songs, psalms and utterances" (398). He knows, in this state of fallen nature reflected in the Ludeyville estate, he has reclaimed that feminine he had nearly lost.

6

RECLAIMING THE ORPHIC

A labyrinthine man never looks for the truth, but only for his Ariadne.

—Friedrich Nietzsche, *Beyond Good and Evil*

Humboldt's Gift

Bellow's dialogue with historiocultural inherited codes of American masculinity begins with *Dangling Man* and culminates in *Humboldt's Gift*. Charlie's deconstruction of his hypermasculine American condition does not begin until he is sixty and begins to contemplate the tragic and ignominious death of his mentor, Humboldt, in terms of his own loss of poetic fire. Von Humboldt Fleisher, Charlie decides, has attempted the impossible synthesis of capitalism and poetry—the hypermasculine with the feminine: "[H]e intended to be a divine artist, a man of visionary states and enchantments, Platonic possession. He got a Rationalistic, Naturalistic education at CCNY. This was not easily reconciled with the Orphic. . . . He wanted . . . to prove that the imagination was just as potent as machinery, to free and to bless humankind. But he was out also to be rich and famous. And of course there were the girls" (*HG* 119).

Contemplating the newspaper obituary of Humboldt, he comments: "He brought Coney Island into the Aegean and united Buffalo Bill with Rasputin. He was going to join together the Art Sacrament and the Industrial USA as equal powers" (*HG* 119). As Charlie sees it, the failure was in trying to join an outer America with inner America, action with contemplation or, symbolically speaking,

109

the hypermasculine world with its estranged feminine counterpart. It is the problem of reuniting the anima with the animus on both a personal and a national scale, as Charlie describes it. Yet mired as he is in typically Chicago "sex malaria," thuggery, threats, scams, divorce lawyers, legal pimps, physical culturists, real estate princes, and minor mafiosi, Charlie realizes that hypermasculine America has overcome that which signifies the feminine, the "school thing," the "skirt thing," the "church thing" called poetry (118).

It is against this Jungian model of regendered inner harmony that Bellow counterposes the mental collapse of the manic, paranoid Von Humboldt Fleisher. He is simultaneously Charlie's alter ego and Bellow's hypermasculine American imago—a giant ruin of overwhelming cultural contradictions who becomes the measure of masculine America's aspirations and failures. *Humboldt's Gift* is the novelistic unfolding of a cautionary tale as well as a romantic lament about a great industrial nation that has all but destroyed the so-called feminine side of its psyche—that side Bellow defines as nature, art, contemplation, imagination, music, family feeling, and true brotherhood.

Recalling his original glimpse of this symbolic feminine, Charlie describes traveling on the Greyhound to New York to meet the author of *The Harlequin Ballads*. It was late spring, the trees were budding, and the music in his ears was that of Beethoven's *Pastorale*. "I felt showered by the green, within" (*HG* 2), he recalls, realizing suddenly how thoroughly in the last forty years that fertile springtime of the soul had been turned to a perpetual winter. Against this lost vision Bellow juxtaposes a prolonged prose mea culpa concerning his lifelong allegiance to many destructively hypermasculine alter egos, most of which become subsumed in Humboldt. As Charlie notes, Humboldt "adored talking about the rich" and was always inspired by money; he loved the scandals of people like "Peaches and Daddy Browning, Harry Thaw and Evelyn Nesbitt, plus the Jazz Age, Scott Fitzgerald, and the Super-Rich. The heiresses of Henry James he knew cold. There were times when he himself schemed comically to make a fortune" (4).

He remembers Humboldt's father as a classic nineteenth-century American adventurer whose imagination encompassed Pancho Villa and the American robber barons. He is associated in Charlie's mind with "boots, bugles, bivouacs," "luxury hotels," "limousines," "girls," "gangsters," and "railroad money" (*HG* 4). The son, he observes, was afflicted with this same expansive nineteenth-century masculine model but felt a compromising defensiveness about his Jewishness and his gloomy, aggrieved, neurotic, immigrant mother. Charlie describes Humboldt as compensating for these imagined masculine deficiencies through his big drinking, monumental pill-taking, Mozartian talent for conversation, Napoleonic scheming, and superhuman bouts of mania.

Charlie identifies another aspect of Humboldt's competitive American masculinity when he makes repeated references to his Babe Ruth belly, football player's shoulders, and rookie appearance. To Charlie he is quintessentially American because he is a composite of the renaissance prince, a thick and heavy man, a beached whale, and a bully who keeps up with sports and night life, the jet set, the Kennedys, used car prices, and the want ads, like any normal American male. Charlie steadily critiques Humboldt's capitalistic and American pretensions by ridiculing his desire to be the first poet in America with power brakes. He likens Humboldt's flamboyant roadster to a primitive communal outhouse, a "four holer," or a "staff car from Flanders Fields" (*HG* 21). For Charlie, Humboldt is smitten with "car mystique" (20), the ultimate sign of American hypermasculine illusions. Charlie comically describes him humped over the huge wheel, clenching a cigarette holder between his teeth, polo boot dominating the accelerator, hyped up on booze or pills, driving maniacally through the Holland Tunnel.

Ironically, the car, one of the chief symbols in the novel of the American masculine transcendence, emerges from the tunnel straight into the industrial wasteland of Scranton, where, Charlie complains, "Tall stacks, a filth artillery, fired silently into the Sunday sky with beautiful bursts of smoke. The acid smell of gas refineries went into your lungs like a spur" (*HG* 22). Scranton is Bellow's visual commentary on the deadly legacy of capitalistic striving and the inevitable destruction of nature, or the maternal ground. Charlie notes that even Humboldt's property in the country is "marginal land" that is "exactly like Bedford Street, here, except that the surrounding slum was rural" (22). Humboldt's and America's loss of the feminine is equated with the simultaneous loss of both nature and the orphic.

This loss, Charlie suggests, has to do with America's and Humboldt's addiction to masculine power. He believes that Humboldt, flattered by being read by Adlai Stevenson, has construed himself simultaneously as Hegel's World Historical

Individual and as the universal Whitmanesque persona. Through his reading of military generals, military history, and his high-flown conversation about "machinery, luxury, command, capitalism, technology, Mammon, Orpheus and poetry" (*HG* 21), Humboldt has inadvertently invoked not the feminine muse, but rather Mammon "himself." The original cause is Humboldt's and America's twentieth-century imitation of the greedy, swashbuckling nineteenth-century fathers: "I saw Humboldt whipping his team of mules and standing up in his crazy wagon like an Oklahoma land-grabber. He rushed into the territory of excess to stake himself a claim. This claim was a swollen and quaking heart-mirage" (155). Even Humboldt himself senses the incompatibility of the masculine quest for power and poetry as he weakly rationalizes: "If I'm obsessed by money, as a poet shouldn't be, there's a reason for it. . . . The reason is that we're Americans after all. What kind of American would I be if I were innocent about money, I ask you? . . . Walpole said it was natural for free men to think about money" (159).

The consequences of this masculine American lust for power and importance Bellow relates to the destruction of the literal and symbolic feminine. As Humboldt develops paranoid jealousies about Kathleen, he probes her childhood attachments to other men, secretly follows her to the supermarket, hides her keys, beats her, and finally tries to kill her with the car—the ultimate symbol of masculine empowerment. It is an overt reminder of the terribly matricidal consequences of such wanton destruction of the feminine.

Charlie accurately identifies the nature of this masculine subjugation and disempowerment of the female other when he puts Humboldt's unspoken message to Kathleen into his own words: "Lie there. Hold still. Don't wiggle. My happiness may be peculiar, but once happy I will make you happy, happier than you ever dreamed. When I am satisfied the blessings of fulfillment will flow to all mankind" (*HG* 23). Charlie equates this with the crazy tyrant's message of modern power and says in stunned amazement: "Wonderful things are done by women for their husbands. She loved a poet-king and allowed him to hold her captive in the country" (25). This eclipsing of female status and power he identifies ironically with the Eastern practice of purdah (26). Both the outcast Kathleen and that lost feminine she represents are depicted as besieged, defeated, and imprisoned in hypermasculine America. It is Bellow's gendered corollary of the tyrannical message of modern power.

As for himself, that other representative feminine presence in Humboldt's life, Charlie complains that in company or alone, he is increasingly "fiddled and trumpeted off the stage" (*HG* 30) by a Humboldt who believes himself such an "exceptional person" he should be put in charge of arranging the lives of others (29). The connection between masculine virility, power, and poetry is neatly summed up by Bellow in the pseudo "Song of Myself" Humboldt delivers to the backstreet prostitute the morning he believes he has secured the Princeton chair. "You don't know what you're missing. I'm a poet. I have a big cock" (139), he shouts, absolutely sure of his drawing power. The woman behind the door merely laughs.

The ultimate rout of the feminine in Humboldt, however, is signified in his competitive jealousy at Charlie's success. As Humboldt cashes the blood brotherhood check, he completes his estrangement from both Kathleen and Charlie. He also loses his poetic powers. "He spilled dirt, spread scandal, and uttered powerful metaphors. What a combination! Fame gossip delusion filth and poetic invention" (*HG* 161), Charlie laments. Corrupt, murderous, and paranoid, Humboldt looks for booby traps in the Buick, fears that the Ku Klux Klan might burn a cross his front yard, and fantasizes about Sewell's imagined anti-Semitism. Bellow presents this condition of paranoia as both mirror and symbol of the insane consequences of masculine power.

With Humboldt as emblematic of the failure of the feminine in the American culture, Charlie systematically measures the strength and style of this hypermasculine American acculturation in both himself and the men who surround him. Each is shown to be a victim of a masculine ethic compounded of European history as well as of the consequences of the unique social experiments of American history—Puritan self-validation, colonization, slavery, mass extermination of the Native American, the rape of the land, westward expansion, the American Dream, robber-baron empire building, and the dubious triumphs of twentieth-century technocracy—in short the capitalistic American masculine experience of decline in the late twentieth century.

Alex Szathmar is a historical blend of both European and American models of masculinity which preclude the feminine. As Charlie's surrogate father, he is lovable, nurturing, and superficially dishonest. Alex too, however, is a victim of American hypermasculine codes which preclude the orphic. He is still smitten with the old West Side "sex-malaria" of their adolescence (*HG* 204). He is a night school lawyer who sports a pretentious office and derives voyeuristic pleasure in pimping for divorce clients. Charlie notes with naive admiration and surprise, that despite his "Roman nose, mutton-chop whiskers, his fat chest wide hips neat feet virile cleft chin," he is stout, massive, and capable of "a clumsy but unshakable sexual horsemanship atop pretty ladies" (206–7). Amused, Charlie tells him that his long sideburns make him look like "the bad guy in an old Western—one of those fellows who sold guns and fire-water to the redskins" (206). He causes Charlie to think of Jung's historical human types and immediately labels Szathmar an eighteenth-century cavalryman or perhaps Rodin's Balzac, "virile, peremptory, craggy, pagan, and Tritonesque" (206). Yet Charlie clearly recognizes in Alex one line of his own ethnic background when he describes them both as a lustful pair of "cunt-struck doddering wooers left over from a Goldoni farce" (204). They are both decaying squaw men, Charlie ruefully concludes, although he confesses, "In Szathmar's breast there was a large true virile heart whereas I had no heart at all, only a sort of chicken giblet" (208–9).

Closely related to Szathmar in vulgarity and old West Side "man-liness" is George Swiebel, an even more "antique" masculine model from Charlie's childhood. Charlie sees him as "hermetical" and straight out of the "Tarot deck" (*HG* 49). Charlie notes with affec-tion and heavy irony: "George feels he can speak for Nature. Nature, instinct, heart guide him. He is biocentric. To see him rub his large muscles, his Roman Ben Hur chest and arms with olive oil is a lesson in piety toward the organism. . . . He holds his own body in numinous esteem. He is a priest to the inside of his nose, his eyeballs, his feet" (42). He sees the bathhouse not just as a contem-porary capitalistic and American phenomenon but as an archaic male ritual celebration masking the primitive underside of modern American male culture. Both George and Charlie realize that "the steam bath was like the last refuge in the burning forest where hostile animals observed a truce and the law of fang and claw was suspended" (195).

Thinking back a generation, Charlie nostalgically remembers Myron Swiebel, George's father, who swore he owed his longevity to "heat and vapor, to black bread raw onion bourbon whisky herring sausage cards billiards race horses and women" (*HG* 194). But unfortunately for poet Charlie, it is an unusable model. George has grafted onto this eastern European model a Jewish-American adaptation by mimicking Walt Whitman and Hemingway, who claimed privileged relationships with draymen and clam diggers, Italian infantrymen and Spanish bullfighters. He sees through George's choice of traditional manly arenas in third-world countries or his searching for lost beryllium mines in the heart of Africa, where "the natives were always his brothers and were mad about him" (445). It is outdated Hemingwayesque theater to Charlie. By comparison, the second-generation Jewish sons raised in the ethnic neighborhoods of American cities have not done too well. A skinny dope addict from the Chicago neighborhoods, Louie has been sent by his mother to learn his American masculine role from George and the African safari experience. George declares his rite of passage into manhood aborted. He literally defrocks Louie as he takes back the safari kit he originally purchased for him and gives him instead a taxi fare and money to buy his mother a present.

Another problematic Jewish-American son and brother is Ulick Citrine, with his overdressed fat body and "fierce false look of innocence" (*HG* 386). He finally strikes Charlie as an even less admirable variation of George's capitalist Darwinian or Hemingwayesque model of masculinity. Decked out in a flame Italian blue silk shirt, which Charlie believes cries out for an ideal American body, Ulick is an updated version of the American robber baron (385–86). His financial schemes Charlie snottily dubs "capitalistic fugues" (402). Charlie identifies Ulick as a *Business Week* face (389), a "demonic millionaire clown," with balance sheets that would "read like Chapman's *Homer*, illuminated pages, realms of gold" (396). Ulick is not a grown man at all, only an aging version of his greedy childhood self, an "obese, choked-looking boy, the lustful conniving kid . . . [who] slugged it out with bullies in the street, and was a bully himself" (385–86). Tossing handfuls of peanut shells into the back seat of his car, forcing ripe persimmons into his dripping mouth and tearing at the smoked marlin with his teeth and hands, he reminds Charlie of a greedy shark who is "[a]rrogant . . . haggard, [and] filled with incommunicable thoughts" (398). His comic bilious attack and subsequent heart surgery are symptomatic of the capitalist ethic of consumption he has succumbed to.

This portrait is Bellow's most direct indictment of the capitalism in America and its corollary—the failure of family feeling. "He was the positive, I the negative sinner" (*HG* 396), Charlie notes when

Ulick admits it would not be "manly" to do business on Charlie's behalf with Charlie's money if he didn't skim a little off the top. By contrast, Charlie's sentimental, brotherly emotions mystify Ulick and fill him with suspicion. He is one of several capitalist entrepreneurs in this novel found without emperor's clothes to go with their hypermasculine illusions. "He might have been wearing sultry imperial colors" (396), says Charlie, who finally dismisses Ulick as "one of Rouault's crazed death-dealing arbitrary kings" (389) and himself as the court remembrancer to Ulick's tribal chieftain act (400).

Bellow effects a further deconstruction of this capitalist hypermasculine model in his unpleasant depiction of the next generation of American entrepreneurs, the high-roller Cuban developers. Charlie sarcastically describes them in terms of their preoccupation with golf, waterskiing, racing, twin-engine airplanes, and horses. He envies their trim bodies, their elegant clothes, and their athletic ability, but he is not blind to the all-too-easy grafting of ancient Latin machismo onto the ancient Caucasian model of the American hypermasculine.

Closely connected to Ulick, only lower on the evolutionary scale of masculine ambition, reach, and criminality, is Rinaldo Cantabile, Charlie's personal demon or agent of distraction. On an evolutionary scale, "[Cantabile] had reached the stage reached by bums, con men, freeloaders, and criminals in France in the eighteenth century, the stage of the intellectual creative man and theorist" (*HG* 174), says Charlie. With his boots made of unborn calf, his minklike furry mustache, stunning good looks, and exquisite broad leather belts, Cantabile seems to be living out a particular conception of a more androgynous masculinity perpetrated by the slightly less swanky male couturiers of the inner city, and by Hollywood gangster movies. However, his histrionic behavior in the toilet at the bathhouse belies even these dubious models. Charlie can compare only him to Kohler, Yerkes, and Zuckerman's apes at the London Zoo— primitive on the evolutionary scale, comic, and vulgar.

What of Cantabile's elegant, rich brown raglan coat and its beautiful oriental buttons, which he calls "treasure buttons" from "Circe['s] . . . sewing box"? (*HG* 86). Is Bellow suggesting that Cantabile has been seduced by a witch who has turned him into a beast? Or does he see Cantabile as a masculine Circe who turns others into swine?

For Charlie, Cantabile is a mirror reflecting his own dangerously high gratification levels and squalling, disengaged hypermasculine soul. Later on, as he views with disdain and amusement the spilt-blood leather of the Thunderbird seats, the flamboyant dash panel, and the flashy mistress, Charlie guiltily recognizes himself as an upscale version of the same kind of American male. He cringes at the comparison when forced to think of himself driving the erotic Renata downtown in the once-elegant Mercedes. To this extent Humboldt, Charlie, and Cantabile are all smitten with an American masculine car mystique.

Lawyers, not entrepreneurs, rank lowest on the modern evolutionary scale of the undesirable capitalist masculine types. As Charlie stands between Tomchek, Srole, and Pinsker outside the courtroom, he realizes he also is associated with this form of dog-eat-dog hypermasculinity. "There we were, three naked egos, three creatures belonging to the lower grade of modern rationality and calculation" (*HG* 221). He provides devastatingly comic portraits of them. Tomchek has "sourly virile" breath and gives off an odor of "old-fashioned streetcar brakes" and "male hormones" (219). Srole is chubby, pale, long haired, and a bully, a type Charlie identifies as a stooge and associate who would willingly "chop [him] into bits with his legal cleaver" (222). "Cannibal" Pinsker is a pure animal and "gut fighter" who only wishes to get his dough (220). But it is Urbanovich, the typical "Chicagoan and a politician," who represents the government of crooked lawyers that runs the country (232–33). The judge is a plump, bald, flat-faced, fatty Serbo-Croatian who represents raw, hypermasculine "hog-butcher" Chicago. His "racket was equal justice under the law" (232), only now "there were no sheaths and it was naked self with naked self burning intolerably and causing terror. . . . History had created something new in the USA, namely crookedness with self-respect or duplicity with honor" (221).

Flonzaley, Koffritz, and Stronson are caricatures of this deadly masculinism who rather unsubtly symbolize the death and burial of the whole culture with their crooked schemes for mausoleum selling and embalming. Stronson is identified as a crooked "fat boy" with "buttocky" cheeks, "page-boy bob," swinging ornaments, chains, and a "pig-in-a-wig appearance" (*HG* 277). Ironically, he is depicted cowering behind his massive Mussolini-type desk, terrified that Charlie and Thaxter might be hit men sent by the mob.

Tigler, Kathleen's second husband, is a sexy, bandy-legged,

tantrum-throwing old Western rodeo rider who delights in denying his guests lights and water at the dude ranch. "[It] gave him keen satisfaction to stick and screw people" (*HG* 367), says Charlie, who dubs him a Rumpelstiltskin. He is a mean, dishonest, broncobuster with a wired jaw who Charlie believes deserved to die of a gunshot wound. Charlie laughs silently at Tigler's stoic silence after his near drowning and is amused at his inability to say thanks or to admit he cannot swim. He represents for Bellow a certain conception of Western American masculinity stripped of its John Wayne glamor and chivalry.

All these comic and mostly unattractive masculine caricatures cause Charlie to recognize parts of his historically constructed American masculine self, but it is Langobardi, the princely, elegant crook-become-gentleman, whose style of masculine command he most admires. He was "rarefied into a gentleman and we discussed only shoes and shirts. Among the members only he and I wore tailored shirts with necktie loops on the underside of the collar. By these loops we were in some sense joined," he boasts, while simultaneously recognizing yet another dimension of his own masculine illusions. Charlie admires Langobardi for keeping his hands clean while he slums and for avoiding rough talk, which "he left to commodity brokers and lawyers" (*HG* 67). With intense awe Charlie, the dandy, observes that Langobardi dresses better than any board chairman with his ingeniously lined jackets and paisley waistcoat backs. Poor, goofy Charlie is still a Chicago South Side kid enough to be impressed by Langobardi's high style and friendship with the Mafia hit men like "late Murray the Camel and the Battaglias" (67). Yet, despite the clowning self-irony involved, the reader senses Charlie's genuine awe at the godlike masculine power in Langobardi's eyes, which Charlie is sure "have the periscope power of seeing around corners" (69). Charlie records his admiration of this masculine mystique: "He was manly, he had power. In his low voice he gave instructions, made rulings, decisions, set penalties, probably" (69). Only ugly, greedy, coarse thugs earn Charlie's total disapproval at this stage. Comparing himself to such a man, however, he comes to the realization that his own pursuits are disappointingly less "manly." He is forced to confess: "Now I saw that Langobardi and I had a relationship in the same way that the Empire State Building had an attic" (70). After all, Charlie's days are not spent in criminal command but rather in reading Hegel on the subject of boredom.

His other "culture Prince," now also dethroned, is his longtime intellectual companion, Durnwald. A cranky bachelor, bully, rationalist, and "professor's professor," Durnwald comes in a slow fifth as a power player when compared to Langobardi. He lives the "manly" life of thought only (*HG* 186), says Charlie, who by now has decided to listen not just to the intellect but also to his body in nature. "I was related to nature through my body, but all of me was not contained in it" (186), Charlie decides. Desiccated academy intellectuals like Durnwald, he sees, have also missed out on poetry, but much less flamboyantly than the racketeers and thieves of the establishment.

But Bellow is not through with parading Charlie's masculine alter egos before him. In Pierre Thaxter Bellow creates another doppelgänger who represents Charlie's androgynous, hedonistic, pretentious, and half-cultured self. Thaxter is a combination King's Road radical, Chicago student bohemian, flamboyant dandy, and pseudointellectual. He is also a con man and literary poseur, qualities Charlie guiltily recognizes in himself. He is a gendered harlequin or trickster character as he combines both masculine and feminine elements. Yet despite his seemingly Jungian admixture of masculine and feminine elements, Thaxter is merely chaotic. He is also Bellow's unkind example of the liberated modern pseudointellectual, or postwar *litterateur* who, having originally embraced the feminine, has abandoned poetry to make capitalistic use of ideas and literature. With his lunatic Christian pacifist anarchism, esoteric reading habits, classical education, and culture mania, he is a jumble of unreconciled opposites, a total parody of the postwar modern poet and earlier renaissance man.

Recognizing in himself elements of all these comically distorted hypermasculine gender ideologies and illusions, Charlie, who is really a small, sensitive, man with Jewish and, according to Bellow, feminine sentiments about familial love, realizes he has been seduced by the values of a hypermasculine American culture that has all but destroyed his feminine self. As a Jew and a poet, he has overcompensated by straining to make himself appropriately masculine in a striving Anglo-Saxon culture that not only confuses wealth and virility with power and grace, but cannot seem to separate physical fitness from salvation. Looking back at himself, Charlie cringes at his bout with health foods, his gambling with crooks, his courtship of gentlemanly Mafia bosses, his fetish for tall, deadly sexual goddesses, his love affair with the exotic Mercedes, his proud cultivation of a reputation in intellectual circles, and his abortive attempts to accumulate money. The summation of this quest for masculine power he offers in a highly ironic picture of himself in company with the American male power elite, "revolving elliptically over the city of New York in that Coast Guard helicopter, with the two US Senators and the Mayor and officials from Washington and Albany and crack journalists, all belted up in puffy life jackets, each jacket with its sheath knife" (112). It is a fragile, artificially elevated, self-inflated, masculinist construction floating in self-congratulatory bliss above the real world, encapsulated in a military machine and armed with pathetically inadequate weapons. A hard-hitting feminist might make much of phallic connotations of the sheathed knives and the general portrayal of masculine impotence. These men dangle also.

Only after the deconstruction of these powerful, wealthy, self-important, hypermasculine, mostly Protestant American models does Bellow show Charlie reaching back into his memory for images of the mostly Eastern European Jewish men from his extended childhood family. To this extent, Bellow's model for Charlie is a regendered and exclusively masculine one that pays only lip service to the accidentally female presence of a "Naomi." His earliest vision of it is the warm memory of Jewish men of his family of childhood who are mostly seen by Charlie as a valuable though endangered male species. He tells Naomi regretfully, "My father became an American too and so did Julius. They stopped all that immigrant loving. Only I persisted, in my childish way. My emotional account was always overdrawn" (*HG* 299). Its other human manifestation was in Naomi Lutz herself. We take less seriously his regret at missing out on her.

This intellectualized account, however, appears gratuitous by comparison with his emotional commitment to family-centered, nurturing Jewish males. The comparison Bellow finally offers is not a world without Naomi as contrasted to one with her. It is a world of the nostalgically conceived family-centered Jewish males contrasted with the world of the hypermasculine Protestant American males. Whereas the former are associated with equally nostalgic memories of home, neighborhood, and family, the latter are repeatedly associated with the denuded natural world, death, greedy excess, and alienation. Inevitably, his vigorous but vain attempts to bond with these non-Jewish males occur not in home or family settings but in company with their sexual priestesses or crooked friends. Note the many references to such social spaces and events as triple sex games, sharing a bathroom stall, threats of violence, cannibalistic financial dealings, one-upmanship, shared voyeurism, nudity, acts of primal aggression, physical daring, and outright sexual combat. Note also the repeated references to high status male toys such as cards, guns, baseball bats, fancy clothes, cars, money, tough talk, and erotic women.

Significantly absent from this world are children, the elderly, mothers, wives, and accounts of bourgeois domestic life. Bonding between men is never shown among these Gentiles, and neither is bonding between women. In fact, women almost always appear as sexual objects competed for by men. Bonding between men and women, such as Charlie experiences only once in early adolescence with Naomi, is nearly always supplanted by a destructive sexual politics signifying the final failure of the hypermasculine American culture to capture and subdue the feminine either literally or symbolically.

The adult male relationships Charlie engages in represent a complete anthropology of unbalanced, overweening American hypermasculinity that has engulfed Jewish and Gentile males alike. Yet beneath this encrustation, the submerged aboriginal self of Charlie's Jewish childhood is still capable of eager, swelling feelings. When he is about his childhood family comprising the boarder, Menasha, and brother Julius, Charlie remembers: "I was all torn up with love. Deep in the heart. . . . At home if I was first to get up in the morning I suffered because they were still asleep. I wanted to wake them up so that the whole marvelous thing could continue" (*HG* 74). Looking at the "mad-rotten-majesty" picture on Humboldt's obituary, he realizes that the American public takes pleasure in "the poets' testimony that the USA is too tough, too big, too much, too rugged, that American reality is overpowering" (118). After all, he reluctantly concedes, "a poet can't perform a hysterectomy or send a vehicle out of the solar system. Miracle and power no longer belong to him." He realizes with disgust that the American public are labeling poets like himself and Humboldt feminine. They call poets the "good and tender and soft men, the *best* of us," while secretly reveling in the fact they themselves are appropriately masculine creeps, thieves, and unfeeling vultures (118).

Significantly, he makes no further progress in deconstructing his own hypermasculinity until he dismisses the deathly feminine erotic, represented by Renata, in favor of the life-giving feminine, represented by elderly Jewish male models. Note that the erotic is not embraced and absorbed as part of the masculine self, as the Jungian model seems to require. Rather, a more misogynistic and puritanical model prevails and the erotic must be exorcized before the recovery of the feminine can be completed. Note also that Naomi has dropped out of sight. Herein lies the central contradiction of the text as it tries to move toward the promise of a Jungian psychic integration of masculine and feminine, or of contrasexual elements within the personality of the questing male. It is a recurrent pattern; Bellow uses it also in *Mr. Sammler's Planet* and *Herzog*. Only in the absence of the literal feminine is each of these heroes able to embark on a prolonged period of meditation and anthroposophical study he expects to lead him to that feminine absent presence.

Assuming the more nurturing role he has previously attributed to the Jewish males of his childhood, Charlie exercises compassion and forgiveness toward the wily Señora, cuts up Roger's food in motherly fashion, takes the child for walks in the park with the other mothers, and meditates alone, upside down in the Madrid hotel room. This is hardly the feminist's dream of the rehabilitated male, even if it is Charlie's deliberate turning away from hypermasculinity and cultivation of a new and more feminized role. After all, the nurturing models from the family of childhood are patriarchal Jewish males.

When he returns to America, these roles are further enlarged through nurturing and regenerative acts toward the elderly males and the significant dead. As he lovingly reburies Humboldt, and joyously reclaims Waldemar and Menasha, he simultaneously renounces his passion for money, cars, awards, fame, and the hypermasculine American thrill of criminality. Taking his financial affairs into his own hands he shows he is "very much in command" (*HG* 469). He resists Cantabile's nonsense and decisively picks up his own legal and financial affairs. The "Romance of Business," which has previously held him in its thrall, he dismisses as mere "pushiness, rapidity, effrontery" (*HG* 469).

This time an older, more chastened Charlie is reminded of his anima or soul by a sign given by the magical crocus growing up through the brutal and cracked city pavement. In this late season of his life, however, it is not a vision conferred by innocence and youth. Nor is it achieved by recovery of the literal feminine. It is attained only through renunciation of both the erotic and the hyper-masculine. Though there is a recovery heralded symbolically by Menasha's song from Aïda sung in tribute over Humboldt's grave and his obvious allusion to home in the Negro spiritual melody "Goin' Home" from Dvorak's *New World Symphony*, it is only the merest beginnings. This nostalgic recovery only leads him to the memory of his own family of childhood, not its recreation. The muse Menasha succeeds in invoking seems to be the now elderly Jewish immigrant surrogate father of Charlie's memory. Charlie at sixty must begin the search where he left off at the end of his childhood. It is represented in his mind as Naomi Lutz and suggests at least the promise of association with the literal feminine. He realizes that the great tragedy of his American twentieth-century masculine experience has been the failure to keep hold of a more vital masculinity and a more compatible feminine presence in the hope of cultivating the poetic.

7

MISOGYNY

A MEA CULPA

The dead sing through her mouth and the cries of infants are clear
to her. But for him this dialogue is over. He says he is not part of
this world, that he was set on this world as a stranger. He sets
himself apart from woman and nature.
　　　—Susan Griffin, *Woman and Nature: The Roaring Inside Her*

M isogyny in literature occurs as both representation of
women and as a rhetorical discourse within Western culture
that employs an antifeminist series of tropes. It is usually staged
through the male gaze and forms one of the enduring deep-seated
mental structures of the Western symbolic economy. As R. Howard
Bloch comments, "[t]he discourse of misogyny runs like a rich vein
throughout the breadth of medieval literature [and contemporary
literature]. . . . [As] Paul Zumthor might suggest, [it is] a 'register'—
a discourse visible across a broad spectrum of poetic types."[1]

I have discussed at length just how the male homosocial and
misogynous specular arrangements of the Bellow text ensure the
foreclosing of the possibility of seeing the feminine. I have demonstrated this very misogynous representation of women and
established the multiple masculinities with which the Bellow protagonist is bombarded. In this chapter I wish to turn my attention to
Bellow's deliberate, and in a couple of cases, comic portrayal of
three misogynists through whom he might be seen to be making
both a concerted study of misogyny and misogynists, as well as a

mild and even comic mea culpa. The two texts suggestive of this authorial intent are *Mr. Sammler's Planet* and *More Die of Heartbreak*.

Mr. Sammler's Planet

In *Mr. Sammler's Planet*, the historical construction of a certain type of misogynous masculinity is carefully laid out. Mr. Sammler critiques Western culture by focusing on its psychosocial construction of a particular type of misogynous masculine personality—that of an early-twentieth-century European scholarly iconoclast who has been acculturated in the late Austro-Hungarian Empire and become an Anglophile. Although he worked with the idea of misogyny in earlier novels, Bellow provides in *Mr. Sammler's Planet* an intimate look at its broadest cultural dimensions and its most intimate personal manifestations.

Early reviewers of *Mr. Sammler's Planet* nearly all made the mistake of conflating author and protagonist, dismissing the novel as Bellow's "self-indulgent effort at creating a thinly disguised fictional persona" and as a misanthropic "failure of nerve," a "disproportionate dis-ease with the present and an avuncular superiority over unwashed radicals."[2] Even Alfred Kazin damned it with faint praise as a "brilliantly austere set of opinions."[3] This is only part of the picture. Actually, Mr. Sammler is Bellow's quintessential wounded misogynist. In him converge the misanthropic and misogynistic Western intellectual traditions of the Greek, Jewish, Roman, Christian, and modern literary establishments. He is carefully constructed as a representative contemporary man of learning who is simultaneously gentleman, scholar, priest, European, American, Asian, Protestant, Catholic, Jew, intellectual, cultural historian, free-thinker, writer, and journalist. He speaks no fewer than seven languages and publishes his articles in the *World Citizen*. In fact he is called a "world citizen." "It was always Mr. Sammler's problem that he didn't know his proper age" (*MSP* 5) "or at what point of life he stood" (6). As one who has climbed out of the grave, he spans both states of Jewish postwar existence, life and death, modern and contemporary life.

Sammler has come to understand part of his acculturation in misogyny, although he remains unaware of other parts of it. Sammler reveals his misogyny in several ways: through descriptions of his intellectual mentors in misogyny, elaborate accounts of the masculine age he spans, descriptions of his childhood upbringing, and revelations about his pathological fear of women. He admits his mother named him for the notoriously misogynistic German skeptical philosopher Artur Schopenhauer,[4] whose first name ironically means alternatively "lofty," "hill," or "noble." He tells us he read Schopenhauer's virulently antifeminist *World as Will and Idea* when he received it as a gift from his doting mother on his sixteenth birthday. He describes reading the nineteenth-century Russian novelists Tolstoy and Dostoevsky while educating himself to be a Polish aristocrat. Sammler also describes how as a child he fed on the works of patriarchal, bourgeois, Victorian, and English establishment authors like Trollope[5] and Bagehot,[6] and how he was acculturated in both the late Austro-Hungarian Empire and in late Victorian English intellectual history.

One of his first adult intellectual mentors was the famous Victorian, H. G. Wells.[7] Although praising the rational Wells for his wonderfully intelligent views, however, Sammler ultimately denounces him as "horny," a "lower class limey" (*MSP* 28). As a reactionary advocate of "free love" and government subsidized motherhood, the famously virile and amoral H. G. Wells ceases to hold his young disciple's admiration. Sammler finally rejects both Wells's abusive sexuality and his misanthropy, failing to see how he himself has been imbued with the same latent pessimism and contempt for women. He comments, though, with unconscious irony, that Wells had been a "sex emancipator, the explainer, the humane blesser of mankind"; he could "in the end only blast and curse everyone" (28).

In summary, the time of Sammler's acculturation is the immediate post-Victorian Age, an era in which British and European nations were still secure as the world's greatest colonizers and still some years away from the fall of empires and the democratizing geopolitical changes of World War II. During Sammler's young adulthood, the racist, white, Anglo, male elitist, and patriarchal social caste systems of Europe still dominated. As part of this privileged caste, he has come of age during a moment of supreme male triumph and vindication—a moment that still lingers briefly after World War II. The narrative voice ironically inserts that in Poland, England, and France at this time "young gentlemen . . . had been unacquainted with kitchens" and that Sammler in his old age "did things that cooks and maids had once done. He did them with a certain priestly stiffness. Acknowledgment of social descent" (*MSP* 7). The loss of male privilege still galls Sammler. "Historical ruin. Transformation of society. It was beyond personal humbling" (7).

Bellow describes the young Sammler as a petted male narcissist, the only son of a "spoiled" female freethinker and aristocrat, and tells how as a child he was encouraged to view women as servile:

> he had covered his mouth, when he coughed, with the servant's hand, to avoid getting germs on his own hand. A family joke. The servant, grinning, red-faced, kindly, straw-haired, gummy (odd lumps in her gums) Wadja, had allowed little Sammler to borrow the hand. Then, when he was older, his mother herself, not Wadja, used to bring lean, nervous young Sammler his chocolate and croissants as he sat in his room reading Trollope and Bagehot, making an "Englishman" out of himself. (*MSP* 60–61)

Pampered and adored by these women, Sammler confesses in his old age that this privileged childhood produced an adult who is "not easily pleased," "haughty," "eccentric," and "irritable," and worse still, "without compassion" (*MSP* 61). He finally acknowledges that his arrogance and chronic misogyny render him unsympathetic, unfeeling, asexual, without tenderness, and unable to bond with family members. Only at the end of this self-examination is Sammler finally able to weep with love when Elya Gruner dies. He describes the beginning of this disintegration of his solitary, masculine ego, as if "irregular big fragments inside were melting, sparkling with pain, floating off" (312). He finally praises in Elya what he lacks in himself, the feminine ability to feel empathy for and connection with others, those qualities Sammler now knows to be the basis of Elya's admirable social contract.

But ultimately Sammler blames Western cultural history for producing this kind of masculinity that has so brutally exorcized femininity. Apart from its obvious roots in ancient Jewish, pagan, and Christian thinking, Sammler's misogyny derives more recently from the Enlightenment and the whole diminishing moral and political structure of nineteenth-century aristocratic society.

In his sexual panic he equates contemporary social chaos with a lawless, pagan, female eroticism. While Sammler fears sharing political privilege with underclass minorities—the great unwashed proletariat—it is women who, in Sammler's emotional imagination, are made to bear the most calumny. He translates loss of male political power into unrestrained female sexuality. The demonic power of the female erotic as the chief source of anarchy becomes for Sammler the ultimate symbol of despised creatureliness.

His morbid and near pathological fear of women is obviously a denial of his own "creaturely" or feminine characteristics. He has presumably interiorized the misogynistic Victorian codes of masculinity historically passed down by the patriarchal Western institutions of church, government, intellectual traditions, family, and public school. His failure to appreciate the democratic principles involved in extending human rights and freedoms to the masses (including women) stems from his nightmare vision of the Dionysian and apocalyptic dimensions of such ideas as they are translated into human behavior in downtown "hippie" New York in the 1970s.

Sammler's chief identification with Western patriarchalism, however, is Bellow's constant designation of him as a priestly celibate and prophet. A sexually disinterested or perhaps sexually frozen man, he neatly sidesteps the issue of his own human sexuality by hearing the confessions of sexually wounded men and licentious women. Elya Gruner calls him a "polite Slim-Jim" (*MSP* 28); his other friends regard him as prophet, priest, and judge, a repository of the values of a disintegrated civilization. Such characterizations grant him a much needed licence to be a professional celibate. Shula regards him as a "prophetic Tiresias," or a Prospero, two other types of the priestly celibate. Sammler describes himself as "confidant of New York eccentrics; curate of wild men and progenitor of a wild woman; registrar of madness" (118), a role traditionally reserved for a religious leader. Although he resents housekeeping, he does it to avoid the dirty, careless, sloppy habits of women like Shula and Margotte, and he does his chores with a "certain priestly stiffness" (7).

Yet, for most of the novel, Sammler is a cruel and detached confessor who does not dispense love and forgiveness from his solitary cell. Rather, he condemns, remains aloof, intellectualizes, and even sneers at his penitents. Sammler the priest is a rather cool synthesizing intelligence who has put his capacity for feeling and social complicity on ice. With part of himself frozen into watchfulness and intellectual reserve, Sammler is apparently no longer motivated by personal desire, homesickness, fear of death, or a need for love, emotions that seem only to humiliate his flock. As Sammler soon discovers in the lecture hall at Columbia, however, this once respectable, asexual, academic, and priestly role has evaporated, its protections gone. As Sammler hears Feffer's student radicals label him effete and impotent, he realizes, "Gone is the living man." He is now "one who had been sent back to the end of the line. Waiting for something. Assigned to figure out certain things, to condense, in short views, some essence of experience, and because of his having a certain wizardry ascribed to him" (*MSP* 274). Actually, he has become like his original mentors, a misogynist and misanthrope like H. G. Wells, a skeptical cultural historian like Schopenhauer, a displaced Victorian patriarch like Trollope and Bagehot, an old player in an even older European culture game reserved for men.

Because of the diseased connection in Sammler's mind between social anarchy and female eroticism, liberating women sexually means opening a Pandora's box of female witchery powerful enough to eclipse the entire Western social order. This is Irigaray's matricide—the denial of the maternal ground and its relegation to corrupt inferior nature. In his mind, loss of dignity and restraint is represented along with the female erotic and images of decay. In his priestly desire for "lunar chastity," he attributes to the earth its archetypal feminine connotations. It is a "grave . . . our mother and our burial ground . . . prolific belly . . . great tomb" (*MSP* 182). He says of his student readers: "poor girls" who "had a bad smell. Bohemian protest did them most harm" (36).

The horror of woman as the devourer of life, as the unruly, despised other, is the dominant component of Sammler's misogyny. Always the contemptuous and superior priestly intellectual, Sammler fears to an unreasonable degree any loss of control, failure of logic, sign of eroticism, or display of female emotionalism. He denounces Margotte's inferior intellect by condemning as ridiculous her "unmasculine" intellectual efforts at impersonating her late husband, Arkin. He laments that there is no one to protect Arkin's ideas from her tormenting and inane conversation. He admiringly describes Arkin's interruptions of Margotte's opinions as "virile." He delights, even retrospectively, at the conspiracy of male intellect ranged against her. Both deride Margotte's "goodness." Both roar over Arkin's insulting witticism that Margotte was "a first-class device as long as someone aimed her in the right direction" (*MSP* 19).

His final exorcism of Margotte as the feared other is to deny her the two most terrible powers ascribed to women, the capacity for intelligence and the capacity to regenerate. Sammler comments patronizingly that her eyes were devoid of wickedness and that she was "a bothersome creature, willing, cheerful, purposeful, maladroit" (*MSP* 17). He condemns her for her haphazard housekeeping, her greasy tableware, unflushed toilets, German wrongheadedness, and constantly damp sleeves. In these accusations of uncleanliness, Sammler is expressing an ancient belief that women are unclean and regularly in need of ritual purification. In a final burst of cruelty, he condemns her for being on the "right side, the best side, of every big human question: for creativity, for the young, for the black, for the poor, the oppressed, for victims, for sinners, for the hungry" (20). Presumably the philosophy of social obligation, faith, hope, and charity, the Sermon on the Mount or the "Golden Rule" is a "female philosophy" that a strong-headed, rational male is proof against. The final blow is his unkind conclusion that to live with Margotte, Arkin must have been driven to "erotic invention" (20).

Because he has valued the friendship with Arkin over his friendship with Margotte, Sammler pettishly resents Margotte's calling Arkin "her Man" (*MSP* 20). In Sammler's mind, Arkin is his man. Castigating her for high-mindedness, the trait that bores him most, Sammler bitterly complains: "She talked junk . . . she bred junk" (21). When her attempt to grow potted plants and vines in the apartment fails, he spitefully attempts to demonstrate her failure as creatrix, germinatrix, and matriarch of the garden bower, the ultimate misogynistic denunciation. While Margotte tries to root forsythia branches in water, Sammler associates lilacs with the smell of garbage and of death. For him, she is a childless "great mother" who offers sanctuary to all. He hates her for her affectionate kisses and for her need to be loved.

But it is her sexual power Sammler fears the most. He notices "her legs in black net stockings, especially the underthighs, were attractively heavy" (*MSP* 17). He is also aware of "her lovely dark grin, dark and tender, with clean, imperfect small teeth, and eyes dark blue and devoid of wickedness" (17). Yet he rapidly expunges his awareness of her physical attractiveness in a flood of panic-stricken contempt. Sammler prefers Arkin, with his rational theorizing, his contemptuously indulgent tolerance for Margotte, his equally misogynistic disdain of her values, and his "tall, splendid, half-bald" head with its "good subtle brain" (16). He is especially taken with Arkin's patronizing and misogynistic assessment of the women he teaches at Hunter College—"charming, idiotic, nonsensical girls. . . . Now and then, a powerful female intelligence, but very angry, very complaining, too much sex-ideology, poor things" (16).

Sammler's pronounced fear of female sexuality, of human emotional needs, of human lack of control, of human lack of dignity, and of human irrationality and slovenliness is also projected onto his daughter, Shula, whom he initially dismisses as "a wavering-witted" creature" (*MSP* 198). He persistently blames her maladjustments on her socioerotically aroused "Victorian" mother and on the community of punishing Roman Catholic nuns who hid her from the Nazis in their Polish convent. Thus, he successfully exonerates himself, and by implication the entire German Third Reich, from any paternal blame when on Ash Wednesday she observes Christian custom and at other times maintains "Jewish connections" (22). The balance of Shula's behavior he attributes to the "hysteria" inherited from her mother. His own hysteria, neurotic disorders, and socioerotic response in the presence of the black pickpocket apparently do not count. He finally commends only one quality in his daughter—her passive obedience. He even blames Antonina for her own Holocaust death and for her daughter's instability because she attempted to assume a male role by returning to Poland in 1939 to settle her father's estate.

But repeatedly, his disdain of Shula turns to the unfatherly subject of her female sexuality. "Who knew how many sexual difficulties and complications were associated with Shula's hair," he comments. He calls her swelling dark red lips "ridiculous" and says of her breasts—"what problems must be there" (*MSP* 22). Like the true Freudian, all psychological difficulties translate for Sammler into sexual neuroses.[8] Later he rejects the obligation to visit Shula's apartment because he fears she is with a lover, apparently a bogey he has invented. Though fascinated by her, he reduces the repugnant adult Shula to a childlike simpleton for whom he is reluctantly responsible. Worse still, he fragments her into her primitive or biological components by persistently imagining her as a combination of hair, legs, breasts, and belly, as he accidentally glimpses her in the bath. He then quickly relegates her to the category of generalized female belonging to the "gender club," and therefore busy undertaking an apprenticeship in whoring.

Sammler has little more feeling for his dead wife, Antonina. His main condemnation of her is that she was socioerotically aroused by her association with the brilliant and famous members of the Bloomsbury set—H. G. Wells in particular. Thus Antonina, and not Sammler, becomes responsible for Shula's crazy fixation with the H. G. Wells project and theft of Lal's manuscript. He is even able to deny his one-time sexual attraction to his wife with no remorse at all.

This fear of the female erotic or other, however, is most clearly projected onto Angela in whom, notes Sammler, "you confronted sensual womanhood without remission. You smelled it, too. She wore the odd stylish things which Sammler noted with detached and purified dryness, as if from a different part of the universe. What were those, white-kid buskins? What were those tights—sheer, opaque? Where did they lead? That effect of the hair called frosting, that color under the lioness's muzzle, that swagger to enhance the natural power of the bust!" (*MSP* 36).

Though Sammler is unkind about Walter Bruch's sexual dysfunctions, he is less brutal with him than with Margotte, Shula, and Angela. Bellow's most overt underscoring of the Victorian-Freudian basis of Sammler's misogyny comes in his near satire of it during the counseling scenes between Bruch and Sammler. Dryly and amusedly dismissing the human dimension of Bruch's distress at his uncontrollable sexual fetishism, Sammler labels the problem as "old fashioned," "Victorian sex suffering" (*MSP* 60). Bruch's habit of responding sexually to the bare arms of Puerto Rican women, while at the same time "having a highly idealistic and refined relationship with some lady" (59), characterizes Bruch as being trapped "in his own Cynara-Dowson fashion" (59).[9] With conscious irony he tells Bruch: "Well you haven't harmed anybody. And really people take these things much less seriously than they once did. . . . Besides, your plight is so similar to other people's, you are so contemporary, Walter, that it should do something for you (60).[10]

Aware of the sarcasm creeping into his tone, Sammler decides that "the sexual perplexities of a man like Bruch originated in the repressions of another time, in images of woman and mother that were disappearing. He himself, born in the old century and in the Austro-Hungarian Empire, could discern these changes. But it also struck him as unfair to lie in bed making these observations" (*MSP* 60).

Bellow carefully builds the image of a Mr. Sammler steeped in the Victorian sex-lore with the reference to Dr. Krafft-Ebing's case histories of Victorian sexual psychopathology, studies that are used today to establish the relationship of such sexual neuroses as fetishism to the taboos of the Victorian age. Through Sammler, Bellow depicts a specifically Victorian misogyny and sexual fetishism in which the locus of sexual attraction for the male is transferred from actual female sexual parts to nonsexual parts of the body, a neurosis that again causes the male dismemberment of the female. Sammler's reference to Freud's rat man further indicates Bellow's awareness of the powerful sadomasochistic component that characterizes both Victorian and modern sexual psychopathology, and hence misogyny.[11]

Bellow obviously has a conscious and primary interest in the theme of misogyny, its cultural roots, and its psychocultural manifestations. He has revealed Sammler's male mentors, his historic age, his personal history, his characterization as a repository of the values of that age, and his designation as a disinterested priestly celibate. He has shown the relationship between Sammler's sexual neuroses and his misogynistic terror of women. Bellow has clearly delineated him as a misogynist for whom woman can function only as the fearful archetypal mother-devourer, scapegoat, bitch-goddess, nurturer, castrator, angel, or whore. She is his Terrible Other, and because of this the feminine eludes him. For the misogynist Sammler, sex is a failed, chaotic, pagan religion.

The final outcome of Sammler's misogyny is his desire for total immunity from women. Early in the novel he characterizes himself as the "old hermit" to Angela's "beautiful maiden" (*MSP* 70). Now he desires disinterestedness and the celibacy of medieval monasticism with its promise of "lunar chastity." He would like to confine himself to his room to read enduring mentors—the Bible and German mystic Meister Eckhardt. While the Bible contains the principle coding of Judeo-Christian misogyny, the other contains sermons of Meister Eckhardt written to exhort Dominican nuns on the necessity of exorcizing their female sexuality. These sermons also contain elaborate accounts of Eckhardt's own self-flagellation, extended fasting, fear of female sexuality, and philosophy of severe detachment from the comforts of human relationship.[12]

Eckhardt is not Sammler's final mentor, however. It is only after his awakening to some of the feminine virtues of Elya Gruner that

Bellow allows the reader to feel hope for Sammler. In Elya, Sammler at last catches a glimpse of another kind of masculinity, which incorporates the feminine.

In summary, we see that Sammler's

> misogyny is bound to the desire to escape the senses, perception, the corporeal, or consciousness, which leads to the inevitable conclusion that it contains a desire for the absolute, or for a totality that is the unmistakable symptom of a death wish. Nor does the paradox end there, since the identification of misogyny with the desire for perfection is the site of another contradiction—a conflict between the keenness of the awareness of woman as flaw and the desire for wholeness, expressed in the persistent exhortation to virginity.[13]

Clearly, Bellow has great affection for Mr. Sammler, and yet for all his remarkable qualities, Bellow is quite deliberate in exposing the misogynist psychohistory that has shaped him. This androcentric novel belongs squarely within the long rhetorical tradition of Western culture and stages of all its tropes. It is a virile, antifeminist novel testifying to how successfully these deep-seated mental structures in Western culture have survived the test of time. But it is also a self-conscious ironic production, and that makes for a kind of mea culpa.

More Die of Heartbreak

Bellow's 1987 novel, *More Die of Heartbreak*, functions as a Prufrockian lament about failed men and absent mermaids. Full of misogynous love-lore, comic characters, botched loves, fatal forays into the danger zones of sex and romance, farcical retreats, and seriocrackpot sexual philosophizing, this text provides an analogue of Bellow's end-of-the-century comic despair over the impasse of heterosexual relations. Misogynous in its narrative construction, the novel unfolds as the self-ironic report of two men exchanging battle wounds with each other and a mock reader or narratee at the expense of women whom they perceive to have failed their romantic expectations.

Bellow's narrational structure provides the first clue that this novel's rhetorical strategies align it with a long Greco-Roman, medieval, and modern tradition of misogynous texts. Other clues include: its male center of perception, its objectification of women, its staging only the scoptophilic male gaze, its sympathetic exoneration of misogynist men, and its framing of stereotypical binary gender patterns. In this text, as in the previous one, the ontological status of woman disappears as she becomes aligned only with the senses. Intellectually passive, metaphysically liable, woman in this text is usually shrewish, depraved, androgynous, or worse still, gender unintelligible. Such a female figure is integral to the misogynous plot, which usually hinges on the dissuasion of men from marriage and the company of women.

What principally stages this text's enactment of misogyny is the location of the center of consciousness in Kenneth. Not only is it an account told by one male character to another, but it creates a sympathetic listener or mock reader within the text who is clearly a male intimate of the narrator. It also creates a sympathetic reader outside of the text who is likewise scripted by the strategies of the text as a like-minded intimate, a reflective sharer of experience or close companion of the writer. What the text forms is a sympathetic male listening circle. If we are unresisting readers, we are compelled to play our role by conforming ourselves to the textual cues, learning the rules of the misogynous reading as we proceed. But what of the resisting reader, say perhaps a woman who finds herself being coerced into an intimate listening circle of male misogynists? Does she abandon her resisting female self and allow some kind of gender transformation to occur? Should she retreat from the men's room in polite puzzlement? Should she allow herself to feel alienated or outraged, or should she perhaps read the text as it was not meant to be read—read it against itself in an act of resistance? Not to do so would be to render herself morally inert or self-divided. A reading that focuses as much on the resisting female reader as it does on the text will, one hopes, yield useful insights into both meaning and the differing effects of the text on its male and female readers. As Judith Butler reminds the would-be gender critic: "The critical task is . . . to locate strategies of subversive repetition enabled by those constructions, to affirm the local possibilities of intervention through participating in precisely those practices of repetition that constitute identity and, therefore, present the immanent possibility of contesting them."[14]

Bellow's schedule of gender complaints in *More Die of Heartbreak* is lengthy: the multiple failures of science, religion, and

belles lettres to illuminate love, modern distortions in human relations, the meaning of sadomasochism, the interconnection of love
and death, the failure of modern marriage, the ironies of biological
sexuality, the contemporary failure of poetry in human relations,
and the comic incompatibility of heterosexual love with the male
quest for higher consciousness.

The genre in which he has chosen to explore these gender
complaints is suggested by his adaptation of the Gogolian farce
"The Bridegroom" with its classic misogynist tale of the flight of
the bridegroom from entrapment by marriage. Hence the fitting
Charles Addams cartoon:

> "Are you unhappy, darling?" [he asks Morticia.]
> "Oh yes, yes! Completely," [she replies.] (*MDH* 10)

The gender anxieties and observations in this late-twentieth-
century text parallel those of late nineteenth-century Anglo-American
writers. As Sandra Gilbert and Susan Gubar argue in *No Man's Land*,
though the plot of sexual battle is timeless, during the late Victorian
and early modern periods the simultaneous appearance of the
woman writer and activist feminists provoked an anxious and sometimes violent male literary backlash.[15] "The Love Song of J. Alfred
Prufrock," a key proof text, offers an interesting parallel with *More
Die of Heartbreak* in its depiction of an emasculated male who is
convinced that the mermaids of fabled romance are dangerous and
will not sing to him. Prufrock's gender anxieties at the beginning of the
century and Kenneth's at the end of it share remarkable similarities.

Between the dual consciousness of Kenneth and Benn, the
narratee, and the listening circle, Bellow constructs a drama about
the male evasion of marriage and the banishment of women from
the male republic of higher consciousness. In this economy, woman
is reduced to the signifier of masculine desire as fantasy object.
Motivated by such an old misogynist agenda and fueled by anger at
his father's libertinage and wasted intellectual gifts, his emasculating
liaison with Treckie, and his childish fear of losing Benn to the
ladies, Kenneth becomes violent in his attempt to dissuade Benn
from marriage. He attempts a search-and-destroy mission targeting
Benn's Poe-like quest for love with the classic beauty, Matilda
Layamon. His explicit goal is to save both of them for the grail quest
for higher consciousness. The upshot of this destructive endeavor is

that both protagonists turn viciously on women for their collective failure to accept, arouse, anticipate, love, minister, or compensate them perfectly enough. It is a devaluation that robs all women of metaphysical value.

The cruel, arrogant, and taunting depictions of women generated by Kenneth for Benn's benefit systematically implicate the narratee and the listening circle in misogynistic depictions of crazy, scheming, chaotic, devouring, sexually rapacious, transvestite, or androgynous women. Erotic teases, whores, rich bitches, or aged hospital inmates, the women are passed around the listening circle for laughter, for horror, or for ratification as flagellating, physically abhorrent, or socially tyrannical demons. Cixous explains why such formulas can only result in obstacles to the compassionate and truthful examination of the subject of love: "In history, the first obstacle, always already there, is in the existence, the production and reproduction of images, types, coded and suitable ways of behaving, and in society's identification with a scene in which the roles are fixed so that lovers are always initially trapped by the puppets with which they are assumed to merge."[16]

It would seem that Bellow is aware of how this works because this consciousness is what fuels much of his comedy. Clearly, the gender club in the listening circle is scripted and cued by the text to see itself, Kenneth and Benn, as a community of unfortunate sexual victims of a droll mortality full of such contaminating women precisely because the roles are already fixed in stereotype. According to Kenneth, sex and women are cruel jokes nature has played on otherwise noble male natures, nurtured in romantic and even chivalric expectations. For these men, however compelling the erotic might be, it is metaphysically devoid of value. Bachelorhood and celibacy are prized as morally and spiritually superior lifestyles to be preserved, if necessary, by deception, abandonment, and flight. Even when Benn finally notes with amazement that "there are more deaths from heartbreak than from atomic radiation" (*MDH* 197), both men fail to see the role misogynous flight from women plays in such massive human misery.

Bellow is perfectly aware of these paradoxes of male gender-ideologies. It is not women's gender sufferings or feminist readers' expectations that interest Bellow, however. He is attempting to measure a set of historically constructed romantic expectations and gender ideologies (male-authored ones) on contemporary men living through the last decade of this most American of centuries. Unfortunately, women characters are used only as objectified fictional creations of Kenneth, Benn, and the listening circle.

Everything builds from Bellow's use of Kenneth as his center of consciousness in the novel. He creates a careful portrait of him as a sexual wraith (*MDH* 40), a failed intellectual, an inept lover, and a disappointing son. Thus, Bellow casts him as the classic unreliable narrator encased in several layers of persiflage and irony, a man whose many masks defy complete identification. The clues to Kenneth's unreliability, however, lie in his relationship with his father. He hates his father for his flair on the dance floor, intimate knowledge of the erotic jungle, and "sex-intoxication" (37). Coupled with this, Kenneth also envies Rudi's sure knowledge of who he is, avoidance of botching, and unpunished debauchery. Most of all, he hates his father's estimate of him as "one of those continuing-education types" who, in Aristophanes terms, has "his head up his ass" (41). Kenneth views Rudi as a force of nature who "couldn't help jamming the broadcasts from other sources" (38). His final assessment: "Dad had all the definition, the finish, of a personage; I was still in metamorphosis" (38). His worst condemnation is his father's lack of family feeling: "If my father had so much family feeling he wouldn't have been such a screwer of other men's wives. And didn't the wives adopt a similar outlook? The world crisis was everybody's cover for lasciviousness and libertinage (two little words you seldom see)" (41).

Bellow suggests that Kenneth's belief that he is cut out for higher things than his father's mere creatureliness derives partly from compensatory mechanisms: "I was determined to go beyond him. [I am] made of finer clay, as they used to put it; smarter; in a different league. Where he outclassed me he outclassed me—tennis, war record (I had no such thing), in sex, in conversation, in looks. But there were spheres (and by this I mean higher spheres) where he had no standing, and I was way ahead of him" (*MDH* 12).

Rudi the roué father must be rejected and the druidical metaphysical quester, Uncle Benn, substituted as a surrogate father who does not jam transmissions from beyond the creaturely sphere. Benn is linked directly to Kenneth through their both being physically ungainly and somewhat Russian. Benn, the spiritual father, possesses a classic Russian face and ancestry, and a body like a Russian church. Like Kenneth, he is also single now and mostly celibate. Kenneth is proud of their spiritual bond: "We were doubly, multiply, inter-linked. Neither of us by now had other real friends" (*MDH* 15).

Benn's new interest in sex, however, provides a major drawback: "Unfortunately he wasn't too old for female entanglements. . . . [I]n the years before his second marriage he had his hands full, dealing with ladies: flirtations, courtships, longings, obsessions, desertions, insults, lacerations, sexual bondage—the whole bit from bliss to breakdown" (*MDH* 49, 50).

While observing Benn's frequent farcical escapes via the airways, Kenneth approvingly comments: "In an age when you have Eros on one side and Thanatos on the other in a jurisdictional dispute, you may as well pack up and head for the airport rather than stand and wait for the outcome. Better to be in motion" (*MDH* 50). Kenneth's absurd gender model for this is Darwin, whose research he believes to have ruined him for larger emotions and directly caused his impotence.

Kenneth's response to Benn's secret marriage is that of a furious, controlling child. "I didn't take his marriage well; he should have given me advance notice" (*MDH* 50). Like a curious schoolboy he still wonders how Benn "made out" with Aunt Lena, who subscribed to Swedenborgian doctrines of human passion. When he tries to visualize the druidical Benn in Eden contemplating his arcana, significantly there is no Eve present in Kenneth's picture, as opposed to Rousseau's famous painting of a forest clearing replete with a nude on a recamier sofa and surrounded by tigers of desire. When Benn confesses his attraction to Matilda Layamon, Kenneth is appalled at Benn's Poesque notions about the child love with "hyacinth hair" and "classic face." After a thunderstruck silence, he explodes: "Christ, what was I supposed to say! I can't bear to have this kind of stuff laid on me, and I was sore as hell" (17). Then he notes: "I never dreamed that he might be so irresponsible, down-right flaky" (17). He nastily likens Benn's comments about Poe's Helen to the equivalent of a Bing Crosby crooning and believes Benn could find no other way to take refuge from the demon of sexuality, which inevitably reduces "the private life [to] . . . a bouquet of sores with a garnish of trivialities or downright trash" (39). It is a small wonder that Kenneth's assessment of Benn's other women is so cruel.

The climax of these misogynistic depictions comes in Dr. Layamon's sermon on the terrible contemporary vision of the literality of the female. Whereas Benn's perception of women is initially a Poe-like idealization of the beloved and Kenneth's is that of the classic misogynist, Dr. Layamon sees women as aged hags. As Dr. Layamon takes the gagging Benn through the female surgical wards, exposing him to the bald old privates of the elderly women patients, he takes the listeners with him in a journey calculated to alienate Benn from women. "When it becomes a matter of limbs, members and organs, Eros faces annihilation" (*MDH* 90), the shocked Benn reports.

On the plane to Tokyo, the occasion of Benn's second bridegroom flight, Kenneth eagerly advances his project to deconstruct woman and romantic love for Benn. He patronizingly explains that Benn's spiritual nature attracts educated women who are affected by these emanations. In his misogynistic discourse, Kenneth classifies a whole category of women he considers unfortunately educated enough to fear they will bore important men. These women are girded up by the expectations of their stage mothers and live in outer metaphysical darkness "where their poor hearts are breaking," he tells Benn. "This feminine disappointment and sorrow is very hard on men [like Benn]. They often feel called upon to restore the self-esteem that's been lost" (*MDH* 93), he concludes. It is a characterization of women as uneducable, metaphysically deficient, parasitic, and in need of fixing.

Within this ideological framework, Kenneth then launches the main attack on the educated and powerful Matilda Layamon. Kenneth imagines for his audience Matilda's morning moods as ferocious, her teeth as sharp, and her acquisition merely a consequence of Benn's absent-mindedness. Once Matilda is resignified as bitch, he constructs Benn as "a Phoenix who runs after arsonists"— the lover who is "burnt to the ground, reincarnated from the ashes" (*MDH* 199).

Kenneth's intellectual agenda is the first clue to his gender hostilities. "Inner communion with the great human reality was my true occupation, after all," he confesses. "I did it out of a conviction that it was the only worthwhile enterprise around" (*MDH* 188). His uncle's habitat was one he had chosen over more attractive settings such as Paris because he hopes that here human life was making essential advances.

Human progress, however, is a celibate male enterprise dependent on the exclusion of the female erotic. For Kenneth and Benn, male-female relations must remain metaphysically devoid of value. "As Uncle Benn's self-appointed guardian spirit, I, too, had to try to interpret their motives and anticipate their plans" (*MDH* 188), he protests as Della Bedell, Caroline Bunge, and Matilda Layamon threaten to contaminate the joint quest with their neuroses, Elavil, and erotic powers. But his quest is more absurdly grandiose than the comparatively modest Benn's—he will do for human beings what Benn has done for botany— brilliant classification and mystic identification of rare states of Being. Bellow is clearly making fun of Kenneth, whom he presents as a sexual wraith who can scarcely cope with ordinary life, love, parenting, sex, and everyday human relationships. Bellow carefully depicts Kenneth as the son of a notorious womanizer and a sexually cheated mother. Kenneth feels robbed of masculine identity by both parents. He calls himself skinny, diffident, passive, politically unambitious, and sly looking. Treckie finds his French palate, talent for high-powered conversation, middle-class sense of responsibility, and low libido inadequate for her sexual needs. He blames his much-abused mother for failing to bolster his male ego and for becoming disenchanted with her female role as petted bourgeois Parisian subjected to habitual infidelity and then denies the validity of her protest by narcissistically focusing only on his own abandonment.

Kenneth's gender hostilities are quite honestly come by, and they are principally staged in his Russian 451 "The Meaning of Love" class. The curriculum is an encoding of a long historical tradition of misogynous love-lore. Included are such European commentators as Gogol, whose bridegroom-to-be in "The Wedding" flees out the window before entrapment in marriage; Dostoyevsky, whose ill-starred lovers die unfulfilled; Rozanov, the critic-historian and Christian mystic who envied the Jews for their fertility cult because he mistakenly thought their ritual baths to be sources of fertility; Rousseau, who argued that human love is a necessary social delusion; Yermelov, a childhood acquaintance who believed that, in the physical body, angelic love becomes mere carnality; Plato, who believed love between men to be the highest expression; Kojeve, his own Russian teacher, who taught of the small glaciers in the human breast that must be melted; Swedenborg, who believed nature, including sexuality, to be mere hell; Stendhal, who thought more than one sexual experience is one too many; Freud, who believed that heterosexual love is merely overvaluation of the beloved; Krafft-Ebing, who posited theories of Victorian male sexual fetishism; Havelock Ellis, who developed an antiromantic sociological model of human sexual behavior; Blake, who presented a dubious model of gender relations in *Marriage of Heaven and Hell* ("Blight with plagues the marriage hearse"); Poe, who made a tragic attempt to defy rationalism and the industrial revolution with poetic myths of female perfection; Philip Larkin, who posed a theory of romantic love as a "deep sleep" that blots out reality; and Benjamin Franklin, who offered the cynical old saw "Before marriage keep your eyes wide open, after marriage keep 'em half closed." It is an antifeminist archaeology whose ultimate effects on the primarily women students is metaphorically suggested by Dita's sadic mutilation at the hands of the dermatologist.

Apparently, this account of the Russian 451 "Meaning of Love" class, with its bizarre encoding of a violent and erroneous tradition of male hatred, is designed to finish off Benn's infatuation with Matilda. Romantic love, Kenneth tells Benn and the listening circle, has been debased by its accommodation within capitalism and merchandising: "natures that could love have become too unstable to do it" (*MDH* 219). Benn's counterthrust, "Through love you penetrate to the essence of a being" (225), panics Kenneth, who begins to despair over trying to resignify Benn's primitive, pre-industrial era views on love. If Benn is questing for a classic beauty as the physical embodiment of his search for earthly perfection, Kenneth is superfluous, unqualified, and in short, powerless. He must reclaim Benn as the priestly celibate— druidical, charismatic, semimystical—a man who is destined to be one of the "Citizens of Eternity" (198). Benn seems instead to be obsessed not only by botany but by female sexuality: "He couldn't leave the women alone. . . . Part of his Eros had been detached from plants and switched to girls. And what girls! A phoenix who runs after arsonists! . . . Burnt to the ground, reincarnated from the ashes. And after all, every return of desire is a form of reincarnation" (198–99).

This misogynous vision of the male sexual adventurer is a fearful index to Kenneth's ancient and outrageous gender ideologies. A soul such as Benn's "demands the abolition of such things as love and art . . . which it can tolerate intermittently if they don't get in its way" (*MDH* 301), he decides. Poe and romantic ideology must be deposed. Blame rationalism and capitalism, he argues:

> Something was wrong here, off the wall with the classic face,
> the grandeur of Rome, the glory of Greece. Poe, this poor

genius nitwit married to a moronic and forever prenubile girl
. . . here was a poet who had run straight into a world rolled
flat as a pizza by the rational intellect (and at a primal, crude
stage of capitalist development—let's not leave out capitalism), and he fought back with whiskey and poetry, dreams,
puzzles, perversions. Then also Baudelaire, Poe's successor,
with his vicious madonnas, taking the field—sickness and
sensibility against mechanization and vulgarity. (209)

Kenneth is identifying not only Poe's but also his own and
Benn's dilemmas as would-be-lovers in late capitalist, rationalistic,
and mechanized America. In such a blasted world, the classic
beauties of Rome have been deposed, chivalry is gone, and romance
is impossible. In their places, only the tyranny of the literal or the
biological now prevails.

Kenneth's rhetorical use of the account of Cleopatra and Mark
Antony is designed as the coup de grâce in convincing Benn of the
mutually exclusive nature of eros and the metaphysical quest.

Pondering it again, I began to consider that a man might
either give women and love what time he had to spare from
his major undertakings (for instance, the struggle for existence, or the demands of his profession; also vainglory,
fanaticism, power—each person would have a list of his
own) or else, released from work, enter a feminine sphere
with its particular priorities and directed towards very different purposes. Here is an example everybody will understand.
If you weren't at war like Mark Antony, you were in love like
Mark Antony; in which case you left the battle and ran after
Cleopatra when her galley fled at Actium. (*MDH* 210)

Entrapped in binary thinking patterns positing the existence of
two mutually exclusive spheres symbolized by activities of war
or love, Kenneth posits a falsely monistic system of desiring that
functions much like Deleuze and Guattari's Marxist and Freudian
description of an economy of individual desire.[17] In such a system,
there is only one libidinal economy of desiring because energy spent
on sexuality is not available for higher intellectual tasks. This sexist,
Freudian paradigm reinscribes the kind of binary thinking that
arbitrarily separates eros and intellect, body and spirit.

Even Kenneth is shocked at his success with Benn, who savagely begins ritually exorcizing Matilda. The beauty that has attracted Benn previously now appears to endanger his life's work. Now a scapegoat for the duplicity, corruption, and glitz Benn associates with the Electronic Tower of modern Babel, she is resignified from a Poe Madonna to a women's lib siren—a sexy, highly educated career transvestite who wants to be the "tough broad in the broker-age world" (*MDH* 293). Matilda, the whore of high finance, has wasted and corrupted his powers to the point that he can no longer distinguish a silk plant from a real one.

Kenneth reports with shock Benn's final belief that Matilda has become a dangerous counterforce: "The case was built that there was a demiurge hidden just under the woman's skin—that while she was sleeping . . . there were exhalations of duplicity from that delicate, straight nose" (*MDH* 326). But even though Kenneth has watched Benn very wickedly resignify Matilda into a demiurge, Kenneth casts Benn sympathetically for the listening circle as "the weary, way-worn wanderer" in the Poe poem (293). He actively encourages Benn's erroneous assessment that because of Matilda he has lost his special powers and has disobeyed the prophetic voice of warning sent via the psychopathic Tony Perkins in the movie house. "A man like me, trained in science, can't go by revelation" (298), rationalizes the well-tutored Benn as he enacts his third bridegroom flight into the perpetual polar night of sterile ice, lichens, and the all-male research team.

Bellow's humor is generated by his awareness of the ironic gender ideologies involved. Hence, when Kenneth switches his desire from the ungrateful Treckie to the truly educated, mature, though facially flawed Dita Schwartz, the resisting feminist reader has to note with amusement the timeliness of Kenneth's facile repentance over Dita. After all, Treckie has permanently rejected him, a beautiful woman seems unattainable, his baby daughter will need a temporary mother, Benn is lost to the Pole, his father is in Paris, his mother is with the starving Ethiopians, and his metaphys-ical quest is on hold. Such a reader would also note how suddenly Kenneth becomes aware of how few women are capable of appreciating his fine palate, egocentric monologism, and low libido. From the image of an anonymous, scabbed-over face beneath the beehive of bandages, Kenneth suddenly presents us with Dita as a true friend, "independent, complex, determined [and] imaginative" (*MDH* 173), "pale-faced, black-eyed, . . . [with] hair that grows with

Indian force" (174), and a still flawed face. "A woman with a well-developed figure, she had lips of the Moorish type, a nose perhaps fuller than my own criterion for noses could come to terms with, and a solid face with nothing masculine in its solidity. Excepting some negligible defects, she was terribly handsome" (249). Does this ambivalent aesthetic response to Dita's physical aspect suggest he is now a repentant Dr. Aylmer, or is mere human necessity in the transcendent?

For Kenneth and Benn, life remains possible only through sexual sublimation or transformation of the female into repulsive, androgynous scapegoat. Eros and intellectual pursuit cancel one another out here as they do in the previous novels. The irony of the title now becomes fully apparent. Is Bellow saying that the quest for the feminine is probably more important than the quest for an end to radiation poisoning, or are both equally deadly? Is the book a witty exposé of the misogynous historical foundations of contemporary gender lore, or is it an elderly and bitter lament intended for a sympathetic male readership? Kenneth and Benn's misogyny remains an ethical problem for enlightened male and female readers, even when they are willing to concede what has inevitably been imported during Bellow's appropriation of a comic historical genre. The problem lies not only in the misogynous narrative strategy outlined previously, but also in the fact that the text unabashedly coopts us to despise women and to forgive Benn and Kenneth's treatment at the hands of less-than-ideal women.

As a classic, though ironic, misogynist text, *More Die of Heartbreak* primarily stages the violation of women through its fictionally constructed male gaze. The text is scoptophilic because it engages in a humorous spectator sport for male readers who are invited to engage with Kenneth in humor based on visual narcissism and a sadistic, misogynist erotics. All of this culminates in one appalling nightclub scene depicting the Japanese female prostitutes suspended in a cage above the heads of the electrified male audience for whom they are displaying their genitals with their fingers. It is the companion scene to the hospital vision of the wasted, asexual, elderly women. This scene invites a male conspiracy (writer, protagonists, and listening circle) against all the women in the text and outside it who threaten the exclusivity of the male gender club and its political imperatives. It is the analogue for the whole text and for Kenneth's Russian 451 class.

Although I do tend to believe that any book is a rough analogue of what its author thought and felt, Wolfgang Iser reminds us that a text does not pop into the world as a neatly finished bundle of meaning. It has an effect upon the reader who must act upon the textual material in order to produce meaning. The reader collaborates and applies a code of meanings to meet those offered by the text. Applying a feminist set of reading codes produces a different reading result than perhaps Bellow intended when he chose as his ur tale Gogol's "The Wedding," with its tale of the flight of the bridegroom. Just as a literary work refers to the outside world by selecting certain norms, value systems, and worldviews, texts adopt repertoires of norms and then suspend their validity within their fictional world. Each norm asserts certain values at the expense of others, and each tends to construct the image of male and female nature. What is preeminent in this unjust and cruel rendering is sympathy for women-hating men.

Both *Mr. Sammler's Planet* and *More Die of Heartbreak* offer a detailed psychological cultural analysis of misogyny, and insofar as they do this they tend to function as Bellow's mea culpa or tacit statement of awareness of the issue. Such clearly autobiographical novels suggest, however, that like most authors who manage such an awareness, this author is implicated in many of the very misogynistic strategies he is capable of identifying and intelligently critiquing.

8

CONCLUSION

Until we can understand the assumptions in which we are
drenched we cannot know ourselves. . . . A radical critique of literature, feminist in its impulse, would take the work first of all as a
clue to how we live, how we have been living, how we have been
led to imagine ourselves, how our language has trapped as well as
liberated us, and how we can begin to see—therefore live—afresh.
—Adrienne Rich, "When We Dead Awaken:
Writing as Revision"

This book is primarily about the construction of masculinity and
femininity in Bellow's androcentric American novels staged
through the consciousness of his self-ironic, mostly male monologists. Out of the singularly masculine scopic economy of these
novels emerges a profoundly ambivalent representation of historical
American masculinity and a disturbing and disturbed account of
woman. The subtle ironies of the Bellow texts demonstrate a
complex double movement in which the texts simultaneously
construct and deconstruct their own grammar of gender. At the
very moment many of these protagonists re-encode misogynist and
demeaning tropes of femininity, they also watch themselves doing it
and even manage to catch a highly intelligent glimpse not only of
their own destructive specular economies, but also of the elusive
feminine they seek. Furthermore, standing outside the text we watch
Bellow, the author, providing a brilliant critique and cultural taxonomy of the many historical modes of American masculinity and
their cultural consequences for the human spirit and for art. It is
obvious that many of these gender constructions and their social
and spiritual consequences are deliberate and self-conscious

147

explorations by Bellow. The historicity of masculinity as well as many of the protagonist's constructions of masculinity and femininity constitute a major and hitherto ignored thematic preoccupation in the novels. The pain, humor, and violence of this masculine scopic economy, along with the deliberate ironic undercutting of these unreliable narrators suggest Bellow's cultural awareness of their predicament, and perhaps even his own.

Even so, the constant staging of misogyny remains an ethical problem for enlightened readers when they are willing to concede what will inevitably be imported by Bellow's use of a monologic narrative strategy, and of comic historical genres such as those which inform *More Die of Heartbreak*, for instance. The problem lies not only in the misogynous narrative strategies I have outlined in the previous chapters, but also in the fact that the texts unabashedly coopt us to despise women and to sympathize with the monologists' treatment at the hands of less-than-ideal women. We are too frequently scripted as Bellow readers to admire the protagonists' idealism and conversational talents, and to believe with them that heterosexual love (women) make(s) such suckers of us all. Through our cooption into the sympathetic male listening circle, we pass only a light sentence on even such farcical misogynists as Kenneth and Benn precisely because they are such fallible, loveable types. It is a cooption that defers what Kristeva calls the "dream of the undistorted relation to the other" and results in what Naomi Schor repeatedly calls the "denial of the objectified other the right of difference."[1]

Numerous Bellow fictions have lamented the failure of relations among the sexes and shamelessly invoked negative stereotypes of women. Behind their comedy, intelligence, sophistication, good fun, and irony lies a virulent hostility to women that calls upon the sympathies of like-minded men. At the very time he appears to be conducting a serious investigation into the contemporary failure of heterosexual relations, Bellow fails to provide proper elucidation of his topic by holding these male protagonists sufficiently accountable for their roles in the travesty of human relations encoded in these texts. After all, "gender is what gender *means*. . . . The process that gives sexuality its male supremacist meaning is therefore the process through which gender inequality becomes socially real."[2]

Critic Drucilla Cornell suggests that literature that is ultimately misogynist not only fails to illuminate the subject of gender relations, it succeeds all too well in reinscribing all the old damaging stereotypes instead of a "newer choreography of sexual difference."[3] All androcentric monologic texts function politically as "incorrigible perpetrator[s]." Their ideological and attitudinal collusion, staged through the sympathetic male listening circle, invokes sympathy and amusement at wilfully destructive male significations of woman. The woman reader is hence forced to watch objectified women characters being passed before her very eyes, between male writer, male characters, and the male listening circle as a medium of misogynous exchange at the very moment she is being coerced textually into sympathetic identification with the male protagonists. The paradox here is that in any discourse of misogyny, while misogyny desires to escape the senses, perception, and the corporeal for higher consciousness, bound up in its very desire for the absolute, for totality, is its death wish.

The very subject of misogyny makes visible some very obvious antagonisms between female readers, male authors like Bellow, misogynous texts, and the female subjects of that very misogyny. It also points up the entire problem with representation when there is opposition between what is perceived and what is endorsed. It demonstrates the limits of idealism and highlights those conflicts between authors and readers that parallel the conflicts between misogynists and the women who are misrepresented by their pervasive but often unrecognized images. I suspect that when he chose to use some of the classic formulas of the misogynist text, Bellow was only too well aware of these issues, but valued the comic possibilities inherent in the formula over its drawbacks.

Annette Kolodny elaborates this intimate relationship between the androcentric text and androcentric methods of reading by explaining:

> Insofar as we are taught how to read, what we engage are not texts but paradigms . . . Insofar as literature is itself a social institution, so, too, reading is a highly socialized or learned activity. . . . We read well, and with pleasure, what we already know how to read; and what we know how to read is to a large extent dependent upon what we have already read (works from which we've developed our expectations and learned our interpretive strategies). What we then choose to read—and, by extension, teach and thereby "canonize"—usually follows upon our previous reading.[4]

In other words, men are women's material and symbolic conditions. The decentered subject, woman, is precisely the subject who cannot within this Bellovian textual economy escape the designations imposed by language. As readers we intersect with the text along a "horizon of expectations" formulated by our own respective cultural environments as we try to discover the questions that the work itself was trying to answer in its own dialogue with history.[5] Small wonder that a reader who claims membership in a feminist interpretive community should fail to intersect with a misogynistic "horizon of expectations." If David Bleich and Norman W. Holland are right in asserting that a reader's most urgent motivation is always to understand self, this text thwarts any female reader's quest for an adequate representation.[6] Gadamer articulates a justification for new reading paradigms such as this: "every age has to understand a transmitted text in its own way, for the text is part of the whole tradition in which the age takes an objective interest and in which it seeks to understand itself."[7] This is doubly valid in an era one of whose primary concerns is gender and the status of women. Feminist readers of these texts likewise have the right to rehabilitate the historical significance of the text for themselves. In doing so, they may well only be rewriting the text of themselves as moral critic. But even if the material text remains untouched and unmoved by such an act, the reader does not.

What allows for a degree of double-voicedness in the Bellow text is the fact that Bellow constructs his egocentric monologists through comic irony and parody. Furthermore, some of these monologists are very self-aware concerning their own imaginative and intellectual limitations. In this way Bellow's contemporary versions of the romantic idealists and the male Victorian autobiographers can be seen framed themselves by their author and others who reflect them back to themselves. This undermining of the authority of the Bellow monologist, however, while it loosens up the possibilities of the text, does not exactly allow for the full staging of the feminine subjectivity. But it does crack the seams of total masculine self-absorption, narcissism, and monocularity, causing the optic to be knocked a little off center and also causing the simultaneous erasure of any imperial subject in the text.

By reading this text against the grain of its androcentricity, it is possible to study the camera, the holder of the camera, the point of articulation and perspective from which the image is constructed, and also the spectator or reader, the point where the image is received, reconstructed, and reproduced vis-à-vis subjectivity. Adrienne Rich has called this re-visioning, the act of looking back, of seeing with fresh eyes, of entering an old text from a new critical direction, which she says for women is more than a chapter in cultural history—it is an act of survival.

Accordingly, such a reading can only suggest further inter-pretations, but it cannot result in closure or any ultimate knowledge about authorial intention, the ultimate nature of the self, its objects, or truth. I do believe, however, that it can produce an enlightening and ethical dialogue about Bellow's articulation or nonarticulation of gender and other difference. Furthermore, it will illuminate the problematic issues of representation surrounding the articulation of femininity and masculinity in the male-authored text of the late modern period in American literature. No object called woman can or should be produced by such a reading— only a horizon, as Alice Jardine puts it, "a *gynema*."[8] It is not stable and it has no identity. Jardine calls such a reading a "tear in the fabric," or the production of "woman-in-effect" (25). She also recites an anecdote from Hegel. In the first volume of *The Aesthetics*, Hegel tells a story about a fish who reproached his painter for not having given him a soul. The problem is that it is unclear who was speaking—the real fish or the painted fish or something in between. Jardine uses this example to talk of reading the "woman-effect" rather than to seek to define woman, man, or any other identity:

> The task of modernity in France, as it has been programmed in France, is to "kill the father" in all his disguises, whatever his function or form. Because it is preeminently narrative whose function is to assure communication between two or more paternally conceived egos, narrative is seen as that which must be disturbed first so that the creation of new breathing spaces in language may be affirmed and valorized. Along with narrative, those systems which support it—from the linguistic sign to the image, from the Cartesian subject to the Truth—must also be dismantled if modernity is to accomplish its parallel task: to name the unnamable. . . . But as we have seen, those new spaces and even that which cannot be named have, nonetheless, been consistently renamed as "woman." . . . When one turns to contemporary American fiction, however, the first thing that strikes the

imagination, if one has been thinking a great deal about the death of the father and its consequences, is that there would seem to be no father—at least not "in" narrative. The father as figure, or as character if you like, is already dead, seems to be absent from most contemporary American fiction, or else is only there as a pre-text: to be explained, ridiculed, parodied or ignored by the son. In any case, he is certainly not there to be sacredly feared or adored; nor is his word there to be transgressed. (229–30)

Jardine argues that this killing of the father in modern French literature, and the apparent absence of the father in contemporary American literature, is a striking difference in male textual experiments between America and France. She then traces France's history through Catholicism and monarchy compared to American history's development from Protestantism and democracy. She notes the absence of the virgin mother in Protestant tradition as opposed to Catholic tradition—two very different symbolic matrixes. She also argues that in a democracy, all sons resemble one another, and the state subsumes the role of the father. Any question of resemblance to the father becomes moot. The son's identity is established not by killing his father but by killing his *semblables*—the copies of his self. She says of the mother in democracy, she is not the sacred, incestuous object to a king but rather the maternal function as replacement for the father as the central locus of phallic power within the nuclear family. Even more interesting is Jardine's designation of American democracy as a matriarchy. Either way, the son's identity is problematic because of his negation in mass culture. Hence the mother is almost always evil, cancerous, vicious, chaotic, uncontrollable, monstrous, phallic, and powerful. Not only is the father dead, but his name is missing. He is a weak or missing father. She goes on to argue that in American writing, there is a total evasion of those spaces internal to signification, spaces that have been gendered feminine, an avoidance strategy mediated by technique. The self, an American obsession, may be caught in a network of uncontrollable forces (both social and maternal), but "I" can avoid confusion with those forces through a sustained cognitive control of and mastery over the signifier: a technical mastery protecting the self from the dangerous power of the signifier. The author avoids at all costs relinquishing control over his material: he remains sovereign, never putting the authority of his discourse into question in a radical way. The problem is the core American belief in the total freedom of the self itself. This American obsession with self goes beyond adversity and informs American pragmatics, empiricism, and pluralism. Most importantly, this conception of the self has engendered an approach to interpretation that is increasingly incompatible with contemporary thought in France. While French writers are emptying out images, narrative, characters, and words in order to reach some erotic core, or some significant core, American male writers add more images, more narrative, more words and characters to cover up the emptiness they fear. This American preoccupation with filling the image of the self connotes a fundamentally different relationship to the symbolic mode. There is a violent refusal of the maternal in American male writers, a refusal to explore the fragile infrasymbolic spaces of language as they have been excavated in France. The American interpretive response to twentieth-century crises in legitimation has not been one of exploding maternal identity, concepts, and narrative to get at their feminine core; rather it seems not to have been touched in terms of its textual genders by gynesis.

Yet perhaps this form of avoidance strategy may participate in a form of "gynesis."[9] The putting into discourse of woman or the feminine as problematic seems to exist here only at the level of representation. It has been externalized rather than internalized, thematicized rather than practiced as the primary problem for any "subject-in-narrative" without necessarily problematizing either one (230–36). It is as if the American literature of modernity has exhausted the resources of its own representative mode and now wants to fold back into the infinite murmur of its own discourse.[10] The utopian hope for a better world not shaped by such ancient and violent gender ideologies is best expressed by Irigaray: "A genesis of love between the sexes has yet to come about, in either the smallest or largest sense, or in the most intimate or political guise. It is a world to be created or recreated so that man and woman may once more finally live together, meet and sometimes inhabit the same place."[11]

Jardine concludes that gynesis at work in the male text and women authors still doing new realism rooted in unproblematized representation at least disrupts the male story. This study takes feminist issue with Bellow and his texts. But it also acknowledges that Bellow, far more than most writers of androcentric American literature, reveals us to ourselves as creatures as capable of truth as well as of error, especially in terms of the historical arrangements of gender. It has not been my intention to manipulate contemporary gender or postmodern theory in order to provide a condemnation of Bellow's texts, but rather to further illuminate their richness and complexity, their aporias, their intellectual assumptions, and their cultural constructions. Nevertheless, as Simone de Beauvoir reminds us, "Representation of the world, like the world itself, is the work of men; they describe it from their own point of view which they confuse with absolute truth."[12]

POSTSCRIPT

RAVELSTEIN

A s this book was about to go to press, Saul Bellow published *Ravelstein* (2000), his first major work of fiction since *More Die of Heartbreak* (1987). Among other things it is an account of a satisfyingly realized Platonic intellectual friendship between two men, one homosexual and the other heterosexual, as well as an account of a successful heterosexual relationship. Furthermore, there seem to be few traces of the kind of misogyny evident in the character of Mr. Sammler, or of the comic impasses of the Kenneth Trachtenberg and Benn Crader male intellectual discipleship. The gender implications of *Ravelstein* are intriguing. What might it mean that the male/male friendship is foreclosed due to the premature death of Ravelstein, or that the relationship between Ravelstein and Chick lives on beyond death through Rosamund, the female student Ravelstein has picked out for Chick? Equally intriguing is the devoted Rosamund, who on the one hand is the least stereotypical, most voiced, and perhaps most appealing of all Bellow's female characters, but who, on the other hand, is young enough to be his daughter and functions as both intellectual companion and biblical helpmeet to the aging, ailing, "great man." In addition, she triangulates and supports the important male intellectual bonding. To what extent then does she function in *Ravelstein* as woman as enigma, whose task it is to keep the androcentric hermeneutic machinery grinding, and to what extent does the Chick/Rosamund relationship represent a significant advance in Bellow's ability to portray both femininity and a viable heterosexuality? Is femininity affected by the fact that Rosamund is bartered between two powerful men in the cementing of that male/male relationship? Is Chick still imprisoned in a room of his own sans the desired male friendship in the pattern of earlier novels, or is he now, ironically in old age, safely in possession of both prizes, an enduring male friendship and true femininity?

NOTES
BIBLIOGRAPHY
INDEX

NOTES

1. Introduction

1. Brigitte Scheer-Schäzler, *Saul Bellow*, Modern Literature Monographs (New York: Ungar, 1972); David D. Galloway, *Absurd Hero in American Fiction: Updike, Styron, Bellow, Salinger* (Austin: Univ. of Texas Press, 1966); Pierre Dommergues, *Saul Bellow* (Paris: Grasset, 1967); Irving Malin, ed., *Saul Bellow and the Critics* (New York: New York Univ. Press, 1967); Earl Rovit, ed., *Saul Bellow: A Collection of Critical Essays*, Twentieth Century Views (Englewood Cliffs, N.J.: Prentice, 1975); Keith M. Opdahl, *The Novels of Saul Bellow: An Introduction* (University Park: Pennsylvania State Univ. Press, 1967); Robert Detweiler, *Saul Bellow: A Critical Essay*, Contemporary Writers in Christian Perspective (Grand Rapids, Mich.: Eerdmans, 1967); John J. Clayton, *Saul Bellow: In Defense of Man* (Bloomington: Indiana Univ. Press, 1968); Nathan A. Scott, *Three American Moralists: Mailer, Bellow, Trilling* (Notre Dame, Ind.: Univ. of Notre Dame Press, 1973); M. Gilbert Porter, *Whence the Power? The Artistry and Humanity of Saul Bellow* (Columbia: Univ. of Missouri Press, 1974); Peter Bischoff, *Saul Bellows Romane: Entfremdung Suche*, Abhandlungen zur Kunst-, Musik-und Literaturwissenschaft 160 (Bonn: Bouvier, 1975); Robert Kegan, *The Sweeter Welcome: Voices for a Vision of Affirmation: Bellow, Malamud and Martin Buber* (Needham Heights, Mass.: Humanities, 1976); Chirantan Kulshrestha, *Saul Bellow: The Problem of Affirmation* (New Delhi: Arnold, 1978); Yuzaburo Shibuya, *Bellow: Kaishin no Kiseki* (Saul Bellow: The conversion of the sick soul), Eibei Bungaku Sakkaron Sosho 28 (Tokyo: Tojusha, 1978); Edmond Schraepen, ed., *Saul Bellow and His Work*, proceedings of a symposium held at the Free Univ. of Brussels, Dec. 10–11, 1977 (Brussels: Centrum coor Taal-en Literatuurwetenschap Vrije Universiteit Brussel, 1978); Stanley Trachtenberg, ed., *Critical Essays on Saul Bellow*, Critical Essays on American Literature (Boston: Hall, 1979); Tony Tanner, *Saul Bellow*, Writers and Critics (New York: Chips, 1978); Eusebio L. Rodrigues, *Quest for the Human: An Exploration of Saul Bellow's Fiction* (Lewisburg, Penn.: Bucknell Univ. Press, 1981); Malcolm Bradbury, *Saul Bellow*, Contemporary Writers (London and New York: Methuen, 1982); Liela H. Goldman, *Saul Bellow's Moral Vision: A Critical Study of the Jewish Experience* (New York: Irvington, 1983); Jeanne Braham, *A Sort of Columbus:*

159

The American Voyages of Saul Bellow's Fiction (Athens: Univ. of Georgia Press, 1984); Robert F. Kiernan, *Saul Bellow* (New York: Continuum, 1989); Ellen Pifer, *Saul Bellow Against the Grain* (Philadelphia: Univ. of Pennsylvania Press, 1990); Peter Hyland, *Saul Bellow*, Modern Novelists (New York: St. Martin's, 1992); and Tetsuji Machida, *Saul Bellow, A Transcendentalist: A Study of Saul Bellow's Transcendentalism in His Major Works from the Viewpoint of Transpersonal Psychology* (Osaka: Osaka Kyoiku Tosho, 1993).

2. Toril Moi, *Sexual/Textual Politics* (London: Methuen, 1985), 8.

3. Jean Baùdrillard, *De la seduction* (Paris: Editions Galilee, 1979), 208.

4. Jacques Derrida, *Writing and Difference*, trans. Alan Bass (Chicago: Univ. of Chicago Press, 1978).

5. Noam Chomsky and Michel Foucault, "Human Nature: Justice Versus Power," in *Reflexive Water: Basic Concerns of Mankind, A. J. Ayer and Others*, ed. Fons Elders (London: Souvenir, 1974), 148–50.

6. Stephen Greenblatt, "Literature, Culture, Politics," in *Critical Terms for Literary Study*, ed. Frank Lentricchia and Thomas McLaughlin (Chicago: Univ. of Chicago Press, 1990), 230. Greenblatt describes how this subversion occurs: "In any culture there is a general symbolic economy made up of the myriad of signs that excite human desire, fear, and aggression. Through their ability to construct resonant stories, their command of effective imagery, and above all, their sensitivity to the greatest collective creation of any culture—language—literary artists are skilled at manipulating this economy. They take symbolic materials from one zone of the culture and move them to another, augmenting their emotional force, altering their significance, linking them with other materials taken from a different zone, putting in their place a larger social design." Art and commentary, then, are not "neutral relay stations" in the circulation of cultural materials.

7. Luce Irigaray, *This Sex Which Is Not One*, trans. Catherine Porter with Carolyn Burke (Ithaca, N.Y.: Cornell Univ. Press, 1985), 31–32.

8. Robert Alter, "More Wrestling with Forebears," review of *Towards a Theory of Revisionism*, by Harold Bloom, *New York Times*, 31 January 1982, sec. 7, p. 8.

9. Alice Jardine, *Gynesis: Configurations of Woman and Modernity* (Ithaca, N.Y.: Cornell Univ. Press, 1985), 42.

10. Irigaray, *This Sex*, 155.

11. Jacques Derrida, *Of Grammatology*, trans. Gayatri Chakravorty Spivak (Baltimore: Johns Hopkins Univ. Press, 1976), 26. According to Heidegger, the object of Man's perception must be released from its bondage before Man as subject can be released. Man must become but a listener and respondent to the speech-thought of Dasein by exercising great care, infinite patience, and wise acceptance. It is Derrida's insistence on "textual life," however, that breaks whatever mirrors are left, and it is Derrida himself who also lays "presence" at the very foundation of Western systems of representation. For Derrida, the text means beyond itself; and writing is that difference which disturbs the self-presence of phonetic theories of language within metaphysical systems of representation. Presence is "being" ousia or parousia, signifying integral unmediated presentness. In its dynamic element, this ousia is physis. This dynamic element deconstructs the fundamental opposition between nature and culture and all other binaries. The myth of presence is the myth of nature before culture, the natural goodness of

the maternal, which has never existed but only been dreamt of. Texts dissimulate and hide the laws and operations of their game. Derrida states, "The horizon of absolute knowledge is the effacement of writing in the logos, the retrieval of the trace in parousia, the reappropriation of difference, the accomplishment of . . . the *metaphysics of the proper* [*le propre*—self-possession, propriety, property, cleanliness]" (26).

12. Luce Irigaray, *Ce sexe qui n'est pas un* (Paris: Editions de Minuit, 1977), 67.

13. Teresa de Lauretis, *Technologies of Gender: Essays on Theory, Film, and Fiction* (Bloomington: Indiana Univ. Press, 1987), 15. The post-structuralist displacement of the unitary subject and the revelation that it is constituted, not constitutive, is one truth—but this is not sufficient for an accurate understanding of subjectivity. As de Lauretis argues, gender difference and the production of subjectivity postulates that what accounts for the content of gender difference is gender-differentiated meanings and positions differentially made available to men and women in discourse.

14. Barbara Johnson, *The Critical Difference: Essays in the Contemporary Rhetoric of Reading* (Baltimore: Johns Hopkins Univ. Press, 1980), 13. Johnson reminds us: "It is not the life of sexuality that literature cannot capture; it is literature that inhabits the very heart of what makes sexuality problematic. . . . Literature is not only a thwarted investigator but also an incorrigible perpetrator of the problem of sexuality."

Clifford Geertz, *The Interpretation of Cultures* (New York: Basic Books, 1973), 16, 29. Furthermore, cultural analysis is always intrinsically incomplete, as Clifford Geertz has noted:

> It is a strange science whose most telling assertions are its most tremulously based, in which to get somewhere with the matter at hand is to intensify the suspicion, both your own and that of others, that you are not quite getting it right. But that, along with plaguing subtle people with obtuse questions, is what being an ethnographer is like.
>
> There are a number of ways to escape this—turning culture into folklore and collecting it, turning it into traits and counting it, turning it into institutions and classifying it, turning it into structures and toying with it. But they are escapes. The fact is that to commit oneself to a semiotic concept of culture and an interpretive approach to the study of it is to commit oneself to a view of ethnographic assertion as ... "essentially contestable."
>
> Geertz concludes that its best outcome is to bring "us in touch with the lives of strangers" (16). He also notes that those strangers are often ourselves. This is, after all, the best spiritual discovery of contemporary feminism—the promise of understanding and the power of transformation that cultural studies offers. Here aesthetics, ethics, and literary and cultural studies are inevitably reoriented in relation to one another.

15. Annette Kolodny, "Dancing Through the Minefield," in *The New Feminist Criticism: Essays on Woman, Literature, and Theory*, ed. Elaine Showalter (New York: Pantheon, 1985), 153.

16. Michel Foucault, *The History of Sexuality: An Introduction*, vol. 1, trans. Robert Hurley (New York: Vintage, 1980), 157.

17. de Lauretis, *Technologies of Gender*, 96. More important, this suggests that novels work somewhat like films in these dynamics: "The spectator's gendered subjectivity is both implicated and constructed (as self-representation) in cinematic [novelistic] representation. That must be stressed again, since gender is not a fact, a datum, but is itself a representation, whose status (truth value, epistemological or moral weight, etc.) and degree of 'reality' (objective to subjective) vary according to the social hierarchy of discourses and representations. Thus one's gendered subjectivity is not only implicated, such as it is, in the spectator's encounter with each film [novel], but also constructed, reaffirmed or challenged, displaced or shifted . . . in each film viewing process."

18. Hélène Cixous and Catherine Clément, *The Newly Born Woman*, trans. Betsy Wing (Minneapolis: Univ. of Minnesota Press, 1986), 71.

19. Judith Fetterley, *The Resisting Reader: A Feminist Approach to American Fiction* (Bloomington: Indiana Univ. Press, 1978), xx.

20. Ibid., xxii.

21. Susan Winnett, "Reading and Sexual Difference" (paper presented at the annual meeting of the Modern Language Association, Special Session 475, New York, Dec. 27–30, 1983).

22. Nancy Miller, "Reading as a Woman: The Body in Practice," in *The Female Body in Western Culture: Contemporary Perspectives*, ed. Susan Rubin Sulieman (Cambridge: Harvard Univ. Press, 1986), 355.

23. Laura Mulvey, "Visual Pleasure and Narrative Cinema," *Screen* 16, no. 3 (Aug. 1975): 7. Furthermore, the discussion of the social contract, our ethical responsibility to the other, which writers and their readers engage in, can be discussed only when those fictional characters we confront, or who confront each other, are not just each other's reflections stemming from the symbolic economy of the masculine selfsame, but are primary and autonomous. Woman then stands within the masculine symbolic order as signifier for the male other, bound by a symbolic order in which a man can live out his fantasies and obsessions through linguistic command by imposing them on the silent image of woman still tied to her place as bearer of meaning, not maker of meaning. In other words, men are women's material conditions. The decentered subject, woman, is precisely the subject who cannot, within this textual economy, escape the designations imposed by language. Feminist readers ought to owe their primary allegiance not to the text and author-centered readings, but to the subject-object relations of the text and the resultant effect on readers.

24. Julia Kristeva, *La revolution du langage poetique* (Paris: Editions du Seuil, 1974), 326.

2. A Room of His Own: Monologists and Male Homosociality

1. M. M. Bakhtin, *The Dialogic Imagination*, ed. Michael Holquist, trans. Caryl Emerson and Michael Holquist (Austin: Univ. of Texas Press, 1981), 12. I am indebted to Bakhtin for the terms *monoglossia*, *heteroglossia*, and *polyglossia*. In particular, I found the fourth essay, "Discourse in the Novel," helpful in the following explanation.

2. Ibid., 24. Bakhtin describes the narrative consequences of this

monologist text when he compares the crucial differences between monoglossias, like Bellow's texts, and heteroglossias, which are not tied to the dominating voice of the male monologist. Heteroglossias, by comparison, are semantically open to dialogic forms (two or more voices). Monoglossias always deny the split and gendered nature of the subject, and attempt, not altogether successfully, to repress those other voices. Bakhtin makes the case for the novel that, unlike poetry, which stages the illusion of a monoglossia, (*odnojazyie*) of unitary, single-voiced language, the novel enacts polyglossia and heteroglossia (*raznoreie*) by being multivoiced. For him, language, and that of the novel in particular, is "dialogic," meaning within it someone is always talking to someone else. Heteroglossia (*raznoreie*) is the master trope governing Bakhtin's fundamental theoretical position. It is a primitive delusion, he writes, to believe in a single, holistic language positing definite boundaries of meaning since there is an immense plurality of experience. Otherness is always automatically constituted by preexisting meanings of words and their historical and social contexts. After all, context always takes precedence over text in these matters. But otherness is also constituted in the intentions of the other person in the dialogue. Heteroglossia is sometimes used by Bakhtin to mean "word-with-a-loophole." Since within the genre of the novel there is always a minimum of two in dialogue, a *Svoj*, (one's own) point-of-view, and *uzoj*, the opposite or otherness of place, point of possession, or person, there is always dialogue because *uzoj* makes dialogue possible. He claims that the novel is that literary art form most indebted to *cuzdost*, or otherness. The single-voiced poetic text (*edinogolosnoe slovo*), which features the voice of the speaking personality or speaking consciousness, always has a will behind it, a desire of its own, a timbre, and special overtones. This is the voice of the poet. Prose, however, is double-voiced (*dvugolosnoe slovo*). Heteroglossia is the condition that produces the primacy of context over text because all utterances are heteroglot in that they are produced by a complex of conditions impossible to recover historically. Thus, when cultures are closed or "deaf" to one another it is because each considers itself absolute. When one language sees itself in the light of another, however, "novelness" (heteroglossia) has arrived. What results is education or enlightenment (*prosvešenie*). Heteroglossia is where centripetal and centrifugal forces collide. Thus, the dialogic imperative, mandated by the pre-existence of the language world to any of its current inhabitants, precludes the possibility of exclusive monologue. These novels also come close to being what he calls *apannemoneumata*, or recollections that function like "transcripts of real conversations among contemporaries; characteristic also is the fact that a speaking and conversing man is the central image of the genre."

3. Luce Irigaray, *Speculum of the Other Woman*, trans. Gillian C. Gill (Ithaca: Cornell Univ. Press, 1985), and *This Sex*, 26. Once in this position, she becomes representative of the excluded social which contains not just a self-generated, self-sustaining autonomous masculine, but a full range of social forces, including those that sustain him. Hence, the monoglossia, which stages the almost seamless masculine point of view, is particularly suited to the production of a seemingly self-created, self-sustaining male homosociality that would appear to have erased its debts to femininity and relegated it to the margins.

That masculine narcissism which is the hallmark of such romantic individualists is best described by Luce Irigaray in *Speculum of the Other Woman* (1985) and

This Sex Which Is Not One (1985). Throughout these two masterworks, she describes well the historical development of androcentricity in Western culture as a result of the narcissistic male gaze into the flattened mirror of self-reference which endlessly reproduces an exact copy of the masculine selfsame. Better to look into the image reflected within the mirror of the concave speculum, she advises, because that is where the viewer might find not only the as-yet-unimagined feminine, but the excess, the surplus, and the multiplicity of the yet-to-be-imagined masculine. She suggests that authors who choose monoglossias and monologists do so because they seek mastery in order to quell the unsettling forces of the contingent.

4. Martin Danahay, *A Community of One: Masculine Autobiography and Autonomy in Nineteenth-Century Britain* (Albany, N.Y.: SUNY Press, 1993).

5. Irigaray, *Speculum of the Other Woman*, 26. Luce Irigaray describes the symbolic construction of Western metaphysics as a development of the economy of the masculine selfsame in which textual representations of both genders reflect this fundamental social dynamic. In Western culture, she asserts, masculinity dominates the representational economy and produces "the desire for the same, for the self-identical, the self (as) same."

6. Ibid., 26.

7. Irigaray, *Speculum of the Other Woman*, 247. Through these functions of blindness, symmetry, and logocentric specularization, such as the erasure of the maternal ground of existence, the debt to the maternal body, and the absence of significant woman/woman relationships, the continuation of logocentrism is ensured. Despite periodic symbolic upheavals during which some surplus, remainder, or other evidence of a feminine "not same" appears, the masculine symbolic economy quickly suppresses its attempts at "presence." All relationships with the Mother, between mother and daughter, sisters, and generations of women, succumb to silence and invisibility within this tautological circle. The founding moment of Western culture, she argues, is not a patricide, but a matricide in which the father obscures from the vision of the son his debt to the maternal.

8. Ibid., 254. It is a small leap from here to her most controversial deconstruction—"Hom(m)osexuality": the desire of male for male established within the male homosociality or patriarchy, in Irigaray's system. This is the origin of homosexual desire, since male/male power relationships are its chief characteristic. In other words, logocentrism itself is hom(m)oerotic. Its desire is constructed via a masculine selfsame, the social function of which is to guarantee that men consolidate relationships with other men. Misogynous attitudes develop from the relegation of women and women/women relationships to the margins for the purpose of reifying of male homosociality.

This construction of the masculine selfsame in turn creates a reification of the male/male relationship causing the subordinate, utilitarian figure of a woman to function as a bodily conduit through which he will triangulate his desire for masculine filiation. This masculine desiring mechanism within patriarchy and heterosexuality insists that men love one another more than they love women, argues Irigaray, and yet simultaneously disrupts any possibility of genital desire or actual sexual expression through its compulsory heterosexuality. What happens to women within this male economy of desiring is the devaluation or erasure of the feminine. Her relegation to the margins, if not her total eclipse, is a perpetual erasure that always forestalls the representation of feminine multiplicity within symbolic representation.

9. Eve Sedgwick, *Between Men: English Literature and Male Homosocial Desire* (New York: Columbia Univ. Press, 1985). I am particularly interested in her description of the other homosocial dynamics of the heterosexual world of men rather than in identifying a repressed homosexual desire between Bellow's male characters. This is work for another gender critic on another occasion.

A review of the classic traits of male homosociality shed much light on the dynamics of Bellow's male homosocial world. As Sedgwick describes these traits, they include: (1) male solipsism and monastic retreat, (2) inevitable pairs of competing men whose relationships are always steadily degenerating (often doppelgängers or brothers), (3) protagonists who are plagued by fears of paranoid persecution by other men, (4) the presence of hypercharged male relationships, (5) male bonding over the ruined or relegated "carcass" of a woman, (6) exaggerated heterosexual conquest, (7) sexual deviations from the heterosexual norm, such as homosexuality, sadomasochism, fetishism, and homophobia, (8) privileging of manly pleasures and society, (9) the formation of male hierarchies, (10) the presence of violence and murderous resentment between men, including cuckoldry as a major means to masculine political dominance, (11) the inevitable mapping of the feminine onto defeated male opponents, or, conversely, onto loved and admired men, (12) homosexual repression, (13) misogyny, (14) the construction by many male protagonists of a pseudopatriarchal family out of the remnants of male friends and male family members, (15) the occasional presence of a shamanistic, feminized, bisexual male who functions as a mediator in male/female relationships, (16) a bisexual designation for the "poetic imaginary," (17) the constant, thwarted desire among men for enduring male friendship, and (18) the presentation of female sexuality as punishing and metaphysically devoid of value. Obviously not all of these characteristics and mechanisms are applicable to Bellow's texts, and I do not wish to enact a procrustean reading without regard for their individual contradictions and complexities.

10. Claude Levi-Strauss provided the original anthropological model of male homosociality by describing how, in primitive cultures, women function as exchange items between men. This conceptual model was set forth in *The Elementary Structures of Kinship* (Boston: Beacon, 1969).

11. Gayle Rubin, "The Traffic in Women: Notes Toward a Political Economy of Sex," in *Toward an Anthropology of Women*, ed. Rayna Reiter (New York: Monthly Review Press, 1975), 157–210, argues that patriarchal heterosexuality (such as that represented in the androcentric monoglossia) can be best understood in terms of one form or another of trafficking in women as exchangeable symbolic property useful for cementing the bonds between men. Its presupposition is that relationships between men structure male desire within patriarchal cultures and therefore constitute the primary motivation for all heterosexual relations. For instance, marriage is seen as an exchange between two groups of men with the women functioning less as a partner than as the object of exchange. The bride then becomes the conduit in a triangular relationship in which the true partner gained by the bridegroom is the man, or group of men.

Clearly, Rubin is building from the work of Claude Levi-Strauss in *The Elementary Structures of Kinship* (1969).

3. Those Dreadful Mothers

1. Maurice Blanchot, *L'entretian infini*, (Paris: Gallimard, 1969) quoted in Jacques Derrida, "Living On/Borderlines," in *Deconstruction and Criticism*, ed. Harold Bloom et al. (New York: Seabury Press, 1979), 75–106. Blanchot observes that in such cases it is as if the masculine subject then acts in response to some felt need to "police" or "enforce" some unspoken order or law which insists that there is in operation some truth of equivalence about male and female subjectivity that must be sustained. In other words, the masculine seeing and speaking subject preserves this male homosocial world by controlling the phallogocentric orthodoxy of feminine representation, lest perhaps this other or feminine escape his verbal containments and wreak havoc within this isomorphic masculine symbolic order. This egocentric male voice then functions to preserve the stage for untrammeled masculine action precisely in order to maintain the illusion of the truth of equivalence. This feminine I am allowing you to see, says the egocentric monologist, is not my construction, but is the very essence or presence of the feminine that precedes existence.

2. Michel Leiris, *L'age d'homme*. (Paris: Gallimard [Folio], 1939). The pain of this "lack" or perpetually reconstituted "absence" is explained by Michel Leiris in a broad postmodern historical paradigm or master narrative similar to Irigaray's. With Irigaray, he describes the founding fantasy of the Platonic and Judeo-Christian tradition as an active negation of the mother or the feminine as the material basis of biological, cultural, and historical life. Both Leiris and Irigaray talk of the relegation of woman to passive matter through an ever-increasing spiral of nonmaterial philosophical abstractions like God, Money, and the Phallus. Leiris in particular talks of the resultant anxiety these substitutions produce in men: the horror of such a lack or absence, the anxiety of presence and absence, the separation of form and content, spirit and matter, value and exchange. He also explains its most tragic accomplishment—the metaphysical separation of Man and Nature, Man and Mother. He calls the results of this matricidal founding fantasy of Western culture the history of the emergence of "Man" and predicts the end of such a history. What follows, he argues, can only be the quest for reunion with the feminine, the exploration of the maternal abyss, and movement towards new access for the feminine, made possible by the collapse of or production of the masculine selfsame in place of other.

3. Jacques Derrida, *Of Grammatology*. As Derrida explains, "Wherever there exists the traditional male subject present to himself in relationship to an object [woman or other], there exists metaphysics and its attendant phallologocentric representations."

4. Hélène Cixous, "Entretien avec Françoise van Rossum-Guyon," *Revue des sciences humains* 168 (1977): 487; and Cixous and Clément, *The Newly Born Woman*, 72.

4. Destructive Wives and Lovers

1. Laura Mulvey, "Visual Pleasure and Narrative Cinema," 17.
2. Ibid.
3. Stephen Heath, "Narrative Space," in *Questions of Cinema* (Bloomington: Indiana Univ. Press, 1981), 53.
4. Mary Ann Caws, "The Female Body in Western Culture," in *The Female Body in Western Culture: Contemporary Perspectives*, ed. Susan Rubin Sulieman (Cambridge: Harvard Univ. Press, 1986), 268–69.

5. The Land Elsewhere

1. It will be of small comfort to feminists to note that Bellow frequently locates the feminine poetic within male/male relationships, and even inside the patriarchal Jewish family of origin. No modern gender critic would gender romantic readiness, the orphic, or the poetic disposition as either feminine or masculine. Bellow, however, gives us an overt reminder that his model for both culture and personality is a male one—Jung's construct of anima and animus. It is a model that feminists have repeatedly rejected for its male bias since the anima, as conceived in this model, is merely an adjunct to the male animus and modeled from it rather than being separately conceived. Its latent misogyny is evident in that he can locate the symbolic feminine within the world of the masculine and thereby render the literal feminine virtually unnecessary in his world of male culture and male poetry. Notice also that at no point does he consider the impact of capitalist culture on the literally female poet and visionary, because for him she does not seem to exist. As he mourns the loss of the archetype, Naomi Lutz, one of its early literal, though one suspects accidentally female, manifestations of the feminine in his life, Charlie Citrine longs for that harmonious, aboriginal, springtime self of his twenties, which Bellow describes as originally replete with both anima and animus. Only this completely constituted, harmonious self, he comes to realize, can encompass the revelations of the orphic. Jung's model is a romantic masculine model with the term "anima" being derived from the Latin for "soul" and the term "animus" representing Eros. Hence, it borrows from late-nineteenth-century stereotypes of the masculine and feminine by characterizing the masculine in relation to the spiritual, and the feminine in relation to passion and emotionality. Since Jung thought women characterized by Eros had a special ability to make connections, whereas men characterized by Logos had special abilities to think analytically and rationally, there is considerable sexual bias and inequity in the binary anima/animus model. The feminine that Bellow seems to court can be achieved without women at all, and he seems to suggest that it is just as readily found in men. Jung never developed the idea of the anima as much as he worked with the idea of the animus. It is clearly a theory that favors men because the soul is conceived as residually male and associated with Logos, while the Eros is associated merely with a posited "unconscious." These are not equally constituted contrasexual elements, and it is interesting that Bellow accepts with

167

out further question the problematic myth of the androgyne, which lies at the heart of this theory. Despite the limitations of this model, however, like so many of the intellectual systems from which Bellow borrows, this one is a generally useful metaphor for something he has no other words for.

2. The term *hypermasculine* derives from contemporary American gender psychology and refers generally to exaggerated traits of masculinity involving excessive violence, competition, misogyny, devaluation of the feminine, and physical competition, as well as obsession with economic power, social status, virility, and physique. It is a pejorative psychological term and not to be confused with biological maleness, since both men and women might possess these traits. It is also a term used by Marxist/feminist critics to describe the evolution of capitalist cultures out of such masculine traits as aspiration for power, competition, sense of social hierarchy, the devaluation of minorities and women, the colonizing mentality, social Darwinism, and the equation of politico-economic power with virility (see Nancy C. Hartsock, *Money, Sex and Power: Toward a Feminist Historical Materialism* [Boston: Northeastern Univ. Press, 1985]). The definitive psychosocial research on hypermasculinity and machismo was done by Donald L. Mosher and Silvan Tomkins, "Scripting the Macho Man: Hypermasculine Socialization and Enculturation," *Journal of Sex Research* 25, no. 1 (Feb. 1988): 60–84.

3. Ralph Waldo Emerson, *The Journals of Ralph Waldo Emerson*, 10 vols., ed. Edward W. Emerson and Waldo Emerson Forbes (Boston: Houghton Mifflin, 1909–14), 9:85.

4. Cixous and Clément, *The Newly Born Woman*, xviii.

5. Susan Griffin, *Woman and Nature: The Roaring Inside Her* (New York: Harper and Row, 1980), 13. Griffin describes the hysteric as woman formed from Adam's defective rib, contrary to him in emotional nature. The word *hysterical* is taken from *Hyster*, meaning womb, and Griffin observes that the womb is the seat of emotions and that therefore women are more emotional than men. It has to do with inordinate affections, passions, crying, over lively imaginations. Thus, the hysteric's mind is weak and her powers of reasoning doubtful because she cries, feels, dreams, and prays. Associated with corrupt nature, the hysteric is the opposite of rational modes of being in the world. But he/she is also the source of the orphic and the lost feminine poetic.

6. Maurice Blanchot, *The Last Man*, trans. Lydia Davis (New York: Columbia Univ. Press, 1987).

7. Michel Foucault, *The Order of Things: An Archaeology of the Human Sciences* (New York: Vintage Books, 1970), 387.

8. Constance Rourke, *American Humor: The Study of National Character* (New York: Harcourt Brace, 1931).

9. Joyce Warren, *The American Narcissus: Individualism and Women in Nineteenth-Century American Fiction* (New Brunswick, N.J.: Rutgers Univ. Press, 1984).

10. Leslie Fiedler, *Love and Death in the American Novel* (New York: Stein and Day, 1966).

11. Warren, *The American Narcissus*, 4.

12. Ralph Waldo Emerson, *Complete Works*, 12 vols., ed. Edward W. Emerson (Boston: Houghton Mifflin, 1903–1904), 4:58, and *Journals*, 9:298. In the world of

the inflated self, other people do not really exist—they are only objects to be ignored or destroyed (if they are undesirable) or to be made use of or absorbed into the self (if they are desirable). When an individual magnifies his own individuality to the extent that he sees all phenomena as relating to himself, there is no room for the independent existence of other people (*Journals* 4:17). For Emerson, society is also crippling and diminishing the individual (*Complete Works* 2:199; 7:9). In "Self Reliance," he urged men to elevate themselves above the demands of the world outside himself: "Friend, client, child, sickness, fear, want, charity, all knock at once at the closet door and say, 'come out unto us.'" But of encumbering relationships he notes: "keep thy state; come not into their confusion" (2:72). "I shun father and mother and wife and brother when my genius calls" (2:51).

In his lecture "Literary Ethics," Emerson tells his audience of students that if they would be great, they must be solitary (*Complete Works* 1:173). In the essay "Experience," Emerson warns that other people will drown the individual if he gives them "so much as a leg or a finger" of sympathy: "The great and crescive self, rooted in absolute nature, supplants all relative existence and ruins the kingdom of mortal friendship and love" (3:77, 81). In his "Lecture on the Times," Emerson explicitly tells his audience that nothing is real but the self: "All men, all things . . . are phantasms and unreal beside the sanctuary of the here" (1:279). In a later essay, "Culture," Emerson describes these phantasms and reflectors in the life of the transcendental self: "I must have children, I must have events, I must have a social state and history, or my thinking and speaking want body or basis. But to give these accessories any value, I must know them as contingent and rather showy possessions, which pass for more to the people than to me" (6:158). In "The Representative Man," he admonishes: "Other men are lenses through which we read our own minds" (4:5). In his journal in 1861 he writes: "A wise man, an open mind, is as much interested in others as in himself; they are only extensions of himself."

Emerson, *The Letters of Ralph Waldo Emerson*, 6 vols. (New York: Columbia Univ. Press, 1939), 4:32. Thus all comes back to this particular historical construction of the masculine self. Whatever is outside the masculine self has no separate identity or function except as it is related to the self. Emerson also merged the concept of Manifest Destiny with a belief in the survival of the fittest and was thus able to explain very comfortably the exclusion of people who did not fit into his view of America. In 1840 he wrote in his journal of the black race, "It is plain that so inferior a race must perish shortly like the poor Indians." And maintaining that the Indians had disappeared because there was no place for them, he concludes: "That is the very fact of their inferiority. There is always place for the superior" (*Journals* 7:393).

For Emerson this was not merely a private stance. He demonstrates in his public writings a concern with the masculine self and a disregard for other people that more than matches the attitudes of the narcissistic American cultural hero. Self-oriented insularity also ruled his private life. "The Trick of solitariness can never leave me. My own pursuits and calling often appear to me like those of an 'astronomer royal' whose whole duty is to make faithful minutes which have only value when kept for ages, and in one life are insignificant."

Emerson, *Journals*, 8:242. His wife, Lidian, commented in April of the year that Emerson died, "Save me from magnificent souls. I like a small common-sized one." She might have been echoing Naomi Lutz's lament over Charlie Citrine.

Emerson's ideologies regarding women are also revealing. They should vote but not lead the life of politics. They are angels in the parlor having virtue in regard to their support of man, and they should occupy themselves with love and marriage and the life of the affections. Women, in other words, should minister to male egotism. His failed relationships with Margaret Fuller and both of his wives provide a testimony of the ruinous effects of such egocentrism.

Henry David Thoreau, *The Writings of Henry David Thoreau*, 20 vols. (1906; reprint, New York: AMS Press, 1968), 2:390. All of Thoreau's writings, according to Leon Edel, were a projection of the self. He observes that there is no Beloved in the *Journal* because the only real person there is Henry David Thoreau. Therefore, the love story is the story of self-love. "May I love and revere myself above all the gods that men have ever invented," he wrote.

Thoreau, *The Journals of Henry David Thoreau*, 14 vols., ed. Bradford T. Allen and Francis H. Allen (Salt Lake City, Utah: Peregrine Smith, 1984), 32. He saw himself as totally divorced from all he saw around him. "If with closed ears and eyes I consult consciousness for a moment, immediately are all walls and barriers dissipated, earth rolls from under me, and I float, a subjective, heavily-laden thought . . . eternity and space gamboling familiarly through my depths. I am from the beginning, knowing no end" (*Writings* 1:53–54).

Thoreau created a persona for the reader (and for himself), a persona who lives alone and likes it. At the beginning of *Walden* he suggests that every man might be better off if he got into a large box, bored a few holes in it for air, and hooked down the lid.

Thoreau, *Writings*, 9:276–78. He complains that the heartaches and involvements that other people bring inevitably "impede the current of my thoughts. . . . They unfit me for my tasks."

Thoreau, *Consciousness in Concord: The Text of Thoreau's Hitherto Lost Journal, 1840–1841*, ed. Perry Mill (Boston: Houghton Mifflin, 1958), 218. Thoreau's ruling principle was: "Though I should front an object for a lifetime, I should see only what it concerned me to see."

Thoreau, *Writings*, 6:194. Like Emerson, Thoreau thought he had a higher mission in life: the development of himself. In 1854 he asserted there was nothing extraneous to himself: "This earth which is spread out like a map around me is but the lining of my inmost soul exposed."

Thoreau, unpublished fragment, "A Sister," written around the time of his sister's death in 1849. Clearly, Thoreau considered life a battle and believed that men were born to succeed, not to fail (5:36). "Human emotions are a sickness, an effect of bad bowels" (3:106). Only his sister Helen features in his journal: "A sister. One in whom you have—unbounded faith—whom you can—purely love . . . Whose heart answers to your heart. Whose presence can fill all space. One who is spirit. Who attends to your truth . . . Whom in thought my spirit continually embraces. Unto whom I flow. . . . Who art clothed in white . . . Who art all that I can imagine—my inspirer. The feminine of me—Who art magnanimous."

Thoreau, *Writings*, 11:204. Like Emerson, Thoreau envisaged himself as the

Man-woman: "Genius is inspired by its own works; it is hermaphroditic." This is particularly important in explaining the androgyny of the American individualist and particularly that of Bellow's characters who frequently combine the masculine and the feminine. One wonders who the Beloved is in the Bellow novel. When looked at from the point of view of the other, the transcendental self leaves much to be desired.

Nathaniel Hawthorne, *The Centenary Edition of the Works of Nathaniel Hawthorne*, 23 vols., ed. William Chavrat (Columbus: Ohio State Univ. Press, 1962), 3:123. The culmination of this narcissistic, misogynistic tradition of the andro-centric nineteenth-century male novel is found in Melville, where there are no women at all—only beautiful abstractions. The prototype of evil is an emasculat-ing witch-woman who uses all her powers to subjugate man. Mardi-Hautia Yillah is the angelic maiden with no will of her own who comes to symbolize the search for Truth, the ideal, the unknown, a search that proved tragic for Pierre and Ahab. Annatoo gets swept overboard when she gets too real. The quest for Pierre and for Ahab ends in destruction, perhaps because of their very self-centeredness. Melville regarded the individual (male, of course) as omnipotent. He creates only one real character; the male protagonist who appears in his various works is essen-tially the same man, even when he is the secondary character. This is a persona, a projection of himself with sympathies like his own. This protagonist, however, exists in a vacuum. Life was a stage for male exploit. He saw his audience only as male and advised women not to read his books. They are classic American gyno-phobic male novels, and they lay the foundation for the codes of masculinity and femininity that the self-ironic heroes of twentieth-century fiction must accept or evade.

The first real break in this tradition of the androcentric novel came with Nathaniel Hawthorne and Henry James, who are notable exceptions to the nineteenth-century American literary portrayal of masculine subjectivity and women. James was more European in his literary depictions of women, and Hawthorne saw the cult of the individualistic solitary male as romantic narcissism. Recognizing, like Bellow, the narcissism of the masculine egotism fostered by the transcendentalist paradigm, Hawthorne comments: "[That] struck me as the intensity of masculine egotism. It centered everything in itself, and deprived woman of her very soul, her inexpressible and unfathomable all, to make it a mere incident in the great sum of man" (Nathaniel Hawthorne, *The Blithedale Romance*. In *The Centenary Edition of the Works of Nathaniel Hawthorne*, 3:123).

13. Philip Slater, *Earthwalk* (New York: Anchor Press, 1974), 55.

14. E. Anthony Rotundo, *American Manhood: Transformations in Masculinity from the Revolution to the Modern Era* (New York: Basic Books, 1993).

15. Cixous and Clément, *The Newly Born Woman*, 72.

16. Antonio Gramsci, *Selections from Cultural Writings*, ed. D. Forgacs and G. Nowell-Smith (London: Lawrence and Wishart, 1985), 355.

17. Friedrich Nietzsche, *On the Genealogy of Morals* (1886; reprint, New York: Vintage, 1967), 43.

18. Ibid.

19. Irving Howe, "Mass Society and Post-Modern Fiction," *Partisan Review* 26 (Summer 1959): 433.

20. James M. Tackach, "Saul Bellow's Dingbat Einhorn, Nails Nagel and the American Dream," *Saul Bellow Journal* 2, no. 2 (1983): 55–58.

21. Sara S. Chapman, "Melville and Bellow in the Real World: *Pierre* and *Augie March*," *West Virginia Univ. Bulletin, Philological Papers* 18 (1971): 51–57.

22. Daniel Fuchs, "*The Adventures of Augie March*: The Making of a Novel," in *Americana-Austriaca: Beitrage zur Amerikunde*, vol. 5., ed. Klaus Lanzinger (Vienna: Universitats-Verlagsbuchandlung, 1980), 27–28.

23. Steven M. Gerson, "The New American Adam in *The Adventures of Augie March*," *Modern Fiction Studies* 25, no. 1 (1979): 117–28.

24. David D. Anderson, "Hemingway and Henderson on the High Savannas, or Two Midwestern Moderns and the Myth of Africa," *Saul Bellow Journal* 8, no. 2 (1989): 59–75. See also: Karl F. Knight, "Henderson and Melville's Ishmael: Their Mingled Worlds," *Studies in American Fiction* 12, no. 1 (1984): 91–98; Eusebio L. Rodrigues, "Saul Bellow's Henderson as America," *Centennial Review* 35, no. 4 (1983): 235–46; Janis P. Stout, "The Possibility of Affirmation in *Heart of Darkness* and *Henderson the Rain King*," *Philological Quarterly* 57, no. 1 (1978): 115–31.

25. Joni Adamson Clarke, "A Negation Offering Possibility: *Henderson the Rain King* and the Paradox of Gender," *Saul Bellow Journal* 10, no. 1 (1971): 37–45.

26. James G. Frazer, *The Golden Bough: A Study in Magic and Religion* (New York: Macmillan, 1911).

27. Gordon L. Harper, "The Art of Fiction: An Interview," *Paris Review Writers at Work* 37 (winter 1965): 480–573 (reprint in *Writers at Work*, ed. George Plimpton [New York: Viking, 1967], 175–96.

28. Ibid., 193–94.

7. Misogyny: A Mea Culpa

1. R. Howard Bloch, "Medieval Misogyny: Woman as Riot," in *Misogyny, Misandry, and Misanthropy*, ed. R. Howard Bloch and Frances Ferguson (Los Angeles: Univ. of California Press, 1989), 1. Any study of misogyny must, it seems to me, begin from two fundamental assumptions. The first is a recognition of the very real disenfranchisement of women historically. Such a premise is based upon careful work over the last fifteen years within the realm of social history. The second is the ritual denunciation of women, which constitutes something on the order of a cultural constant, reaching back to the Old Testament as well as to Ancient Greece and extending through the centuries and on into the modern age. It dominates ecclesiastical writing, letters, sermons, philosophy, theological tracts, discussions and compilations of canon law, and scientific works in the fields of biology, gynecology, and medicine. Stemming from Platonic, Stoic, Jewish, Gnostic, Roman, and Christian traditions, it has to do with the recurrence of tropes linking the feminine with ornamentation, artifice, the materially contingent, nature, chaos, and domesticity, or with commodification, eroticism, contamination, riot, gossip, uncontrolled speech, deception, tricksterism, emotionality, transgression, lack of reason, instability, verbal indiscretion, ambiguity, false logic, and incompletion. In summary, she is also synonymous with the senses, offensive, unclean, perverse, and seductive.

The misogynist is he who, in his representation of she, invariably speaks of her in terms that bespeak otherness, and this through the voice of the other. This defining tautology emphasizes the elusiveness of misogyny as well as the pertinence of the question of reading. To be more precise, I think that it can be shown that where antifeminism is concerned, the question of reception is crucial, and in attempting to identify misogyny, one is to some degree always dealing with a problem of voice, the question of who speaks and of localizing such speech. An interesting question arises: if misogyny is a topos, a virtual element, found potentially in almost any work (including those that are overwhelmingly profeminine), how ascribable is it to something on the order of individual authorial intention? It is a moot question if we are primarily interested in the *effects* of reception.

Misogyny's effects on women are perhaps more pertinent. When his gaze entails a coercive desire to fix women in a position of constant determination so that she is synonymous with matter, nature, body, secondariness, the collateral, the supplemental, the inessential, loss, lack, exhausted simulation, and aporia, he has placed her outside history. At this point she is merely one who is made-up. In the misogynist rhetorical tradition, then, the masculine represents itself as being, unity, form, and soul; while conversely, it represents woman as formlessness, chaos, and ontological emptiness. Rather than *being*, woman is accident, becoming, and temporality. She is she whose nature is supervenient.

Much of the discourse of misogyny has to do also with the aesthetic tradition that has descended to us from Kant, which emphasizes the primacy of an aesthetic experience in which the reader or viewer can claim validity for his or her perception, despite its open contradiction of statements of authorial intention or historical possibility. The implications of this discourse for self-determination are obvious. To be so "defined is to be powerless, [while] to show the limits of definition can provide access to power" (xiii). I have made much in this study of how the specular arrangements enacted in the Bellow text follow from Bellow's choice of the first-person monologist, the implied narrator, and narratee, both of whom demonstrate this kind of power. Literature and misogyny alike arise from a specular relationship to rhetoric as well as to women, whereby both are viewed not as a condition of perceptibility but as an appendage. "The gaze, as the mechanism of seduction . . . forecloses all future possibility of seeing" (15).

2. David D. Galloway, "Mr. Sammler's Planet: Bellow's Failure of Nerve," *Modern Fiction Studies* 19, no. 1 (1973): 28.

3. Alfred Kazin, "Though He Slay Me . . . " *New York Review of Books* 15, no. 3 (3 Dec. 1970): 3–4.

4. Artur Schopenhauer (1788–1860), a German philosopher, has been described as notoriously antifeminist and pessimistic. Though D. W. Hamlyn, in his *Schopenhauer* (London: Routledge, Kegan and Paul, 1980), describes his attitudes towards women as a matter of personal idiosyncrasy, it can be argued that they are central to his thesis concerning the power of the human ego. In a damning remark, Schopenhauer commented that women may have talent but never genius (*The World as Will and Representation*, trans. E. F. J. Payne [New York: Dover, 1966], 11, 231). In *On the Basis of Morality* (Indianapolis, Ind.: Hackett, 1995), he notes that women are deficient in justice (17, 148). In *The World as Will and Representation*, he dismisses men's love for women as merely the immortal part of man, which longs for her; the mortal part always longs for everything else (11, 44,

373, 559). The paraphernalia of love and matters of the heart have really no end other than the persistence of the species. He even provides a rationale for homosexuality (pederasty in his terminology) along the same lines, hence equating and effectively dismissing the value of heterosexual relationships beyond procreation. Sammler certainly shares some of these attitudes.

5. Anthony Trollope (1815–1882), whose popular fame rested on his six Barsetshire novels, dealt with themes centering on the conflict of love versus property, the activities of squirearchy and clergy, and clerical ambition versus piety. In general his works tended to show a weakening of the moral fiber of English aristocracy. He is accused of having provided adult fairy stories, and for the average reader, a pleasant sojourn in a secure world, disturbed by only petty problems and minor disappointments. For the young Sammler, his novels would have supplied an easy masculine gloss on most levels of English society and a fairly smug air of English patriarchal self-satisfaction with the status quo.

6. Walter Bagehot (1826–1877), known principally for *The English Constitution*, was acclaimed by G. M. Young as "the greatest Victorian," a Victorian personality who reflected the best aspects of the Victorian period. Young describes him as remarkably energetic, genial, immensely influential, and essentially masculine. Young adds that he was as "thoroughly immersed in the Victorian matter as the most pugnacious, self-satisfied, dogmatic business man of his day" (*Victorian Essays* [London: Oxford Univ. Press, 1962], 127).

7. H. G. Wells, a Bloomsbury intellectual, was the intellectual impresario and mentor of Sammler's young days. Sammler later perceives him as a vulgar and oversexed man who no doubt suffered from and overcompensated for a considerable number of Victorian sexual repressions common to his age. According to his son and biographer, Anthony West, H. G. Wells was in fact a great appreciator of women, who, far from exploiting them, seems to have complied rather willingly with their requests as often as he made his own. An early Fabian Society member, he earned early infamy with that group by recommending "free love" and government-subsidized maternity. Sammler remembers that even in his seventies, Wells was still obsessed with girls. "He had powerful arguments for a total revision of sexual attitudes to accord with the increased life span" (*MSP* 68). West makes much of his sexual innocence after having been closeted, like the young Sammler, primarily with women. In many ways, Wells was typical of his age in his traumatic shift at a fairly young age, from a closeted female world to the masculine world of action and sport. Significantly, the young Wells was brought up to think of his father as being somehow inept as a man. The young Wells felt constantly disloyal to his mother as he moved into his father's world and, at the same time, was afraid of his father. On his first trip with his father to the cricket bowler, he was thrown up in the air and dropped. He associated the resultant broken leg for the next fifty years with guilt for his "disloyalty" to his mother and increasing identification with his father. This guilt concerning his developing masculine identity was compounded in 1877 when his father broke a leg, an event that seems to have brought about the dissolution of the household and his parents' marriage. Later, Wells described his own sexual upbringing as both fearful and irrelevant to the real world. He concludes that "the world was never so emasculated in thought, I suppose, as it was in the Victorian time"

(Anthony West, *H. G. Wells: Aspects of a Life* [New York: Random House, 1984], 210).

8. For a complete treatment of Bellow's lifelong familiarity with the thinking of Sigmund Freud, see Daniel Fuchs's definitive article entitled "Bellow and Freud" in *Studies in the Literary Imagination: Philosophical Dimensions of Saul Bellow's Fiction* 27, no. 2 (1984): 59–80. Sammler denounces this mentor in his later years for "having raised the diaper flag" and for importing psychoanalysis to American culture. In context Freud also stands condemned for his notorious misogyny. Writing to his colleague, Marie Bonaparte, Freud once confessed, "The great question that has never been answered and which I have not been able to answer despite thirty years of research into the feminine soul is, 'what does a woman want?'" (in Ernest Jones, *The Life and Work of Sigmund Freud: Years of Maturity*, vol. 2 [New York: Basic Books, 1953–57], 421). In Freud's view, women were essentially "breeders and bearers," potentially warm-hearted creatures, but often simply cranky children with uteruses, forever mourning the loss of male organs and male identity. Says Freud, "Women refuse to accept the fact of being castrated and have the hope of someday obtaining a penis in spite of everything. . . . I cannot escape the notion (though hesitate to give it expression) that for woman the level of what is ethically normal is different from what it is in a man. We must not allow ourselves to be deflected from such conclusions by the denials of the feminists who are anxious to force us to regard the two sexes as completely equal in position and worth. We say also of women that their social interests are weaker than those of men and that their capacity for the sublimation of their interests is less. . . . The difficult development which leads to femininity seems to exhaust all the possibilities of the individual" (*New Introductory Lectures in Psychoanalysis* [New York: W. W. Norton, 1933]).

9. Cynara Dowson was the young girl whom English poet Ernest Dowson immortalized as "Cynara." She was apparently rather stupid and not even very pretty, the daughter of a refugee Frenchman who ran a third-class café at which the dissolute young Dowson ate nightly for two years. After his meal he would play cards with the girl, for whom he developed a deep love. Shy and reserved, Ernest Dowson never spoke to her of his love. At the end of the two years, she married her father's waiter. But she did inspire his most famous poem, "*Non sum qualis eram bonae sub regno Cynarae*" with its haunting refrain, "I have been faithful to thee, Cynara, in my fashion." More to the point, Ernest Dowson was a man who spoke French like a native, had exquisite manners, and became the archetype of the disorderly young poet who sings from a dung heap, escaping into insanity and drunkenness. His biographer, Arthur Symons, characterized him as "a demoralized Keats." Shy, delicate, and refined on the one hand, he was also miserably unkempt, violent, obscene, promiscuous, and angry when drunk. He seemed attracted to the most degraded women in the manner of an arrested adolescent. In short, he seems to be a model for the dual personality of Walter Bruch, whom Sammler accuses of having the same kind of Victorian adolescent personality disorder with regard to women.

10. Dr. R. V. Krafft-Ebing was a professor of Psychiatry and nervous diseases at the Royal University of Vienna and author of *Aberrations of Sexual Life: The Psychopathia Sexualis*. The book was brought up to date by Dr. Alexander

Hartwich in 1951 and published by Panther Books, London in 1965. The major section of this book is a lengthy series of case histories on sexual fetishism, most of which focus on the patient's abnormal sexual arousal through a fixation—usually on a female body part other than breasts or genitalia. Krafft-Ebing indicates that the source of such a neurosis is frequently an exaggerated fear of the woman as adult sexual being and fear of normal sexual intercourse as contaminating and forbidden to the arrested and childlike male. Bellow is clearly referring, through Sammler, to a very common sexual disorder during the late Victorian period, a disorder he sees as stemming from misogyny and fear of women engendered in an age given to covering women's bodies from neck to wrists to ankles—and placing women in either one of two categories—angel or whore.

11. Freud's rat man is described in *The Complete Psychological Works of Sigmund Freud*, 24 vols., trans. James Strachey (London: Hogarth, 1900). This case history describes a patient suffering from obsessional sadomasochistic fantasies about rats gnawing into the anus of both his father and a woman he loved and hoped to marry. This convoluted case history documents a worst-case scenario of an aspect of male misogyny or exaggerated fear of women. It documents the sadomasochistic delight the patient took in obsessively imagining the punishment and sexual degradation of the woman he loved because of his own repressed childhood terror and sexual guilt with regard to both his father and women. Freud had learned of this Eastern punishment from a military officer of known sadomasochistic preference for corporal punishments whom he met on a train.

12. Johannes Eckhardt (1260–1327), was a German philosopher and mystic who becomes for Sammler the archetypal celibate, quietest thinker, mediator, and priest, whose repudiation of women becomes the precondition of his approach to God. Significantly, part of Meister Eckhardt's pastoral duties as a Dominican friar included preaching and providing spiritual guidance to nuns of his own order and other orders. Many of his sermons were directed to women and included counsel on such matters as the feminine weakness of women in prayer, love of fine clothes, gaiety, irresolution, particularities in food, excessive austerity, and love of private property. It is also to be noted that Eckhardt was given to such sadomasochistic practices as wearing a hair shirt, flagellation to the point of bleeding, and severe and frequent fasting.

13. Howard Bloch and Frances Ferguson, eds., *Misogyny, Misandry, and Misanthropy* (Los Angeles: Univ. of California Press, 1989), 15.

14. Judith Butler, *Gender Trouble: Feminism and the Subversion of Identity* (New York: Routledge, 1990), 147.

15. Sandra M. Gilbert and Susan Gubar, *No Man's Land: The Place of the Woman Writer in the Twentieth Century*, vol. 1 of *The War of the Words* (New Haven: Yale Univ. Press, 1988), 5.

16. Cixous and Clément, *The Newly Born Woman*, 113.

17. Gilles Deleuze and Felix Guattari, *Anti-Oedipus: Capitalism and Schizophrenia*, trans. Robert Hurley, Mark Seem, and Helen Lane (Minneapolis: Univ. of Minnesota Press, 1983).

8. Conclusion

1. Naomi Schor, "This Essentialism Which Is Not One: Coming to Grips with Irigaray," *Differences* 1, no. 2 (1989), 24.

2. Catherine A. Mackinnon, *Toward a Feminist Theory of the State* (Cambridge: Harvard Univ. Press, 1989), 24.

3. Drucilla Cornell, *Beyond Accommodation* (London: Routledge, 1991), 35.

4. Kolodny, "Dancing Through the Minefield," 153.

5. Hans-Robert Jauss, *Toward an Aesthetic of Reception* (Brighton: Constance, 1967).

6. David Bleich, *Subjective Criticism* (Baltimore: Johns Hopkins Univ. Press, 1978); and Norman Holland, *Reader's Reading* (New Haven: Yale Univ. Press, 1975), 5.

7. Hans-Georg Gadamer, *Truth and Method* (London: Sheed and Ward, 1975), 63.

8. Jardine, *Gynesis*, 25.

9. Jardine, *Gynesis*, 15.

10. Here Jardine seems to be borrowing her argument from Gerhard Genette's *Figures of Literary Discourse*, trans. Alan Sheridan (New York: Colombia Univ. Press, 1982), 143.

11. Luce Irigaray, "Sexual Difference," in *French Feminist Thought: A Reader*, ed. Toril Moi (New York: Basil Blackwell, 1987), 127.

12. Simone de Beauvoir, *The Second Sex*, ed. and trans. H. M. Parshley (New York: Knopf, 1953), 143.

BIBLIOGRAPHY

Primary Sources

Bellow, Saul. *The Actual*. New York: Viking, 1997.
———. *The Adventures of Augie March*. New York: Viking, 1953.
———. *The Bellarosa Connection*. New York: Penguin, 1989.
———. *Dangling Man*. New York: Vanguard, 1944.
———. *The Dean's December*. New York: Harper and Row, 1982.
———. *Henderson the Rain King*. New York: Viking, 1959.
———. *Him with His Foot in His Mouth*. New York: Harper and Row, 1984.
———. *Herzog*. New York: Viking, 1964.
———. *Humboldt's Gift*. New York: Viking, 1975.
———. *It All Adds Up: From the Dim Past to the Uncertain Future*. New York: Viking, 1994.
———. *The Last Analysis*. New York: Viking, 1965.
———. *More Die of Heartbreak*. New York: William Morrow 1987.
———. *Mosby's Memoirs and Other Stories*. New York: Viking, 1968.
———. *Mr. Sammler's Planet*. New York: Viking, 1970.
———. *Ravelstein*. New York: Viking, 2000.
———. *Seize the Day*. New York: Viking, 1956.
———. *Something to Remember Me By: Three Tales*. New York: Viking, 1991.
———. *A Theft*. New York: Penguin Books, 1989.
———. *To Jerusalem and Back: A Personal Account*. New York: Viking, 1976.
———. *The Victim*. New York: Vanguard, 1947.

Secondary Sources

Alter, Robert. "More Wrestling with Forebears." Review of *Towards a Theory of Revisionism*, by Harold Bloom. *New York Times*, 31 January 1982, sec. 7, p. 8.

Anderson, David D. "Hemingway and Henderson on the High Savannas, or Two Midwestern Moderns and the Myth of Africa." *Saul Bellow Journal* 8, no. 2 (1989): 59–75.

Bakhtin, M. M. *The Dialogic Imagination*. Edited by Michael Holquist, translated by Caryl Emerson and Michael Holquist. Austin: Univ. of Texas Press, 1981.

Baùdrillard, Jean. *De la seduction*. Paris: Editions Galilee, 1979.

Beauvoir, Simone de. *The Second Sex*. Edited and translated by H. M. Parshley. New York: Knopf, 1953.

Bischoff, Peter. *Saul Bellows Romane: Entfremdung Suche*. Abhandlungen zur Kunst-, Musik-und Literaturwissenschaft 160. Bonn: Bouvier, 1975.

Blanchot, Maurice. *The Last Man*. Translated by Lydia Davis. New York: Columbia Univ. Press, 1987.

———. *L'entretian infini*. Paris: Gallimard, 1969.

Bleich, David. *Subjective Criticism*. Baltimore: Johns Hopkins Univ. Press, 1978.

Bloch, R. Howard. "Medieval Misogyny: Woman as Riot." In *Misogyny, Misandry, and Misanthropy*, edited by R. Howard Bloch and Frances Ferguson. Los Angeles: Univ. of California Press, 1989.

Bradbury, Malcolm. *Saul Bellow*. Contemporary Writers. London and New York: Methuen, 1982.

Braham, Jeanne. *A Sort of Columbus: The American Voyages of Saul Bellow's Fiction*. Athens: Univ. of Georgia Press, 1984.

Butler, Judith. *Gender Trouble: Feminism and the Subversion of Identity*. New York: Routledge, 1990.

Caws, Mary Ann. "The Female Body in Western Culture." In *The Female Body in Western Culture: Contemporary Perspectives*, edited by Susan Rubin Sulieman. Cambridge: Harvard Univ. Press, 1986.

Chapman, Sara S. "Melville and Bellow in the Real World: *Pierre* and *Augie March*." *West Virginia Univ. Bulletin, Philological Papers* 18 (1971): 51–57.

Chomsky, Noam, and Michel Foucault. "Human Nature: Justice Versus Power." In *Reflexive Water: Basic Concerns of Mankind, A. J. Ayer and Others*, edited by Fons Elders, 133–98. London: Souvenir, 1974.

Cixous, Hélène, "Entretien avec Francoise van Rossum-Guyon." *Revue des sciences humains* 168 (1977): 479–93.

Cixous, Hélène and Catherine Clément. *The Newly Born Woman*. Translated by Betsy Wing. Minneapolis: Univ. of Minnesota Press, 1986.

Clarke, Joni Adamson. "A Negation Offering Possibility: *Henderson the Rain King* and the Paradox of Gender." *Saul Bellow Journal* 10, no. 1 (1971): 37–45.

Clayton, John J. *Saul Bellow: In Defense of Man*. Bloomington, Ind.: Indiana Univ. Press, 1968.

Cornell, Drucilla. *Beyond Accommodation*. London: Routledge, 1991.

Danahay, Martin A. *A Community of One: Masculine Autobiography and Autonomy in Nineteenth-Century Britain*. Albany, N.Y.: SUNY Press, 1993.

Deleuze, Gilles, and Felix Guattari. *Anti-Oedipus: Capitalism and Schizophrenia*. Translated by Robert Hurley, Mark Seem, and Helen Lane. Minneapolis: Univ. of Minnesota Press, 1983.

Derrida, Jacques. "Living On/Borderlines." In *Deconstruction and Criticism*, edited by Harold Bloom et al., 75–106. New York: Seabury, 1979.

———. *Of Grammatology*. Translated by Gayatri Chakravorty Spivak. London: The Johns Hopkins Univ. Press, 1976.

———. *Writing and Difference*. Translated by Alan Bass. Chicago: Univ. of Chicago Press, 1978.

Detweiler, Robert. *Saul Bellow: A Critical Essay*, Contemporary Writers in Christian Perspective. Grand Rapids, Mich.: Eerdmans, 1967.

Dommergues, Pierre. *Saul Bellow*. Paris: Grasset, 1967.

Emerson, Ralph Waldo. *Complete Works*. 12 vols. Edited by Edward W. Emerson. Boston: Houghton Mifflin, 1903–4.

———. *The Journals of Ralph Waldo Emerson*. 10 vols. Edited by Edward W. Emerson and Waldo Emerson Forbes. Boston: Houghton Mifflin, 1909–14.

———. *The Letters of Ralph Waldo Emerson*. 6 vols. New York: Columbia Univ. Press, 1939.

Faulkner, William. *The Lion in the Garden: Interviews with William Faulkner 1926–62*. Edited by James B. Meriwether and Michael Millgate. New York: Random House, 1968.

Fetterley, Judith. *The Resisting Reader: A Feminist Approach to American Fiction*. Bloomington: Indiana Univ. Press, 1977.

Fiedler, Leslie. *Love and Death in the American Novel*. New York: Stein and Day, 1966.

Foucault, Michel. *The History of Sexuality: An Introduction*. Vol. 1. Translated by Robert Hurley. New York: Vintage, 1980.

———. *The Order of Things: An Archaeology of the Human Sciences*. New York: Vintage, 1970.

Frazer, James G. *The Golden Bough: A Study in Magic and Religion*. New York: Macmillan, 1911.

Freud, Sigmund. *The Complete Psychological Works of Sigmund Freud*. 24 vols. Translated by James Strachey. London: Hogarth, 1900.

———. *New Introductory Lectures in Psychoanalysis*. New York: W. W. Norton, 1933.

Fuchs, Daniel. "*The Adventures of Augie March*: The Making of a Novel." In *Americana-Austriaca: Beitrage zur Amerikunde*, Vol. 5, edited by Klaus Lanzinger, 27–28. Vienna: Universitats-Verlagsbuchhandlung, 1980.

———. "Bellow and Freud." *Studies in the Literary Imagination: Philosophical Dimensions of Saul Bellow's Fiction* 27, no. 2 (1984): 59–80.

Gadamer, Hans-George. *Truth and Method*. London: Sheed and Ward, 1975.

Galloway, David D. *Absurd Hero in American Fiction: Updike, Styron, Bellow, Salinger*. Austin: Univ. of Texas Press, 1966.

———. "Mr. Sammler's Planet: Bellow's Failure of Nerve." *Modern Fiction Studies* 19, no. 1 (1973): 17–28.

Geertz, Clifford. *The Interpretation of Cultures*. New York: Basic Books, 1973.

Genette, Gerhard. *Figures of Literary Discourse*, translated by Alan Sheridan. New York: Columbia Univ. Press, 1982.

Gerson, Steven M. "The New American Adam in *The Adventures of Augie March*." *Modern Fiction Studies* 25, no. 1 (1979): 117–28.

Gilbert, Sandra M., and Susan Gubar. *No Man's Land: The Place of the Woman Writer in the Twentieth Century*. Vol. 1 of *The War of the Words*. New Haven: Yale Univ. Press, 1988.

Goldman, Liela H. *Saul Bellow's Moral Vision: A Critical Study of the Jewish Experience*. New York: Irvington, 1983.

Gramsci, Antonio. *Selections from Cultural Writings*. Edited by D. Forgacs and G. Nowell-Smith. London: Lawrence and Wishart, 1985.

Greenblatt, Stephen. "Literature, Culture, Politics." In *Critical Terms for Literary Study*, edited by Frank Lentricchia and Thomas McLaughlin, 225–32. Chicago: Univ. of Chicago Press, 1990.

Griffin, Susan. *Woman and Nature: The Roaring Inside Her*. New York: Harper and Row, 1980.

Hamlyn, D. W. *Schopenhauer*. London: Routledge, Kegan and Paul, 1980.

Harper, Gordon L. "The Art of Fiction: An Interview." *Paris Review Writers at Work* 37 (winter 1965): 480–573. Reprint in *Writers at Work*, edited by George Plimpton, 175–96. New York: Viking, 1967.

Hartsock, Nancy C. M. *Money, Sex and Power: Toward a Feminist Historical Materialism*. Boston: Northeastern Univ. Press, 1985.

Hawthorne, Nathaniel. *The Centenary Edition of the Works of Nathaniel Hawthorne*. 23 vols. Edited by William Chavrat. Columbus: Ohio State Univ. Press, 1962.

Heath, Stephen. "Narrative Space." In *Questions of the Cinema*, edited by Stephen Heath. Bloomington: Indiana Univ. Press, 1981.

Heidegger, Martin. "La Doctrine de Platon sur la vérité." In *Questions II*, 142–44. Paris: Gallimard, 1968. Quoted in *Gynesis: Configurations of Woman and Modernity*. Ithaca, N.Y.: Cornell Univ. Press, 147.

Holland, Norman. *Reader's Reading*. New Haven: Yale Univ. Press, 1975.

Howe, Irving. "Mass Society and Post-Modern Fiction." *Partisan Review* 26 (summer 1959): 420–36.

Hyland, Peter. *Saul Bellow*. Modern Novelists. New York: St. Martin's, 1992.

Irigaray, Luce. *Ce sexe qui n'est pas un*. Paris: Editions de Minuit, 1977.

———. "Sexual Difference." In *French Feminist Thought: A Reader*, edited by Toril Moi, translated by Seán Hand, 118-30. New York: Basil Blackwell, 1987.

———. *Speculum of the Other Woman*. Translated by Gillian C. Gill. Ithaca, N.Y.: Cornell Univ. Press, 1985.

———. *This Sex Which Is Not One*. Translated by Catherine Porter with Carolyn Burke. Ithaca, N.Y.: Cornell Univ. Press, 1985.

Jardine, Alice A. *Gynesis: Configurations of Woman and Modernity*. Ithaca, N.Y.: Cornell Univ. Press, 1985.

Jauss, Hans-Robert. *The Critical Difference: Essays in the Contemporary Rhetoric of Reading*. Baltimore: Johns Hopkins Univ. Press, 1981.

———. *Toward an Aesthetic of Reception*. Brighton, England: Constance, 1967.

Jones, Ernest. *The Life and Work of Sigmund Freud: Years of Maturity*. Vol. 2. New York: Basic Books, 1953–57.

Kazin, Alfred. "Though He Slay Me . . . " *New York Review of Books* 15, no. 3 (3 Dec. 1970): 3–4.

Kegan, Robert. *The Sweeter Welcome: Voices for a Vision of Affirmation: Bellow, Malamud and Martin Buber*. Needham Heights, Mass.: Humanities, 1976.

Kiernan, Robert F. *Saul Bellow*. New York: Continuum, 1989.

Kofman, Sarah. *L'enigme de la femme dans le textes de Freud*. Paris: Galilee, 1981. Quoted in *Gynesis: Configurations of Woman and Modernity*. Ithaca, N.Y.: Cornell Univ. Press, 200.

Kolodny, Annette. "Dancing Through the Minefield." In *The New Feminist Criticism: Essays on Woman, Literature, and Theory*, edited by Elaine Showalter. New York: Pantheon, 1985.

Krafft-Ebing, R. V. *Aberrations of Sexual Life: The Psychopathia Sexualis*. London: Panther, 1965.

Kristeva, Julia. *La revolution de langage poetique*. Paris: Editions du Seuil, 1974.

Kulshrestha, Chirantan. *Saul Bellow: The Problem of Affirmation*. New Delhi: Arnold, 1978.

de Lauretis, Teresa. *Technologies of Gender: Essays on Theory, Film, and Fiction*. Bloomington: Indiana Univ. Press, 1987.

Leiris, Michel. *L'age d'homme*. Paris: Gallimard [Folio], 1939.

Levi-Strauss, Claude. *The Elementary Structures of Kinship*. Boston: Beacon, 1969.

Machida, Tetsuji. *Saul Bellow, A Transcendentalist: A Study of Saul Bellow's Transcendentalism in His Major Works from the Viewpoint of Transpersonal Psychology*. Osaka: Osaka Kyoiku Tosho, 1993.

Mackinnon, Catherine A. *Toward a Feminist Theory of the State*. Cambridge: Harvard Univ. Press, 1989.

Malin, Irving, ed. *Saul Bellow and the Critics*. New York: New York Univ. Press, 1967.

Miller, Nancy. "Re-reading as a Woman: The Body in Practice." In *The Female Body in Western Culture: Contemporary Perspectives*, edited by Susan Rubin Sulieman, 354-62. Cambridge: Harvard Univ. Press, 1986.

Moi, Toril. *Sexual/Textual Politics*. London: Methuen, 1985.

Mosher, Donald L., and Silvan Tomkins. "Scripting the Macho Man: Hypermasculine Socialization and Enculturation." *Journal of Sex Research* 25, no. 1 (Feb. 1988): 60-80.

Mulvey, Laura. "Visual Pleasure and Narrative Cinema." *Screen* 16, no. 3 (Aug. 1975): 6–18.

Nietzsche, Friedrich. *On the Genealogy of Morals*. 1886. Reprint, New York: Vintage, 1969.

Opdahl, Keith M. *The Novels of Saul Bellow: An Introduction*. University Park: Pennsylvania State Univ. Press, 1967.

Pifer, Ellen. *Saul Bellow Against the Grain*. Philadelphia: Univ. of Pennsylvania Press, 1990.

Porter, M. Gilbert. *Whence the Power? The Artistry and Humanity of Saul Bellow*. Columbia: Univ. of Missouri Press, 1974.

Rich, Adrienne. "When We Dead Awaken: Writing as Revision." *College English* 34, no. 1 (1972): 18-30.

Rodrigues, Eusebio L. *Quest for the Human: An Exploration of Saul Bellow's Fiction*. Lewisburg, Penn.: Bucknell Univ. Press, 1981.

Rotundo, E. Anthony. *American Manhood: Transformations in Masculinity from the Revolution to the Modern Era*. New York: Basic Books, 1993.

Rourke, Constance. *American Humor: The Study of National Character*. New York: Harcourt Brace, 1931.

Rovit, Earl, ed. *Saul Bellow: A Collection of Critical Essays*. Twentieth Century Views. Englewood Cliffs, N.J.: Prentice, 1975.

Rubin, Gayle. "The Traffic in Women: Notes Toward a Political Economy of Sex." In *Toward an Anthropology of Women*, edited by Rayna Reiter, 157–210. New York: Monthly Review Press, 1975.

Scheer-Schäzler, Brigitte. *Saul Bellow*. Modern Literature Monographs. New York: Ungar, 1972.

Schopenhauer, Arthur. *On the Basis of Morality*. Indianapolis, Ind.: Hackett, 1995.

―――――. *The World as Will and Representation*. Translated by E. F. J. Payne. New York: Dover, 1966.

Schor, Naomi. "This Essentialism Which Is Not One: Coming to Grips with Irigaray." *Differences* 1, no. 2 (1989), 38–58.

Schraepen, Edmond, ed. *Saul Bellow and His Work*. Proceedings of a symposium held at the Free Univ. of Brussels, Dec. 10–11, 1977. Brussels: Centrum coor Taal-en Literatuurwetenschap Vrije Universiteit Brussel, 1978.

Scott, Nathan A. *Three American Moralists: Mailer, Bellow, Trilling.* Notre Dame, Ind.: Univ. of Notre Dame Press, 1973.

Sedgwick, Eve Kosofsky. *Between Men: English Literature and Male Homosocial Desire.* New York: Columbia Univ. Press, 1985.

Shibuya, Yuzaburo. *Bellow: Kaishin no Kiseki* (Saul Bellow: The conversion of the sick soul). Eibei Bungaku Sakkaron Sosho 28. Tokyo: Tojusha, 1978.

Slater, Philip. *Earthwalk.* New York: Doubleday/Anchor, 1974.

Tackach, James M. "Saul Bellow's Dingbat Einhorn, Nails Nagel and the American Dream." *Saul Bellow Journal* 2, no. 2 (1983): 55–58.

Tanner, Tony. *Saul Bellow.* Writers and Critics. New York: Chips, 1978.

Thoreau, Henry David. *Consciousness in Concord: The Text of Thoreau's Hitherto Lost Journal, 1840–1841.* Edited by Perry Mill. Boston: Houghton Mifflin, 1958.

———. *The Journals of Henry David Thoreau.* 14 vols. Edited by Bradford T. Allen and Francis H. Allen. Salt Lake City, Utah: Peregrine Smith, 1984.

———. *The Writings of Henry David Thoreau.* 20 vols. 1906. Reprint, New York: AMS Press, 1968.

Trachtenberg, Stanley, ed. *Critical Essays on Saul Bellow.* Critical Essays on American Literature. Boston: Hall, 1979.

Warren, Joyce W. *The American Narcissus: Individualism and Women in Nineteenth-Century American Fiction.* New Brunswick, N.J.: Rutgers Univ. Press, 1984.

West, Anthony. *H. G. Wells: Aspects of a Life.* New York: Random House, 1984.

Winnett, Susan. "Reading and Sexual Difference." Paper presented at the annual meeting of the Modern Language Association, Special Session 475, 1983.

Young, G. M. *Victorian Essays.* London: Oxford Univ. Press, 1962.

INDEX

190